from RECOLLECTION *to* RECIPE

ONE MAN'S JOURNEY IN RECREATING THE FLAVORS AND MEMORIES OF THE PAST

ROBERT E. VENDETTI

Lemon Leaf Press
PLAINSBORO, NEW JERSEY

Lemon Leaf Press
10 Schalks Crossing Road, Suite 501-211
Plainsboro, NJ 08536

Visit our website at www.LemonLeafPress.com

Printed in the United States of America

10 9 8 7 6 5 4 3 2 1

Design by Brian P. Jordan

Disclaimer and Terms of Use: Any person using the recipes within this book, and the ingredients thereof, is solely responsible for making sure that all ingredients used are fresh and within the dietary limits of the consumer. Reliance upon information and content obtained through this publication is solely at your own risk. Lemon Leaf Press, its principals, or its authors assume no liability or responsibility for damage, illness, or injury to you, or other persons, as a result of using/reading this publication. The author has no financial interest in, and receives no compensation, from manufacturers of products, services, celebrities, or other people mentioned in this book.

For anyone out there that has ever wished that they could cook like my mother, here is your chance

—REV

FROM RECOLLECTION TO RECIPE

This book is dedicated to my mother, Anna, who spent most of her adult life preparing the traditional dishes of our family and making a wonderful home for us. She was my first and foremost culinary educator and so much more than she had ever imagined she could be. Being the inspiration for this endeavor, I only wish that she was around to see her favorite recipes in print.

Anna Vendetti
1929 - 2006.

ABOUT THE AUTHOR

Born in September of 1958, Robert E. Vendetti was raised in the northeast New Jersey city of Clifton, located just 14 miles west of New York City. Both of his parents were American born, as direct descendants of Italian-American immigrants, and both from a long line of good cooks. Growing up, he spent many hours around the dining room table, where he learned about his family's past and acquired the knowledge and appreciation for their culinary traditions.

This cookbook is Robert's first public culinary endeavor, but he is no stranger to the kitchen, a place where he proudly carries on the food traditions of his past. He has no formal culinary education or training, other than watching his mother work in her small kitchen where she turned out everything from the daily family meals, all the way to holiday buffet spreads. In fact, the closest Robert has ever gotten to a commercial kitchen was when he worked in the campus cafeteria while away at college in Manchester, NH. There, he was the grill cook who prepared breakfast and lunch for hundreds of students, as well as provided kitchen prep assistance.

Robert received a Bachelor of Science degree in Accounting from that same college. He went on to work in Accounting for 5 years and later enhanced his technical skills by completing Computer Technology/ Programmer training. He then worked in Information Technology for 25 years supporting various accounting and securities compliance systems. Although he was exceptional at what he did, his passion for cooking grew. This love for cooking, in conjunction with an appreciation for homes, architecture, and home own-

ership, has made Real Estate a perfect career parallel. He enjoys helping people discover the joy and prestige of home ownership, as well as offering up delicious food for his family and friends.

With the recent meltdown in the securities and real estate markets, Robert seized that time and took the opportunity to do something that he has always wanted to do. . . document the family recipes he knows so well and recreate family recipes that have been taken to the grave. He encourages others to do the same thing with their own family recipes before they are lost forever. To that end, he has put together this unique collection of his family's traditional recipes for all to enjoy. Over the years, Robert has created other recipes and someday hopes to publish some of his own creations.

Robert currently resides in the Kendall Park section of South Brunswick Township, NJ. He shares a home with his longtime domestic partner, Chris Ondrak, who is a brilliant and talented floral designer, in his own right. Chris is the founder of the Gilded Lily Floral Studio in Flemington, NJ, and a Northeast Region Past President for the American Institute of Floral Designers.

Robert, held by brother, Randy (1958), as cousins Allen and Ronnie look on.

(When his mother was expecting Robert, his 5-year-old brother told her "this baby will be nothing but trouble." He was right!)

TABLE OF CONTENTS

ACKNOWLEDGEMENTS

Chris Ondrak, my better half, for his support and spending a better part of a year tasting and eating cold food (because I had to stop and photograph everything before we ate it).

Ronald Vendetti, my father and key living resource from a bygone era, who actually witnessed most of these foods being prepared by my grandmother and great grandmother, first hand.

Randall Vendetti, my brother, for his inspiration and advisement.

Judie (Krietz) Vendetti, my sister-in-law, for also inspiring, advising, and help with the *Classic Sponge Cake* recipe.

Jon Vendetti , my nephew, for loving his grandmother's food and inspiring me to keep the recipes alive for generations to come.

Angela "Angie" Cuzzi, for making that terrific pizza that inspired my quest to create the ultimate homemade pizza, and for her longtime friendship with my mother over the years.

Mary Mastropietro, my Aunt Mary, for not only being a good sister to my mother, but also her closest friend, and for being like a second mother to me.

Sue Hantson, my cousin and "Nana protégée," for her interest in this project and providing me with some of my grandmother's recipes, and especially for her advisement on *Nana's Poultry Stuffing*.

Brian Jordan (friend), for all his help in editing and formatting the design of this book.

John Daidone (friend), for helping with the final editing and advice.

Anna Vendetti, my mother, for always having a camera in her hand and being responsible for most of the old photos in this book. Had she not done that, we would not have had all of these great pictures documenting our existence.

And most importantly, to anyone else, past or present, that has inspired, encouraged, advised, helped, tested, tasted, anticipated, and has had to put up with me for the sake of this book. To all of you, I say, "Thank you."

INTRODUCTION

What my conception of this cookbook is NOT, is for it to be just another list of recipes. Instead, I bring family recipes back to life by talking about the life and times behind them. Keep in mind, this is my first attempt as a book author. Beginning a book is always the most difficult part. I guess the best place to start is by cutting right to the chase and define my purpose:

The purpose of this book is to document longtime, traditional, family recipes that had been lost when the primary creators passed on. It is the beginning of a quest to recreate recipes for foods remembered only by way of flavors and key ingredients, but no formal recipe or instructions are available to create them. Also, to introduce something different to the eating public and, quite possibly, teach some basics that can be used for any recipe, and most importantly, to entertain and generate some laughter from a crazy story or two.

Some of these recipes have been plucked from my mother's recipe box, but the instructions were sketchy, at best, and lacked additional details on how to prepare them. Like my mother, I am the type of cook that, for the most part, has lists of ingredients either stored in my head, or jotted down on paper. These "lists" of ingredients are just that. . . lists, with no regard for measurements. I just developed the knack for knowing how to do it. Unfortunately, my grandmothers cooked the same way. I say "unfortunately" because there are recipes that were locked away in their own minds and they have since passed on. I want to breathe some life back into these recipes. I want to start enjoying the foods again that I remember enjoying as a kid, but I also want these recipes to live on, somehow, after I am someday gone myself. You see, I have no children to pass them on to. Well, there is my nephew Jon, who I love to feed, as did my mother. However, he is young, starting a new career, and has no interest in cooking. I'm thinking that when I am no longer around, and he has a hankering for a stuffed vinegar pepper or a hunk of risotto, this book will be there for him.

This whole idea of resurrecting lost recipes started when, one holiday season, I wanted to make a chestnut/chocolate filled, honey-coated, cookie that my grandmother, Victoria (My mother's mother, who I refer to as "Grandma"), used to make. Mind you, Grandma passed away in 1963 when I was just 5 years old. For me to remember these cookies from that young age, you know that they had to really be something special. As a matter of fact, nobody ever bothered to get Grandma's recipe for this flawless confection while she was still alive. A written version was nowhere to be found. Years later, my mother and I decided we wanted to try and make them. We were able to dig up a similar recipe. We tried it, but they were just not the same. It was a good start, though. Over the years, my mother gave up trying, but I have been able to hone that recipe down. I practiced with it enough where I can now present them to family members and they will say, "Bingo! I think you have it." That recipe, by the way, can be found in this book as *Victoria's Castagna Dolce*.

Mom next to her new 36" Caloric, with double ovens (c. 1970).

Most of her married life, my mother worked her magic in a very small kitchen. The kitchen in our small, post WWII, Cape Cod style house could not have been bigger than 10' x 10'. Even though it was a small kitchen, it was big enough to accommodate (and always had) a 36-inch-wide stove. Some serious cooking can be done with a stove this size. There was a small table in the center of the room where we ate informal meals and was also used for additional work space. I can remember sitting at that very same table watching her cooking techniques and enjoying the foods she lovingly prepared. It was out of this small kitchen that some mighty big flavors emerged.

Right off the kitchen, there was a small formal dining room which further opened up into the living room. Thinking back, I can't even fathom the number of times our family and friends gathered around that table. I mean, we really crammed them in there. If there were not enough extension leaves for the table, we brought out the kitchen table and tacked it onto the end, extending into the living room.

Not to belabor the point, but to bring the *big food from a small kitchen* concept to another insane level, my grandmother, Angelina (my father's mother, who I refer to as *"Nana"*) spent her twilight years living in a senior citizen's high rise apartment complex on Franklin Street in Newark, NJ. Her small apartment had an efficiency style kitchen with a 24-inch electric stove, a bar-sized sink, and about

My small, but very stylish, kitchen (c. 2010).

2 feet of counter space. I loved going to Nana's apartment for Sunday dinners where she would put out a spread for the entire family (Her four children, plus their spouses, and up to 11 grandchildren). A large extension table was set up in the middle of the living room and everyone would sit around gorging on mass quantities of food. The refrigerator, one of those apartment-sized ones with the freezer on the inside, did not even have enough space. In winter months, she would keep "overflow" food cold outside on her terrace, 10 floors up from the street.

So you do not need a big kitchen to be big on your food, as my mother, Grandma, and Nana have proven. My own kitchen has been recently updated to 21st century standards, but it is still quite small. Even though I would love a huge, gorgeous kitchen to entertain in, I find my small kitchen gets an A+ for efficiency, and I am generally happy in there. I can stand in the center and touch the sink, the stove, and the refrigerator without even moving more than

How did we ever get so many people around that table? Mom (standing) with her sister, Mary, seated (foreground left) and brother, Tony (foreground right).

one step. The counter workspace is conveniently located between the sink and the stove, and the refrigerator is directly on the opposite wall. The close proximity of these essential areas makes cooking a breeze.

When I was growing up, we ate meals at home everyday in our house. We rarely ate out or ordered in. We certainly could afford to eat out, but we just didn't. Back then, eating supper at home around the dining room table was not a novelty. It was just what people did. Dad brought home the bacon and Mom stayed home to cook it. Everyday at 6:00 PM, we ate our supper. . . yes, supper! *Supper* is what we had every evening from Monday through Friday. Now dinner, that was a different thing altogether. *Dinner* is what we ate on Sunday afternoons, usually around 2:00 PM.

For as much as we ate at home, it was never like a restaurant, in that we had a choice. You ate what was cooked that day. If you did not care for the dish, you tried it anyway and you eventually ended up liking it. Gee, imagine that. This, I believe, is how grown-up taste buds are cultivated. Anyone that had the pleasure of living back then, and knows those routines, can plainly see that the *home preparation and eating food around the table* concept has become watered down over the years. What I am seeing, nowadays, are people getting lazy about

A new house (Clifton, NJ – c. 1955).

keeping up the old cooking traditions and, consequently, the eating together part is waning.

Even though we have busier schedules than our parents did, Chris and I eat dinner (umm. . . I mean "supper") at home every day of the week. Nowadays, the time that we eat will vary because of the crazy schedules we keep. No matter how busy we get, I always make it a point to make dinner at home and, like our parents before us, it's *just what we do.* My day would not be complete without that quiet time.

Throughout this book, you will find that I give my mother high praise in the kitchen, but she wasn't always perfect culinary-wise. Some of her techniques are best forgotten. Let's take vegetables, for instance. She always felt the need to overcook them. I learned later in life that broccoli is not the color gray. I often found myself asking, "If they are called green beans, how come they aren't green?" And, let's talk about her steak. She cooked steak in the broiler of our kitchen stove, which was the lower broiler "drawer" type (I'm sure you know the kind), and it was always cooked within an inch of its life. One time, the steaks actually caught on fire with black smoke billowing up to the ceiling. Never mind calling the fire department, many times I thought of reporting my mother to the *Beef Police.* I've envisioned them busting in, with guns drawn, exclaiming, "Okay lady. Step away from the beef!" Truthfully, I did not experience the joys of a properly cooked steak until well into my 20s, when I moved out on my own and discovered what *medium rare* was.

I can also think back about the things that my mother had in her kitchen that I would never have. I have a good chuckle when I think about it. One of those things I crack up most about was her adamant use of "gas station" steak knives. You see, back in the 1960s, for the benefit of those that were not around at that time, gas stations used to give away items with every fill up. Steak knives and glass tumblers were some of those items and, yes, we had both. Those glasses seemed to disappear over the years (via general breakage or garage sales), but those steak knives live on to this day. Once we gave her a beautiful set of knives, but she would continue to use her gas station knives instead. She just liked them for various tasks. I'd be working in her kitchen and I often said, "Ma, these knives, please. . . When the heck are you going to get rid of these things?" But now she is gone and, for that reason, I think I need to save at least one of those knives for posterity's sake. That being said, it will be no surprise to you that I definitely recommend a good set of knives (for sanity purposes).

In addition to good knives, I also believe that quality cookware is important, to the extent that you can afford it. You don't need to spend money on state-of-the-art cookware to be a good cook. A good cook can find a way to do magic in any kitchen, with the most archaic of equipment. My own personal cookware is made up of favorite pieces I've extracted from miscellaneous cookware sets I have purchased over the years. Some pieces were even dug up out of my parent's basement when I moved out. I have one baking pan of my mother's that I still make *Chicken Parmesan* in because that is the pan she always used to make it. Seeing my *Chicken Parmesan* served out of the same pan my mother used just reminds me of those simple, happy times. Don't get me wrong, I do have many pieces that are of high quality and, I will not lie to you, it can make a difference in the final outcome of some dishes. My point is, don't miss out on an opportunity to cook just because you cannot spend a lot of money to equip your kitchen with state-of-the-art cookware. Good food comes from the heart. If the spirit is willing, a cooking vessel will be found to nurture that spirit.

Most of the recipes I am presenting here are very economical, as they were executed by my grandmother's during the *Great* Depression (You know, the BIG depression that occurred during the 1930s, not to be mistaken with the one occurring in 2010). Since most of the ingredients are low cost, these recipes translate very well for use in the more recent economic times. They are inexpensive because they are home-cooked. The ingredients are fresh and they are better for you than pre-processed foods. For example, a whole pot of *Pasta e Fagioli* can be made for less than the cost of one can of the stuff from the store. It is also a great source of fiber and protein. If you are a busy person, you will like that most of these foods can be frozen in portions, which ups the convenience factor.

There are some very unique recipes in this book that you may have never seen before. There are also some dishes in this book that you can find recipes for anywhere, but presented here with an end result that may have a different twist than what you may have seen before. In my opinion, they are different tasting (for the better). Let's take lasagna, for instance. Why would anyone need another recipe for lasagna? The answer to that lies within the techniques and elements used to create it. For example, I have seen many lasagna recipes, but where will you find one that does not make you fumble with boiling wide strips of pasta, layered with loose, ground beef sauce? The lasagna I present in this book incorporates tiny meatballs instead. They are suspended within regular curly egg noodles and ricotta cheese. As for "no-boil" lasagna sheets, easy yes, but I'm not such a fan (sorry).

How many times have you made something from a cookbook and said, "Hey, mine doesn't look like the picture" (although it probably tasted the way it should have). You are going to find that the illustrations in this book are not air-brushed, food studio glamour shots, made picture perfect for the sake of a book. I did this so you can see what a realistic outcome looks like (I also want to, hopefully, keep the production cost of the book down). They show the real deal, with all possible flaws included, because even mine had flaws, but I knew they tasted right.

Speaking of "tasting right," when recreating recipes that you have not tasted in a long time, you will discover that your taste buds are the best asset in determining if success or failure has been achieved. I always say, *"Your taste buds don't expire."* Even if you haven't eaten that food in years, as soon as the flavors hit the taste buds, a message is sent to the brain saying, "That's it. . . That is grandma's cookie!" People from my own family, that may be reading this, have already tasted most of these dishes before and will know if I got it right or not. For the majority of the readers, you will be trying these recipes for the first time and will not have that same frame of reference. It is to you I say, "Tell me if these are really, truly good, or have I just become bias to them over the years." Please feel free to provide me with any feedback that you care to offer about this book and the recipes contained within. I welcome all comments you may have; for contact information, visit my website at www.lemonleafpress.com.

Most of these recipes are quite easy to make. There are a few challenging ones tossed in, but I encourage you to try them. My hope is to instill a sense of tradition in your own mind so you can become motivated to document, recreate, or resurrect the lost recipes of your own family. If you have been shying away from the kitchen, get back in there, ask your mother questions, get your grandma's recipe box out, and wow your family and friends at the table with things they have not had in a long time (more importantly, I think you will "wow" yourself). You may even start creating some new memories and traditions of your own.

Before I close my introduction, I just want to forewarn you of one thing. When writing these recipes for this book, I thought of things that I hadn't thought about in years. I felt compelled to discuss these

memories and sometimes, just the memory itself, sent me off on writing tangents. When I read them back, I was in a quandry about whether these "brain dumps" were necessary for a cookbook. I mean, who would care about the personal memories of a *no-name-home-cook-wanna-be-cookbook-author?* I thought about editing them out, but my final decision was to leave them in. Who knows? They may become interesting someday, if I become a *BIG-name-home-chef-ACTUALLY-IS-a-cookbook-author!* My decision to leave the stories in was also swayed by the nature of the whole "recipe recovery mission" premise, where I think the stories are an inherent part of the recipe. Many of the incidents and people in the stories have made some type of impact or impression on me, and I wanted that fact to shine through. And that is how the Recipe/Memoir theme evolved. I think there will be more people, than not, that can relate to similar situations in their own lives and will enjoy it. So with that I say, even if you are not interested in making a recipe, read the book and allow the stories to speak for themselves.

Robert E. Vendetti

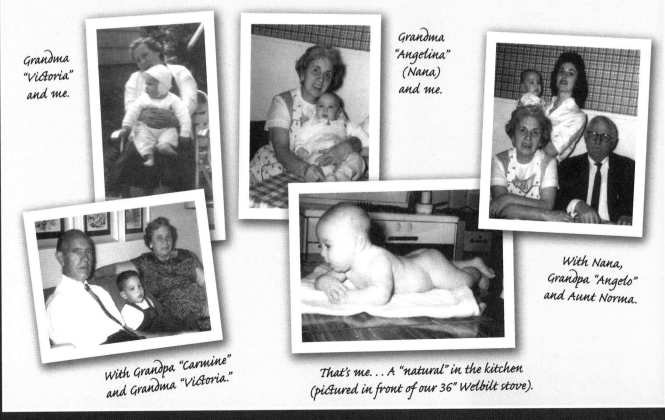

Grandma "Victoria" and me.

Grandma "Angelina" (Nana) and me.

With Nana, Grandpa "Angelo" and Aunt Norma.

With Grandpa "Carmine" and Grandma "Victoria."

That's me. . . A "natural" in the kitchen (pictured in front of our 36" Welbilt stove).

MY CULINARY RÉSUMÉ

Chef versus Cook: For some, there is no apparent difference. To them, good food is good food, no matter who cooks it. However, for many, there is a very real and distinct difference between a *chef* and a *cook*. Over the years, some people that have tasted the foods I prepare refer to me as a "gourmet chef." Am I really, though? No. However, this notion of *gourmet chef* vs. *good cook* raises an interesting discussion point, which I feel deserves a little attention, and a topic in which I have some personal beliefs and opinions I would like to share.

I want to set the record straight from the get go. I do not claim, by any means, to be a gourmet chef. I suppose to anyone that has limited knowledge and experience in the kitchen, I seem like a gourmet chef. I think that I am someone you would classify as a good cook. (And, notice I did not say *"just* a good cook," which I almost wrote. Being a "cook" is in no way subordinate to being a chef and does not warrant anyone putting *just* in front of it.)

So, who exactly is a *chef* and who is a *cook*? The first obvious place I went to was the dictionary to get a working definition of the two (and, both being under "C," made this research very easy). Per Webster's:

> **Chef** — 1: *noun* - a skilled cook who manages a kitchen (as of a restaurant); 2: *noun* - Cook
>
> **Cook** — 1: *noun* - one who prepares food for eating; 2: *verb* - to prepare food for eating by means of applying heat.
>
> (There were other forms of the verb found that imply unsavory behavior, such as "cook the books" or "cook up a scheme," but that is a path we need not go down at this juncture.)

In looking at both of these definitions, one can conclude that a chef is a cook, but a cook is not necessarily a chef. Besides "Cook" being the #2 definition for "Chef," the two words that make this distinction for me are *skilled* and *manages*. "Manages," as in a restaurant kitchen, has an obvious meaning. In the definition, "Skilled" is meant to mean "professionally trained," I'm sure. However, "skilled" can also be interpreted as just plain old *knows how to do it well,* which technically does not require a degree or professional training. My mother, grandmothers, and great grandmothers before me, possessed the natural ability and passion to create great things in the kitchen. They did this on a daily basis. They were not professionally trained, but they were extremely skilled and, theoretically, it was their occupation (so to speak). They created culinary masterpieces, not in a restaurant, but they certainly were the bosses of their kitchens. Were they chefs or cooks?

After watching many culinary experts on food television, and by general observations I have made over the years, I developed my own personal conception of the difference, regardless of the dictionary definitions. Interestingly, I think the number of people you are cooking for has nothing to do with it. A home cook can prepare food for 30 people, and a chef can cook a meal for two (as would a personal chef). So when a culinary expert says, *"Sure, he is a good cook, but he is NOT a chef,"* I hear the words, *"He does not have the passion, nor the formal culinary training, that a person has achieved to qualify him/her as a chef."*

By eating in fine restaurants and/or watching chefs orchestrate their dishes on television, I've come to the conclusion that "art" also comes into play, somehow, when distinguishing between a "cook" and a "chef." Whether food is presented vertically, as opposed to horizontally, seems to further establish one's culinary status. If the food is placed on the plate, triangularly, on the geometric plane (entrée next to starch, next to vegetable). . . Cook! If you stack those same exact elements, vertically on top of each other, and stick in a sprig of rosemary. . . Chef! Filling large platters with food to be passed around the table for the taking. . . Cook! Serving that same food from a chaffing dish or carving station. . . Chef! Wearing an apron. . . Cook! Wearing a white coat. . . Chef! (Okay. I think you get the idea.) But one last distinction (if I may): The term "Chef" seems to be an acceptable replacement for a chef's first name when addressing them in a professional setting.

You might hear someone say, "Excuse me, *Chef,* where is the butter?" However, you would never hear someone say, "Excuse me, *Accountant,* where are the pencils" and the same holds true for *"Cook."*

To all the chefs out there, please do not misinterpret what I am saying. It is not my intent to get you mad at me, nor for me to insult your accomplishments in any way, as you've worked very hard to achieve them. I enjoy frequenting many a fine restaurant in a given year, and I pay a great deal of money for the dining experience you provide. A good chef is always appreciated here. Keep doing what you do by wowing us with your creations.

My only reason for bringing up the whole *chef vs. cook* topic, in the first place, is to segue into establishing my credentials as a cookbook author (for those that like to read books written by people with credentials). If, within these pages, you are expecting the creations of a culinary genius who is well versed in the arts of the craft, I'm sorry to say that you may have purchased the wrong book. On that note, if you were also expecting the writings of an award-winning author, whew, I'm sorry to say you really got taken, although I am *extremely* appreciative that you bought it, and super duper ecstatic that you have read it this far. I assure you that you will be pleasantly surprised and happy with it. If not for a few chuckles, here and there, I hope you will use this book often, even if only for a favorite recipe or two that you stumble upon.

So what exactly is my culinary résumé? Well, it is not so much an actual résumé, as it is more of a culinary history, which is best explained by a story (hey, I warned you stories would be forthcoming). I seem to be very happy when I am in the kitchen creating good food, especially the traditional foods and flavors of my past. I feel blessed to have inherited the passion of cooking from my ancestral roots and I feel obliged to carry these food traditions forward into the future. As already established, I will never claim to be a gourmet chef. However, I do have a teeny, tiny bit of culinary training and background.

First and foremost, as mentioned in my introduction, my mother is responsible for shaping my culinary foundation. For whatever its worth, I enhanced that culinary base by taking a Foods class in my senior year in high school. It was part of the school's Home Economics Department. Here, we learned about good nutrition choices and how to prepare the most basic of recipes for survival. If my memory serves me correctly, there were quite a few boys in that class. Being the high school boys that we were, we only were there because we needed an elective, and where else could you actually get to eat in the middle of the day (Oh boy, Oh boy!). What ended up happening was I excelled in that class, which I can attribute to my coming from a home where cooking was a natural thing. I think I may have even given that teacher a few pointers, if I remember correctly.

After high school, it was on to college where, for a good part of my four years there, I worked in the campus kitchen. I would get up early on a Sunday morning (and in New Hampshire, those were COLD mornings), walk over to the student center, don my kitchen whites and paper hat, and prepare for breakfast grill duty. There was a whole team at work to put this all together. After turning up the heat on the grill, I'd start cracking eggs into a large pot, two at a time, one egg in each hand. I'd add some milk and beat those eggs into submission with a large, wire whip. I'd separate out some into another large pan and mix with some sugar and cinnamon (for French toast). I'd lay rows of bacon and breakfast sausage onto parchment paper on large baking sheets and slide them into the convection oven. Meanwhile, the lead chef would convert potatoes into home fries, mixing up the pancake batter, and chopping vegetables. The girls readied the serving line by adding the scalding water to the warming cart, stocking trays, dishes, and utensils. Cooked bacon, sausage, and potatoes were transferred to metal pans and inserted into the warming cart for serving.

At 7:59 AM, after one final inspection of my grill area, making sure I had my eggs, pancake batter, cheese, ham, vegetables, sliced bread and all my necessary utensils, we waited for the queue at 8:00 AM. . . "Okay, open up the doors." Massive amounts of hungry college students fell into the cafeteria line. I'd take their orders down the line, about five or six at a time. They'd request custom

Off to work on a cold, snowy morning in NH (1977).

... and, more snow on NHC campus (1977).

ers of beer (the most popular grill items were cheese steaks and California-style cheeseburgers).

I have to say that I created quite a good reputation for myself while working in that snack bar. . . the closest I've ever come to celebrity status in my life (well, on campus, anyway). People would see me on campus and say, "Hey, you're that snack bar cooking guy." Every once in awhile, someone would come in and say to my co-worker at the sandwich station, "I would like a ham, cheese, lettuce, tomato, and mayo sandwich. . . but I want *HIM* to make it for me," pointing toward me, as I was already frantically working at the grill. "Dude, I can't do it at this very second," I would say. (Thinking back, I most likely did not use the term *"Dude"* back in 1977. I am just exercising a little creative license to keep the story "up to date" for my more contemporary audience.) "No sweat, I'll wait," they would reply.

So why, exactly, did they want to wait for me to make that sandwich for them? I mean, it's just a sandwich, right? Because they knew I was the type of person that made the food behind that counter as if I was making it for myself. The other students that worked in the snack bar were there on program called *"work study,"* which required them to be there. I, on the other hand, applied for the job myself and wanted to be there. They were not interested in what they were doing and it showed in their food. You don't make a sandwich by taking the pre-portioned out meat, cheese, and veggies and just slapping them onto the bread, without any regard for placement of these elements, dousing them with mayo, and tossing it on a plate. I would take the pre-sliced meat, peel off one slice at a time, and pile it onto the bread, deli style, as if the meat was being sliced directly onto the bread, spreading the meat, cheese, lettuce, and tomato out evenly throughout the sandwich, so that you get some of each in every bite. If the bread was toasted, I'd be careful not the break off the corners as I was cutting. All this makes the difference between a flat, skimpy looking sandwich, and a tasty, attractive looking sandwich that someone would actually want to eat. Eventually, the customers caught onto this. People actually noticed. As with anything in life, it's all in the details that matter.

omelets, scrambled eggs, French toast, pancakes, etc. That grill was humming. As I turned their orders onto the plates, they moved down to the next station where the girls supplied them with the sides of their choice from the warming cart. We did this for three hours straight.

Meanwhile, back in the kitchen, cold cuts were sliced into portions, lettuce chopped, tomatoes sliced, onions chopped, salads made, all in preparation for my move at 11:30 AM to the snack bar, where I ran the grill, as well. The snack bar was an offshoot of the main kitchen and cafeteria, where the students could order a lighter, more informal fare, enjoy a pitcher of beer amongst friends, and play a friendly game of pinball. Sunday lunches were served from the snack bar until the dinner crew took over in the cafeteria at 4:00 PM. I cooked hamburgers, hot dogs, cheese steaks, grilled cheese, and anything you can dream up on a grill. There was a deep fryer where we made French fries, onion rings, fried chicken, and fish. I occasionally moved over to the sandwich board to make sandwiches and *"grinders,"* or the ice cream station to make cones, or *"frappes"* (a "grinder" is what they call a submarine sandwich in New England; a "frappe" is what they call a milk shake). I even served up pitch-

My college, although mostly a Business and Accounting school, had a Hotel, Restaurant, and Tourism (HRT) curriculum. I was majoring in Accounting, although, with my love of food and cooking, I often think I should have majored in HRT studies. Under the HRT curriculum, they had a wine tasting class. During my senior year in college, some of my fellow seniors and I took this wine class, as we needed elective credits, and where else could you actually get "sloshed" in the middle of the day. (Hey, where have you heard that before? I guess *Wine Tasting* was the college man's equivalent to the high school boy's *Foods* class.) Aside from the obvious free libations, this actually turned out to be a serious class, with exams and everything. We learned about the various wine regions and the types of wines that should be paired with various foods. It definitely elevated me from that all familiar scene of my grandfather, with his jug of Burgundy at his side at the dinner table. Growing up, that is the only wine I ever knew about. We drank it with everything.

Fast forward about 15 years. It is the mid 1990s and Chris and I are now together. Chris, being an accomplished florist and me, with my cooking skills, went through a phase of doing fabulous yearly theme parties. We did them in January because it was a slow time for florists and it was just a great time to get people out of the winter doldrums. We'd clear all the furniture out of the living room, set up tables and decorate them to the hilt with specially rented linens and lavish, over-the-top flower arrangements. Of course, we had a cocktail hour with extensive hors d'oeuvres. Our dinner menu was planned from soup to nuts, which I would prepare and serve up on individual plates out of our small kitchen. We invited all of our friends and we mixed up the seating, separating couples, to form interesting table dynamics and personality mix. We'd even do them at different houses. People had a fantastic time at our dinner parties.

Now that I think of it, these parties were probably the closest I have ever gotten to being an actual chef, as earlier defined by Mr. Webster. Even though they were not held in a restaurant, I was the boss of the kitchen in planning the menus, executing them, stylizing the plates, and serving them up with the

Winter "White" Party.

"Beyond Blue" Party.

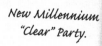

New Millennium "Clear" Party.

2000 Presidential "Balls" Party.

help of Chris and other volunteer table "runners." We did this every year, for about 10 years, but because of expense, indoor space issues (yes, the guest list kept growing), and just plain old getting tougher to execute, we eventually stopped the madness. We changed the party to an outdoor summertime party instead, with a buffet dinner which I cook entirely.

Lastly, another experience that emulated chef-like activities for me took place at my last place of employment. I was a member of a committee whose responsibility was to plan and execute an onsite company breakfast. The purpose of the breakfast was to celebrate company milestones and reward the employees with something special for their efforts. In an adjacent vacant office space, we set up three "omelet to order" stations using hot plates and omelet pans. We also had a pancake/waffle, tater tots, and breakfast sausage station, along with a separate fruit salad/juice and condiment station. We set up tables, with tablecloths and flowers, for people to sit, eat, and socialize while playing upbeat background music. The managers served the employees side dishes from chafing dishes. Many people later admitted that they thought it was just going to be bagels and juices that they would just grab and take back to their desk. Instead, we served an actual breakfast and created an environment that invited people to want to stay, socialize, and get to know their colleagues.

All team members worked very hard in putting together this successful event, but I was told that it was my ideas on preparation and extra touches that really made the event something more than what people expected. I can only attribute this to my college days, working those Sunday breakfasts, as the preparation for much of the corporate event was exactly the same as I used to do 30 years prior. Because of this special recognition, there was no escaping when it came time to do a second break-

Company "Milestone" Breakfast Team
From Left: Winsor, David, Carol, Kim, Bob (me), & John.

fast. Since then, we have put together lunch time "cultural pot lucks," where people participate by preparing a special dish of their culture. I helped in setting up buffet and dining tables for these cultural eat-fests. Our office had a lot of cultural diversity, and the people really enjoyed talking about their dishes and trading recipes.

So that's about it. What you have read is the extent of my culinary experience, at this point in my life. Add to that my personal culinary experience, and that should give you a pretty good picture of where I am at. I sure hope these are suitable credentials for someone that is writing a cookbook. I hope it qualifies me (somewhat) as a culinary resource for you and allows me to prosper (somehow) from this endeavor. We are living in a world where reality shows prevail and celebrities are made of people we ordinarily would not consider particularly smart or intelligent. Having said that, the fact I am a person of intelligence and common sense, and with the little culinary knowledge that I do have, I just might have a pretty good shot at success with this.

MY TIME IN ITALY

One of the things I am most happy I got a chance to do in my life was visiting the country of my origin. For me, I found that the trips to Italy filled in a lot of blanks when it came to understanding my background and the culture. This was especially true regarding the foods I grew up with. It was interesting to see the similarities and dissimilarities to what I was used to. It is even more interesting just how "washed out" the traditions got when they transitioned to the USA.

Some examples: The simple American tradition of eating salad prior to a meal, let alone served as an individual portion, never occurred to me until later in life (when I started frequenting more restaurants). My family always served salad in a large, family style bowl for passing around at the table. Most times it was lettuce only in light wine vinaigrette. It was eaten after the main course, sometimes during. While in Italy, we experienced the exact same thing in most of the restaurants we went to. The bowl of salad was brought to the table for everyone to share and, ironically, lettuce only with a little onion in there, at best. This shows how that tradition came to be in our house and explained to me why we did that. It also proves how Italian restaurants here have been Americanized into serving a dinner salad as a precursor to a meal. Something we did not see in Italy.

In looking at a typical restaurant menu in Italy, a further connection was made between the Italian dining process and our family's traditions, regarding the order of the dinner courses. Not so much every day, but more so with a holiday or company meals, our family would eat insane amounts of food. Case in point: A typical holiday dinner for us was antipasto, soup and/or pasta, main course (accompanied by the salad), fruit, and dessert (finally!). The menus in Italy were structured in exactly the same way: antipasi (appetizers), primi (soups or pastas), secondi (main course, accompanied by the salad), and dolci (sweets/desserts). I now understood why we ate the way we did at home and in the order in which the food came out.

Now, to anyone (even in Italy), that seems like a lot of food. Although, in Italy, the courses are more sensibly sized and paced so that you felt satisfied, and not stuffed, when you got up from table. If we ate that many courses in an American restaurant, we wouldn't be able to move, which brings me to my next point. . .

The Italian people are very physically fit, with slim waistlines. They also wear stylish, every day clothing. As a matter of fact, we noticed that the people were always impeccably dressed. Italian men always wear long pants (nice jeans or trousers) with shoes (no sneakers), and the women wear skirts with a stylish blouse or sweater (at least while they are out on the town anyway). The whole time there, I don't think I saw one obese person. If I saw anyone that could tip the scale, it was us, and the other tourists.

With all the talk about "green" these days, I found Italy to be a very energy conscious country. Energy comes at a premium there, so certain measures are in place as a result. The obviously small diesel cars which, as an American used to big powerful engines, I found to be quite peppy and comfortable. The home refrigerators are small, as they do not draw a lot of power. More interestingly, they are designed small as to not overstock them with food. The Italian people go to the market for fresh food often, sometimes every day. The refrigeration is only necessary for the perishables and to keep a small amount of food cold/frozen for the short run, until it is used. There, plastic supermarket bags need to be purchased at the checkout, if you do not bring your

own to reuse (smart). It is a better incentive for people to reuse bags than we have here in the USA. Here, if people had to pay for the bags at the checkout line, they would definitely make a conscious effort to reuse their own. Instead, we still give the plastic bags out for free and pay the customer a nickel for ever bag they reuse (dumb).

Speaking of food markets, I am envious of the food stores that they have over in Italy. The food is so fresh and authentic, and all right there under one roof. At home, we need to scout and travel far for places that carry that same quality, authenticity, and selection. I was in all my glory shopping in those stores over there. Loaves of bread, stacked in baskets, looked as if cutting them would be like cutting a rock. When you actually cut one, the crust was crispy and the inside was light and airy, like a feather. Pot cheese (ricotta) was piled high on a marble slab where the clerk would scoop up and package as much as you asked for. Meats, like prosciutto, capicola, sopressata, and mortadella hung from above. Cheeses, too many varieties to list here, were also prominently displayed.

There was an abundant selection of wine at the supermarkets, and so inexpensive (by American standards, anyway). I know that is to be somewhat expected, seeing as most of that wine is produced right there. However, when we saw the *Santa Margherita Pinot Grigio* at 7 Euro a bottle (which, at the time, was equivalent to about 10 American Dollars) we piled it into the shopping cart. The natives must have thought we were crazy, but we knew better. That same wine was going for about $25.00 a bottle back in New Jersey. Back at the villa, our housemates would ask if it was okay to open another bottle. "Oh, sure, go right ahead. We'll just go get more tomorrow," we said.

Eating establishments in Italy close at ambiguous times of the day. Depending on what town you were in, or the will of the proprietor, they closed anywhere from 1:00 to 3:00 PM, and either stayed closed for the day, or reopened after 5:00 PM. If we didn't get out until after 1:00 PM, we were hard pressed to find someplace to have lunch. One afternoon, Chris and I were so hungry (yes, it is possible to be in Italy

AND be hungry!). There was not one restaurant open to eat at, so we got the idea to go over to the supermarket and buy some bread, deli meats, and cheeses and have ourselves a little picnic. It turned out to be one, great, delicious idea. One glitch, though. . . the environmentally conscious Italians do not

Our "Italian" Fork.

sell plastic utensils (that explains why you get a little wooden spoon with your gelato). What they had was a gadget wall with stainless steel eating utensils, sold individually. We bought one fork and shared it for our picnic. We kept it as a memento of the occasion. Tossed in with our everyday flatware, every once in a while it surfaces to the top of the pile.

I've been to Italy three times (so far). The first trip to Italy took place in 1995 and was more of a passive one, in that there were various ports of call there for a Mediterranean cruise we were on. Starting with a two-day stay in Paris, we traveled to Nice, France, where we boarded the ship to start our journey. During that cruise, we only got a chance to see some main attractions in Italy, or wherever the tour bus was going that particular day. Although Florence and Rome were two of the more significant ports of call, I must say that our favorite port was the island

Trevi Fountain – Rome, Italy (1995).

of Capri. In Capri, the large ships can not pull right up to the dock, so our ship was anchored a distance off the cost. We had to be transported by dinghy from the ship to the dock.

Once on the island, we took a funicular up a steep incline. As we ascended upward, the views got more and more magnificent. The town at the top was kind of touristy (I thought), with expensive shops and restaurants, but very pretty and quaint just the same. It was when we ventured off the beaten path that we discovered the more down to earth shops and eateries. We found a friendly, open air restaurant along one route. I recall having a very nice carpaccio there. The only problem I had with Capri, as with the other ports of call, was that the visit there was too short. I would have loved to have experienced more of what the island had to offer, perhaps travelling to other parts of it. Someday, I hope to do that.

The following two trips to Italy (July 2006 and October 2008), were land lubber trips, in that we stayed ashore and shared a rented villa with a group of friends. Both trips were in the Tuscan province: the first was on the outskirts of San Gimignano, located mid way between Florence and Siena; the second was in a town called Bucine, located in the Chianti region of Tuscany. We had our own car so, unlike with the cruise, we were free to go wherever we wanted and whenever we wanted.

I anticipated the worst about driving in Italy. I actually found that it was not as bad as I thought it would be. On the *Autostrada,* which is the highway system, the cars travel fast. However, as long as you stay to the right, they are able to pass. Once I got used to the roads, I even did some passing of my own. I must admit, I was less confused getting around over there than, I would imagine, an Italian person would be trying to get around over here. All the roads there are well marked with clear-to-understand direction signs. I am still amazed that I understand the Italian *Autostrada* better than the NJ Turnpike exchange for Newark Liberty International Airport!

One day during the 2006 trip, three of us took a leisurely ride through the Chianti region. We wanted to get something to eat before the establishments

Base of the Eiffel Tower (1995).

Paris, France – View from the Eiffel Tower (1995).

Traveling via dinghy from the ship to Capri Island.

Chris and Me in Capri (1995).

closed for the afternoon, so we stopped in this quaint little town of Radda in Chianti. Little did I know, at the time, that this was going to become one of my favorite places on Earth. There was a little town square, across from which was a wine shop. They had a small menu posted outside. The proprietress did not understand a word of English, so we just pointed to "Lasagna" on the board and held up three fingers. She motioned for us to go sit across the street in the little square and she would bring our wine and food order. We chose a small table in the shade, next to a bubbling fountain. When our food arrived, we were pleasantly surprised to see three dishes of what I call *lasagna perfection*. Each one had a dollop of fresh ricotta cheese on top. The lasagna was light as a feather. I have had some good lasagna in my life, but this was by far the BEST lasagna I have ever had, hands down (yes, "roll your eyes into the back of your head" good).

View outside our villa room (2006).

Wine Shop - Radda in Chianti (2006).

The BEST Lasagna I ever ate (2006).

With happy bellies, we were able to continue our journey through this fabulous wine country. We made it a point to stop back in Radda during our 2008 return trip.

Most days, all the guys in the villa would split up and go on their own daily adventures. Then we all met back at the villa later in the afternoon. Everyone would bring back cheeses and meats to share and savor with various wines. We'd sit out on the veranda and tell stories about our day, all while marveling at the magnificent view. Some days we would take a dip in the pool. Definitely a life anyone can get used to very easily. I found that life in Italy is so laid back, by design. The people in Italy are very hospitable and willing to talk to us, even if we didn't understand exactly what they were saying. There was never a question in my mind as to whether someone was trying to pull our leg, or hustle us (as I felt like in Paris). They always went out of their way to make sure they understood us, and us them. Consider the following case in point:

On the first day of the 2008 trip, Chris and I were looking for the villa in Bucine. The directions said to turn left by a sign and pass the "Carabinieri" on your right. All the directions clicked to that point, except this last piece was very sketchy. After driving back and forth, replaying the directions over and over again, Chris saw a guy getting out of his car and insisted that I stop so he can ask directions. I said, "Are you nuts? This guy is not going to understand a word you're saying." Well, at this point I was

The villa we stayed in – Bucine, Italy (2008).

View from the Villa – Bucine, Italy (2008).

willing to try anything, so I conceded. Chris began, "Excuse me. . ." The guy cut in immediately, "Ah! Buon Giornio! Blabity, blabity, blabity, Blaaa. . ." Chris turned and looked at me for help and I just shrugged. Chris turned back and handed the guy the directions, which were in English, and pointed to the word "Carabinieri" as I shouted from the car, "No capisco Italiano. . . parla Inglese." The man, nodding in understanding, eyed the paper for a few seconds. "Ah! Si, Si. Carabinieri", he replied back, while shaking his head in a "yes" fashion. The guy hand gestured at us. (No, people, not the infamous Italian hand gesture you are thinking about. He gestured directions!). He pointed down the hill and indicated a right turn, saying in the best English he could muster, "eh, right-a. . ." then gesturing a dome with one arm, with his other arm going under (yes, yes, go right and then under the trestle, got it). . . "eh, one-a, two-a," as he counted with his fingers and indicated to turn "left-a. . ." (Okay, second left after the trestle, got it.). Then, pointing right and making a gesture of a house or building. . . "Carabinieri, Carabinieri" (indicating the Carabinieri building will then be on our right). Bingo! We did it. We made contact. We said our "grazie" and our "prego" ("thank you" and "you're welcome"), and off we went. Turns out, there was a small "Carabinieri"

sign on the main road, just off to the left, that we must have driven past a dozen times. Once we made that left, we could see the villa at the top of the hill (By the way, "Carabinieri" means "constable," "sheriff," or "police").

That man could have just as easily shrugged us off, but he didn't. Despite the few glitches that occurred while traveling, now that we have the chance to look back at them, they turned out to be quite funny. Point being, even with the glitches, I wouldn't have missed this opportunity for anything. If you are someone that has roots stemming from another country, I would highly recommend traveling there. Scrimp, save, scratch, claw, do whatever you can to make that journey, at least once in your life. It will help you better understand your culture and, more importantly, yourself.

We loved it in Italy and there is more of it that we need to see. Since we visited the Tuscany region twice, we would like to visit other regions and cities there. Chris would like to experience Venice, and I would like to see more of the southern regions, specifically those that line up geographically with Naples and Rome, which are the regions of my grandparents' origins. So Italy, we WILL be back!! Hey, you know what I say folks. . . enough with the chit-chat and let's get a cookin'!

Bucine, Italy – A walk
through the town (2008).

Pomegranates growing in
a local garden (2008).

Persimmons growing
in a local garden (2008).

Florence, Italy –
A city deli/butcher shop.

Pisa, Italy (2008).

Florence, Italy (2008).

Castellina in Chianti –
Vintage Wine Museum.

Castellina in Chianti Vineyard (2008).

The Villa Petrea pool
at sundown (2008).

1

STARTERS & SNACKS

ANTIPASTO

Growing up in an Italian family, I was always mesmerized by some of the things that the cooks in our family brought to the table. One of the things we had as a first course to every holiday meal was antipasto. I hesitate to call it an "antipasto salad," which I have heard it called on many occasions, because our version really stands apart from anything salad-like. There is no bed of lettuce. There is no tomato. It is just a medley of marinated delights, partnered with other mild and salty elements that, when paired with a good Italian bread, really do tantalize the taste buds.

Before reading any further, the reader must understand something. In our family, there are certain foods that take on attributes based on the personality of its maker. This antipasto is a perfect example of one those foods (See later, the "Great Struffoli War of the 20th Century"). My mother, grandmother, and aunts all made this same style of antipasto, but each put their own spin on it. This phenomenon has brought about somewhat of a subtle food challenge among the lady chefs in our family. Who makes it with provolone cheese; who makes it with mozzarella cheese; who makes it with anchovies; who doesn't like it with this; who likes it better with that; who uses this brand of peppers and who uses that brand. . . Blah, blah, blah. . . the list goes on. Having tried them all, I always knew I was eating the same thing, but I also knew there was something inherently different about each one. To me, they were all good in their own way.

For this appetizer, a good Italian bread is a must have. The quality of the bread has always been very important in our house. My father would travel for miles to get bread from a specific bakery. The best

Italian bread to dunk into the juices of an antipasto like this is one that is crusty on the outside, but light on the inside (not gooey). One thing I can guarantee, you will not find a recipe for baking bread within these pages. Living in northern New Jersey, we always had good Italian bakeries around and it was not necessary to make our own bread.

This antipasto is also terrific as a leftover. It seems the longer it sits, the better it tastes. Leftover antipasto is best stored in the refrigerator, in a plastic or glass covered container. Take it out about 10 minutes before you plan to eat it (to let the oil relax). We always ate leftover antipasto alongside a sandwich. Nothing helps a dry turkey sandwich go down easier at Thanksgiving time. If I remember correctly, I think one time I even added it directly into the sandwich (sort of like a rough version of a muffaletta, I suppose).

When making this antipasto, it is best to combine most of the ingredients together in a large work bowl. Then, turn the contents into a deep platter just before finishing with the rest of the ingredients. The recipe presented here is closest to, and most represents, my mother's version of antipasto. One thing to note, use a packaged mozzarella cheese from the dairy case and not the fresh, wet variety. When adding the cheese directly into the antipasto the packaged type will hold up much better when mixed in, and it will absorb the flavors without breaking down from the oil. If you prefer to use the fresh mozzarella instead, that's fine. I would suggest adding it just before serving, or slicing it onto its own serving plate and allowing each individual to spoon their antipasto on top, right at the dinner table.

ANTIPASTO

FOR MAIN MIX:

32 oz. jar of sweet vinegar peppers
(red and green mixed)

6 oz. can medium, pitted black olives

6 oz. jar small, pimento stuffed green olives

(2) 6.5 oz. jars marinated artichoke hearts
(reserve marinade)

8 oz. jar marinated mushrooms

1 medium onion, chopped semi-fine

2 tablespoons capers

Olive oil (as needed)

Fresh ground pepper, to taste

FOR FINISHING:

8 oz. package mozzarella cheese
(from dairy case, either whole milk or part skim)

Ham, thinly sliced from deli (about 10 slices),
or use prosciutto or salami +/- the ham

1 can rolled anchovies (optional)

Drain the vinegar peppers and remove the stems and seeds. Cut the peppers into about ½ inch slices. Add the sliced peppers to the bowl. Drain the black and green olives well, and add to the same bowl. Drain the mushrooms and add to the bowl. Remove the artichoke hearts from the jars and add to the bowl (reserving the marinade from the artichokes). Add the chopped onions, capers, and ground black pepper. Gently mix the entire contents of the bowl, adding some of the artichoke marinade and olive oil, just a little at a time (do not drench it). Cover and place the mixture into the refrigerator overnight.

The next day, remove the mixture from the refrigerator and stir. If it looks dry, add a little more olive oil and stir again. Remove the mozzarella from the package and cut into ½ inch cubes. Add the mozzarella cubes to the mixture and gently stir in. Turn this entire mixture into a deep platter and arrange the elements uniformly on the platter. Roll individual ham slices and cut crosswise into thirds. Arrange the small, rolled meats evenly over the top. If adding anchovies, nestle evenly into the mixture. Finish with some more fresh ground pepper. Using a large spoon, serve with crusty bread. Makes 6 servings.

STUFFED ARTICHOKES

One of the most weird and wonderful things I remember my mother preparing for us was stuffed artichokes. I remember always getting very excited when I walked in after school to smell them cooking. To this day, my favorite part is the heart, located at the base of the artichoke. What I love even more is the anticipation of arriving to the bottom. Plucking each leaf, one by one, stripping all the delicious stuffing and artichoke goodness off the base of the leaf using the lower teeth. At the point where you get down to the tender, inner leaves, you can actually eat the whole leaf. There is that one part, in the very center (the "choke"), that you need to avoid. These are the thorny, purplish, leaves just above the artichoke heart. These leaves, and spines, can be removed carefully with a spoon, unveiling the heart, which is the prize. The bigger the artichoke, the bigger the heart (and the thornier the spines). Add a little salt and you will find that the heart of the artichoke has a flavor and a texture that compares to nothing else you've ever tasted.

Stymie, of *The Little Rascals* fame, may have said, "It may have choked Artie, but it ain't gonna choke me!," but artichokes are interesting to eat. I remember, during my teen years, one of my neighborhood friends stayed for supper. This friend was not Italian and definitely a stranger to the artichoke. I'll never forget the look on his face when my mother served up this oddity. I don't think I recollect anyone whose eye bugged out more than that. I don't remember if he actually got up the nerve to try it, but I do remember the incident. My mother's chicken parmesan saved the meal for him. Her chicken parm made up for the artichoke, as far as he was concerned. When relaying this story to my brother Randy, and his wife Judie, she said that the same thing happened to her when she started dating my brother. Being Polish, she knew nothing about artichokes. Randy had to teach her how to eat one.

Even though I put stuffed artichokes in the "appetizer" section, we often ate them after the main meal. Since most restaurants classify this as an appetizer, I do the same. You can decide yourself if you want to serve them before or after the meal. If the artichoke is big enough, you can even have it as your meal. Years ago, I took Chris to a well known restaurant in Newark called Vesuvius. I saw stuffed artichoke as an appetizer and told him he had to try it. They were almost as big as the plate and we each ordered one. By the time the meal came, we were stuffed just like a couple of artichokes ourselves. Vesuvius, a great restaurant I remember from my youth, no longer exists.

I have seen artichokes prepared many different ways. I've seen them grilled, baked, braised, and broiled. Some quarter them before cooking. While visiting Italy, we had a version that was halved and included a long stem. It was dissected lengthwise through the heart and the stem, and lightly breaded. This was one of the best artichokes I ever had. A local restaurant once served them as an appetizer where the outer leaves were already plucked for you. They were steamed in some type of lemony broth and served with a small bowl of that same broth for leaf dipping.

These recipes are all good. However, our "family artichoke" (if you may) is the preparation that I am most familiar and fond of. Mom used a seasoned breadcrumb stuffing between the leaves and steamed them in a large, covered pot in a small amount of salted water. Cook time depends on the size of the artichoke, but a good test for doneness is when a center leaf comes out with little effort. If you've never had artichokes this way, be brave and give it a try!

STUFFED ARTICHOKES

4 medium artichokes

2 cups plain bread crumbs

2 tablespoons fresh parsley, chopped fine

2 teaspoons dry oregano

1 teaspoon garlic powder

1 teaspoon salt

1 teaspoon pepper

Olive oil – 1/3 cup (for stuffing);
2 tablespoons (for drizzling)

Fill a 5 quart pot with about 1 inch of water, cover, and bring to a slow boil. With a large serrated knife, "flat top" each artichoke about 1 inch from the top. With kitchen shears, trim the points off of the side petals, making them flat across the top. Remove the stems from the base of the artichokes, cutting flat across, allowing the flower portion to stand upright (if stems are long enough, retain them, as you can cook and eat these too).

Place the trimmed artichokes, top down, into the boiling water. Blanch for about 3 – 4 minutes (this will allow the petals to soften and make them easier to spread open when stuffing). Remove the blanched artichokes and set aside to cool. Turn off the heat under the pot, but retain the water in there.

In a large bowl, combine the bread crumbs, parsley, oregano, garlic powder, salt, and pepper. Add ⅓ cup of olive oil and mix into the mixture until it is just moist (crumbs should hold together when squeezed in the palm of your hand). Working inside the bowl, spread the petals open with your thumb and forefinger of one hand, while working the bread crumb mixture in between all of the petals with the other hand. Do this from the top and all the petals on the sides, as well. Continue this process until all of the stuffing is used up evenly among the 4 artichokes.

Turn the heat back up under the 1 inch of water. Put a little salt in and place the artichokes in the water, side by side, top up. It is okay to butt the artichokes up against each other to fit them. Drizzle olive oil over the top of each, cover, and simmer. If cooking the stems, just throw them right into the water. Keep the pot covered and let them steam. About half way though the cook time, use a small ladle to baste the top of each artichoke with some of the water, allowing the water to seep into the top of each, moistening the stuffing. You will know the artichokes are done when one of the thicker petals pulls free easily. Cook for at least 1 hour.

This can be made in advance. You can let them cool down right in the pot, or remove them to a serving plate and cool completely before eating. They are good cold, too. Eat by scraping the tender base of the petal with your bottom teeth, as they should be nicely covered with breading. When you get to the center, use a spoon to scrape the thorny "choke" from the top of the heart. When you get there, salt and eat the heart. Serve with a little side bowl for the leaf refuse.

Pictures represent a halved recipe.

Stand upright in shallow water. Cover and Steam.

Stuffed Artichokes.

STUFFED VINEGAR PEPPERS

If you recall, from my last recipe, I called stuffed artichokes a "weird and wonderful" food. Well, brace yourself. I actually have something here that is even weirder and more wonderful than artichokes. What other recipe pairs up vinegar peppers with grape jelly? Yes, you read that correctly. This recipe was handed down to us from Nana. How far back it goes before her, I do not know. I do remember Nana talking about "putting up" her own peppers and, as I would imagine, my great grandmother did this as well. This is probably why vinegar peppers are a key ingredient in many of our family recipes (e.g. *Antipasto, Pork Chops*, etc.).

Of course, you are not expected to put up your own peppers. Vinegar peppers can be purchased in jars from your local supermarket. They come in two flavors. . . hot and sweet. They also come in two colors. . . red and green, which has nothing to do with the heat of them, but more so to do with the ripeness. Most of these recipes call for the sweet version, but there are some recipes that benefit from a little kick and the hot versions are definitely an option. It depends on your taste.

This recipe is based on the principle of "sweet and sour." Grape jelly is used in the stuffing, as well as a topping. The pungent flavor of the vinegar pepper, along with the sweetness of the jelly, produces a unique flavor that is unmatched by anything else I have ever tasted. It is one of those odd food pairings that just works well together. The pignoli and walnuts provide a nice added crunch inside the stuffing. They are meant to be eaten cold, not hot, so make them well in advance of when you plan to serve them. Like the antipasto, they are best days later, right out of the refrigerator, alongside a sandwich or with a piece of good Italian bread.

My mother was really funny when it came to sweet and hot peppers. If they were supposed to be sweet and even had a speck of heat to them, she would freak out, "Ooh, ooh, these peppers are hot! They aren't supposed to be hot. I have a good mind to take them back!" Meanwhile, we are already sitting there eating them and she is talking about taking them back to the store. Now, it's not that she didn't like hot, because I vaguely remember her eating the *Hot Potato Salad* (A recipe found later in this book). I think it was just the surprise of them being hot when they were supposed to be sweet. With my mother, it was always a matter of principle.

Yes, she was a woman of principle, indeed. Did I ever tell you about the time my mother took back something to a dollar store? In Florida, she bought something at a dollar store and it broke. She actually brought it back (who does that?). The storekeeper would not give her the money back, so Mom demanded a credit slip. The lady, not accustomed to giving credit slips, had no such thing. Probably just to get rid of my mother, the lady wrote the name of the store and "$1.00" on a blank piece of paper. I found out about this when I was visiting Florida. I mentioned that I needed something from a dollar store and she handed me this paper, "Here, go here and use this. Make sure they honor it." I was like, "What the hell is this?" When she told me, I couldn't believe it.

Oh! Oh! And then there was the time that my mother met some neighbor ladies for lunch at a local eatery and they had to call in the police. My mother ordered a grilled cheese sandwich. What she got was two slices of toast with some American cheese (not melted) in between. When she called the waiter over and told him that she wanted "grilled cheese" and not a "cheese sandwich on toast," he refused to fix it. Well, she was not eating that and refused to pay. An argument ensued and the owner called the police. They showed up, lights flashing. Imagine. . . all this over a grilled cheese sandwich. Our tax dollars were definitely put to good use that day. I'm not sure if she actually ended up paying or not. This happened while I was in school. Just think how interesting our dinner conversation was that day. "So, anything interesting happen today, Mom?" That was my mother for you. Trust me. I can go on all day with stories like this.

Anyway, on Christmas Eve, we would always have these stuffed peppers just prior to our fish dinner. It is a very festive dish for Christmas because of the red and green colors of the peppers. Mom would make extra to give us to take home. In fact, my nephew Jonathan loved these peppers so much that he would actually eat them for breakfast on Christmas morning. This is a practice that I have never personally witnessed, mind you, but can be attested to by my sister-in-law, Judie. Incidentally, Judie, being of Polish descent, brought a little more of an eastern European influence into our holidays. Judie's mother, Jane, was a wonderful cook and an expert seamstress. Jane, in addition to making us clothes, introduced the Vendettis to wonderful dishes such as, "Kielbasa and Sauerkraut," "Galumpkis" (stuffed cabbage), and "Pierogi." We, on the other hand, introduced her and Judie to the Italian five-course meal.

For Judie, a pre-Vendetti holiday meal consisted of two courses, at most. It's no wonder why, at her first Christmas dinner with us, she was overwhelmed with the amount of food and number of courses we had. In talking with her recently, she recalls (in her own words), "We started with antipasto, then we had stuffed escarole soup, then we had a stuffed capon (with all the sides), then we had fruit and nuts, then finally the dessert." After eating all of that food, the entire family retreated to the living room. According to Judie, she just happened to mention how stuffed she was and my mother blurts out, in front of everyone, "So, Judie, how much do you weigh?" Judie was mortified, needless to say. Mom definitely had this way of expressing her inner thoughts, outwardly.

When my parents moved to Florida in 1997, it was difficult for my mother to travel back to New Jersey for the holidays. I insisted on learning this stuffed pepper recipe so we could continue the tradition of having them with our Christmas meal. And, yes, I do make extra and give them to Jon so he can carry out his Christmas breakfast tradition. Jon, this recipe is included in this book for you, because when I'm gone, and you want stuffed vinegar peppers at Christmas, you're it kiddo!

Italy meets Poland:
A circa mid-1980s Christmas Eve buffet (From front to back: Kielbasa and Sauerkraut, Meatballs, Lasagna, Baked Chicken, Glazed Ham, Stuffed Vinegar Peppers, Potato Salad).

Stuffed Vinegar Peppers.

STUFFED VINEGAR PEPPERS

Two 32 oz. jars of sweet vinegar peppers
(red and green mixed)

16 oz. can of plain bread crumbs

3 teaspoons garlic powder

½ cup chopped walnuts

3 tablespoons pignoli (pine nuts)

4 tablespoons fresh chopped parsley

10 oz. jar of grape jelly

1 teaspoon salt

¼ teaspoon black pepper

¾ to 1 cup of olive oil

Olive oil (for drizzle)

Preheat oven to 350 degrees.

Drain the vinegar peppers and remove the stems by cutting a circle around the base of the stem and creating a small, round opening at the top of the pepper. With your finger, remove the seeds, being careful to keep the rest of the pepper intact and not rip it open.

Add bread crumbs to a large bowl. Add parsley, garlic powder, walnuts, pignoli, salt, and pepper. Mix in well. Add just enough olive oil to moisten the bread crumb mixture. Start with ¾ cup and add an additional ¼ cup, if dry. (Do not drench with oil. Bread crumbs should just hold together when squeezed in the palm of your hand.) Add ¼ cup of the grape jelly to the bread crumb mixture and mix in well.

Use a non-stick baking pan. Pack the peppers, somewhat tightly, with the bread crumb mixture, one at a time. Make a little indentation in the stuffing at the top with your thumb to create a little well (this will be for the jelly later). Arrange each in the baking pan. Loosen up the grape jelly by mixing (so it is less jelled and easy to spoon). With a teaspoon, top each pepper with a little grape jelly, filling the little well just enough to completely cover the opening so no stuffing is exposed.

Drizzle a little olive oil over the top (important) and place in the oven for about 30 to 40 minutes, or until the jelly is nice and bubbly. Remove from the oven and cool before transferring to a serving platter or storage container. Chill completely before serving.

Two jars will yield about 24 to 30 peppers, depending on size.

Remove stem and seeds. Arrange in a baking pan. Mix the bread crumbs with spices and olive oil.

**Mix some of the grape jelly to the bread crumbs.
Stuff tightly and make a little well with the thumb.**

**Drizzle with a little oil and bake
until jelly is bubbly. Serve cold.**

EASTER SALAD

Here is an interesting salad. Interesting because of the combination of ingredients you do not see very often and how well all the different elements play nice together in one place. (Perhaps it should be nicknamed "diversity salad" and the world can learn a lesson from it.) You have the sweetness of the orange, which also adds some acidity. You have the black oil cured olives, which introduces saltiness and bitterness at the same time. The onion makes it savory and the black pepper adds a kick. Finally, all of this is tied together with some extra virgin olive oil.

According to my father, this recipe was handed down to Nana from her mother, Carmella (my great grandmother). He told me that his grandmother used to add dried, whole hot peppers to the mix. I could not imagine biting into one of those. However, I can imagine a small dash of crushed red pepper flakes in there, just enough to add another level of interest.

I remember Nana making this for us on Easter Sunday. We always had this as an appetizer in accompaniment to her *Pastiera Di Grano (Grain Pie)*, the recipe of which can be found following this one. Not only is this salad diverse in its ingredients, but it is colorful as well, which makes it a natural for serving on Easter. The orange of the orange, the purple of the red onion, and the deep color of the olives, go nicely next to the colored eggs. Of course, you can serve it anytime you like, not just Easter.

One thing is true: You are at the mercy of the oranges, which can make or break the success of this salad. If you get dry ones, naturally, it will not be so good. The oranges need to be nice, sweet, juicy, cold, and refreshing. Stick with seedless naval oranges, as they won't be as pithy (or pitty!). Enjoy!

EASTER SALAD
(ORANGE, OIL CURED OLIVE, AND ONION)

3 seedless naval oranges, chilled, peeled, and sectioned

½ medium red onion

½ cup of black oil cured olives, pits removed

¼ teaspoon of black pepper

1 tablespoon olive oil

Pinch of salt

OPTIONAL: ½ teaspoon crushed red pepper flakes

Cut the orange sections in half, crosswise and place in a bowl. Slice the red onion thin and then rough cut the slices. Add onions to the bowl. Add the pitted olives to the bowl (if the olives are not already pitted, remove the pits by making a slit in the olive and squeezing the pit out). Sprinkle on the black pepper (and crushed red pepper, if using). Add salt and olive oil and toss. Serve immediately. Can serve in the bowl (family style) or arrange individual portions on top of a lettuce leaf. Makes 4 servings.

Peel, section, and cut sections in half.

Slice red onion thinly.

Remove pits from the oil cured black olives.

Toss together with oil and seasonings.

PASTIERA DI GRANO (GRAIN PIE)

Easter was always interesting at our house. I remember my mother would drag us down to Levy Brothers' department store to sit on the Easter Bunny's lap (similarly to what we would do with Santa Claus). I was always mortified by this oversized "bunny." It scared the bejesus out of me. Once they even dressed ME as a bunny. One year, my parents actually bought us a live chick. We named him Rudy-Kazudy. I was very young, and all I remember is that Rudy-Kazudy lived in a cardboard box and pooped a lot. One day, soon after we got him, poor Rudy-Kazudy kicked the bucket. You cannot keep a chicken in a suburban home. I don't know what my mother was thinking.

Me as the Easter Bunny.

Randy with the Easter Bunny at Levy's ("It scared the bejesus out of me.")

Anyway, back to the recipe. This one is solely my grandmother Nana's, as she is the only one that ever made it for us, and only at Easter time. This is a recipe that my mother never attempted to make, nor have I ever had the benefit of witnessing its preparation. I only had the pleasure of consuming it. Nana's *Grain Pie* was not a pie, in the true sense, in that it was made in a pie dish. It is folded similar-

ly to a large turnover. I only had one living resource (my father) that I could ask about the exact contents of the filling. Luckily, he was able to locate the list of ingredients. We were not sure of the measurements, but having the list of ingredients was half the battle in recreating the recipe.

He said that the filling consisted of wheat grain, which has to be soaked overnight, eggs, ricotta cheese, and another ingredient I was unfamiliar with. . . *basket cheese.* The conversation:

> **Me:** Basket cheese! What the heck is basket cheese? Where do I get it?
>
> **Dad:** Basket cheese. . . yea, basket cheese! You buy it. It comes in a basket.
>
> **Me:** I have never seen this before. Do I buy it at a supermarket. . . where do I get it?
>
> **Dad:** Well, wherever they sell it. You have to find out.

I could see this conversation was going nowhere. Little did I know, this basket cheese was going to become a thorn in my side. As it turns out, I did some research and I found that it gets the name "basket cheese" because it is actually formed in a basket (go figure). Made from cow's milk, it is of Middle Eastern origin, but commonly used at Easter in Italian cooking as a binder for other ingredients. It began to make more sense to me. *Pastiera Di Grano* was something that we always ate as an appetizer at Easter dinner. As a matter of fact, I don't ever remember my grandmother making it for any occasion other than Easter. We ate it with our *Easter Salad*, the recipe that I included just prior. Interestingly, other recipes I have stumbled upon for this Easter tradition are sweet versions, whereas my grandmother made hers savory, with no sugar.

Basket cheese. . . I cleared up the "what" question, but I did not clear up the "where" [to buy] question. The local supermarket does not carry it. My sister-in-law Judie, who is a fantastic cook herself, said she knew where I could probably find it. However, I did not want to drive that far. I found basket cheese on a few gourmet websites, where it can be ordered and shipped (yeah!). Only problem is that it was out of stock on every site (boo!). I thought to myself, "This *basket cheese* thing is really starting to *piss me off!!*" Turns out, this is a seasonal item (according to one website, it is a "winter" cheese, not found easily during warmer months). I refused to be beaten down by a mere cheese! I know that nobody will make this if one key ingredient is so hard to find.

Having the need to move on, I shelved the basket cheese quest for a later time. When my father came to visit us from Florida over the Thanksgiving holiday, I took him up to north Jersey to place a blanket of holiday greens on my mother's grave. We just happened to be in the vicinity of where Judie told me I might be able to find basket cheese, so we took a ride over to that store. It is a large market that sells produce, meats, and dairy, but it carries mostly a large inventory of Italian specialty products. After closely perusing the entire dairy case, lo and behold, there it was. Sitting among its other relatives, pot cheese and mozzarella (I'm not sure, but I think I heard the sound of a divine chorus when I saw it). I'll be damned if it wasn't actually in a basket. Who knew? I was also able to ask the butcher there to cut me up some pork fat (which you will understand, once you read the recipe). By the day's end, I had the wheat grain a-soakin', for tomorrow we make *Pastiera Di Grano!*

Voila! Basket Cheese (at last)!

PASTIERA DI GRANO (GRAIN PIE)

CRUST:

2 cups all purpose flour

½ cup liquefied pork fat (rendered from pork fat)

2 eggs

1 teaspoon baking powder

½ teaspoon salt

Dash of black pepper

In a large bowl, mix flour, baking powder, salt, and pepper together. In a separate bowl, beat eggs well. Add the beaten eggs and the liquefied pork fat into the flour mixture until moistened and somewhat crumbly (you can add a little water to the dough if it seems too dry). On a floured surface, knead into dough, form a ball, wrap in plastic, and set aside to rest for about 15 minutes.

FILLING:

¼ lb. wheat grain,
soaked overnight and drained well

8 oz. of ricotta cheese

½ cup basket cheese

½ teaspoon salt

¼ teaspoon black pepper

2 eggs (separated into 2 whites and 1 yolk, together, and 2nd yolk reserved for brushing)

In a bowl, mix the ricotta, basket cheese, salt, pepper, 2 egg whites, and 1 egg yolk together well, but do not over work it. Fold the soaked wheat grain in evenly with the cheese mixture.

TO CONSTRUCT:

Preheat oven to 375 degrees.

On a floured surface, roll the dough out into an oval about 12 x 14 inches in size (should be on the thick side). Spread the filling out on one half of the oval, leaving a 1-inch border. Brush the border with some of the reserved egg yolk and fold over the crust, turnover style. Secure with the tines of a fork and trim the excess to create a nice clean edge (if you have any extra dough and filling, you can make another, tiny one).

Using a large spatula, transfer to a greased baking sheet pan and brush the entire surface with the remaining egg yolk. Bake it for 30 to 35 minutes, or until just golden in color. Cool completely and refrigerate. Take out of refrigerator and allow it to reach room temperature before serving (this is not meant to be served hot). Slice as you eat, cutting across into 1-inch slices. Refrigerate any leftovers.

Add the pork fat to a hot pan and render into a clear liquid.

Add beaten eggs and pork fat to the flour, salt, and pepper and knead into dough.

Wrap in plastic and allow the dough to rest. Meanwhile, mix all the filling ingredients.

Roll out on a floured surface. Spread filling at one end, leaving a 1-inch border.
Brush the border with egg and fold over the crust, turnover style. Secure with tines of a fork.

Trim the edges clean and transfer to a greased sheet pan.

Brush with egg yolk and bake until golden in color.

Pastiera Di Grano.

TARALLI

Taralli is what I like to describe as an Italian pretzel. There are two varieties of taralli. Just plain old, regular, taralli (soft) and "hard" taralli (What we always called "hard tack"). Allow me to explain the difference between the two . . .

The hard tack uses all purpose flour, and more of it, whereas the soft taralli uses self rising cake flour, and less of it. The hard tack calls for salt, yeast, and eggs. The soft taralli does not. The rest of the ingredients are basically the same for both. Aside from ingredient differences, the main difference is the cooking process. The hard tack is boiled before it is baked. The soft taralli is just baked directly. My favorite is the soft variety, but I actually like them both.

Being one that is more inclined to cooking regular meals, and not a baking guru, I had to find out what exactly "self-rising cake flour" was. I've only ever kept all purpose flour in my pantry. If you are an experienced baker and already know all about self-rising cake flour, I don't want to bore you, so now would be a good time to leave the room, pick up something else to read, or simply just skip one paragraph, while I tell the *not-so-well-seasoned* bakers about this *amazing* product.

Self-rising cake flour is all-purpose flour with salt and baking powder already in it. Supposedly, these elements are more evenly distributed within the flour, thus generating more height in the end result. Knowing this, if you have a recipe that calls for self-rising cake flour, and you only have all-purpose flour on hand, you will need to sift in the missing baking powder and the salt. Vice versa is true. If your recipe calls for all purpose flour, and also includes baking powder and salt in the ingredients list, using the self-rising flour, you will need to eliminate the baking powder and salt because they are already in there.

I'm amazed how writing can be so educational to the author, as it is informational to the reader. The fact of the matter being, you may have had the same reaction I did when I found out what self-rising cake flour was ("Oh!?"). I do suppose it is a pretty important detail that a cook needs to know, at that.

(Oh, by the way, you experienced bakers can come back to the conversation now.)

In a recent discussion with my father about taralli, he told me an interesting story about what taralli means to him. When he was 8 years old (around 1931) his grandmother (my great grandmother) would make fantastic hard taralli. She made them big, about 3 inches in diameter, boil them at home, put them in a basket covered with a cloth, and send my little 8-year-old father off to the neighborhood bread bakery to have them baked in the brick oven. Turns out, this was the infamous Paramount Bakery in Newark, NJ, where the baker/owner, at that time, was my father's-mother's-mother's-brother's-wife's-brother (I hope you got that because there is going to be a pop quiz later). Later, back at home, they enjoyed the hearth-baked taralli with a glass of wine.

My mother made good taralli, but the real taralli queens of the family were the grandmothers. During my own childhood, when visiting Grandpa and Grandma, there would always be freshly made taralli to munch on. When they visited us, taralli was a common "bring-along" food. They were also standard issue, along with Biscotti, in our college care packages. I like to eat them alone as a snack, but they can be used anywhere you would use a breadstick. They are very complimentary of Italian meats, cheeses, and wine. Try them at your next party for something a little different.

Dad (child, right) with his brother, Eddie, his Dad (Angelo), and his Mom (Angelina).

TARALLI (SOFT)

3 cups self-rising cake flour

¾ cup oil

1 teaspoon black pepper

2 teaspoons fennel seed

1 cup water

OPTIONAL: If you do not like fennel seed, try making them with garden herbs, like rosemary or dill.

Preheat oven to 350 degrees. Mix all ingredients together thoroughly into a dough. Roll a little dough in your hands and form into a long, thin strand (about 7" - 8" long). Form into a ring on an ungreased baking sheet. Vary the shapes of the rings for interest (do them sort of rustically, as they do not have to be perfect circles), overlapping and pinching the ends together, forming a closure.

Bake for 35 minutes, or until just golden brown. Do not burn or allow them to get too dark in color. Cool before eating. Makes 3 - 3 ½ dozen taralli.

Roll dough and form irregular rings.

Place on a baking sheet.

Taralli (soft).

TARALLI (HARD TACK)

3 cups all purpose flour

⅓ cup oil, any type
(use ¾ cup of oil if doubling the recipe)

½ teaspoon black pepper

1 tablespoon fennel seed

¾ teaspoons salt

⅔ cup of lukewarm water (use 1 ¼ cups
of lukewarm water if doubling the recipe)

½ teaspoon dry yeast

1 egg

Bring a large pot of water to a boil. Mix all ingredients above together thoroughly (including the ⅔ cup water) and knead into a dough. Roll a little dough in your hands or on a board. Form into perfect circles, no bigger than 2 inches in diameter, by pinching together to form an almost seamless closure. Preheat oven to 375 degrees. Lightly grease a large sheet pan. Boil the rings (do half at a time, as not to crowd them in the pot). When they float to the top, remove with a slotted spoon and arrange on the sheet pan. Bake them for 45 minutes or until they turn a golden brown. Cool thoroughly and enjoy with wine, beer, or a soft drink. Makes 2 ½ dozen hard taralli.

Knead ingredients into a dough.

Roll out a small piece.

Pinch ends together to form a circle.

Drop in boiling water and when they float, place on a baking sheet and bake 45 minutes.

Enjoy Taralli (Hard Tack).

2

SOUPS & STEWS

PASTA E FAGIOLI / PASTA E CECI

I am going to tell you about both *Pasta e Fagioli* and *Pasta e Ceci* at the same time because, even though they are different recipes, the basic concept is the same. Of course, both soups contain pasta as a key ingredient. However, the differences are that the "*e Fagioli*" version is made with cannellini beans and has a tomato base, and the "*e Ceci*" version is made with garbanzo beans (chick peas) and is bianco (White, with no tomato sauce). Growing up, both varieties of these soups were a staple in our house. They were a quick and inexpensive meal. To this day, I still enjoy these dishes and I think of home every time I do. They are great if you want a meal high in protein, but want to break up the monotony of eating meat, chicken, or fish. When other kids were eating Spaghetti-O's, I was eating "Pastafazool."

"Pasta e Fagioli" is the correct spelling for what laymen Italians have come to know as *"Pastafazool."* To be honest, I don't even know if "Pastafazool" is even a word, or has a proper spelling, as it is basically *Pasta e Fagioli* spoken with a dialect. I am just spelling it phonetically, as my ear has always heard it spoken. "Pastafazool" is a defining term for a symbol, if you will, for what we Italians have come to know as a very basic and inexpensive dish. We have used this incorrect term in our house for so long that the correct pronunciation did not come natural to me until much later in life.

This term, "Pastafazool," has now become very odd sounding to me. It actually is a very funny sounding word, when you think of it. It's even more funny when I remember my father and how he would always slip the term "Pastafazool" in when bickering with my mother, even though it had nothing to do with the topic at hand. ". . . Oh yeah?. . . you and your damn Pastafazool, too. . .!" Ah, life was grand. But, all kidding aside, there are times when I am out and about and I still hear people refer to this dish as "Pastafazool." I guess some old habits die hard.

Whenever I give out these recipes to people, they find it interesting that neither of the soups contain stock, of any sort, as its base. The flavor in these soups is derived directly from the use of the various other ingredients. What makes it soupy is the use of the pasta water, right after the pasta has been cooked. The water's flavor comes from the added salt and from the pasta itself. What gives the soups additional flavor is the garlic, celery, parsley, and the tomato sauce (in the case of *Pasta e Fagioli*). Another element that adds flavor is the juice from the cannellini or garbanzo beans, as the beans are not drained after opening the can. Instead, the entire content of the can is used.

Once you make this, it just might become one of your regular recipes. It is great in a pinch, as the contents are easy to keep in your pantry, and you can dress it up for guests. My mother always served *Pasta e Fagioli* to guests from a soup tureen, one that I still have. She served it in white, rimmed soup dishes. What was originally considered peasant food has now become something fancy, similar to what has happened with the biscotti cookie. You'll find that most fine Italian restaurants include *Pasta e Fagioli* on their menus. You will also find that our version is a little heartier, whereas the restaurant versions tend to be a bit more on the soupy side. With either the bean or the ceci versions, the longer leftovers are kept in the refrigerator, the heartier they get. Over time, the pasta absorbs the liquid and it gets thick, but that is what I always loved about this dish.

Pasta e Fagioli (shown here with small shells, white, & red beans).

Pasta e Ceci.

PASTA E FAGIOLI

(2) 15 oz. cans cannellini beans (white kidney beans) + juice

3 garlic cloves, minced (2 if they are bigger, or use more if you like it)

8 oz. can tomato sauce

½ cup chopped celery (or 1 stalk)

⅓ cup fresh chopped parsley, plus a few tablespoons set aside for garnish

¼ cup olive oil

1 cup dry pasta (ditalini, small shells, elbows, or plain old linguini broken up into 1-inch pieces)

Salt and pepper to taste

OPTIONAL:

Substitute one can of cannellini beans for one can of dark red kidney beans (one can of each)

The celery can be omitted

Fill a medium-size pot with water and add enough salt, as you would when making pasta. Bring to a boil and begin cooking the pasta. In another larger pot (approximately 5 quart), add olive oil so it coats the entire bottom and heat. Open the beans, but do not drain. Open the tomato sauce. When oil is hot, toss in the garlic and cook, BUT DO NOT BURN (watch it carefully). Also, add the celery now and sauté with the garlic, if using. Just as the garlic looks like it is about to turn color, pour in both cans of the beans, juice and all. Add the parsley. Add some salt and pepper and stir. Bring this mixture back to a boil, lower flame, and cover. Cook this for about 10 minutes. After the 10 minutes, pour in the whole can of tomato sauce, stir, and simmer for about another 10 minutes.

Meanwhile, check the pasta for doneness (should be very al dente, as it is going to continue to cook in the soup). Drain the pasta through a strainer into a heat-safe bowl or another pot, reserving ALL of the pasta water. Stir the pasta into the beans and sauce. Add just enough pasta water to make it a little soupy. Simmer with the pasta and pasta water for another 10 minutes. Shut off the gas and allow to rest before serving. Taste and add more salt and/or pepper, if needed.

If it looks like the liquid has absorbed, and you want it a little soupier, add a little more of the pasta water. Serve in individual bowls and sprinkle on some of the chopped fresh parsley as a garnish.

Serves 6 (if serving as a soup before a meal);
Serves 4 (if eating as a meal).

Cook pasta separately.

Sauté the garlic and celery.

Add the beans with the juice.

Stir in chopped parsley.

Add the tomato sauce.

Strain pasta, reserving the water.

Add strained pasta to the beans and gradually add some of the pasta water until desired soupiness.

PASTA E CECI

(2) 15 oz. cans garbanzo beans (chick peas) + juice

3 garlic cloves, minced (2 if they are bigger,
or use more if you like it)

1 cup chopped celery (or 2 stalks)

⅓ cup fresh chopped parsley,
plus a few tablespoons reserved for garnish

¼ cup olive oil

1 cup ditalini pasta

Salt and pepper to taste

OPTIONAL:

Substitute ditalini pasta with small shells, elbows,
or plain old linguini broken up into 1-inch pieces

Fill a medium-size pot with water and add a little salt, as you would when making pasta. Bring to a boil and begin cooking the pasta.

In another larger pot (approximately 5 quart), add olive oil so it coats the entire bottom and heat. Open the chick peas, but do not drain. When the oil is hot, sauté the celery with the garlic, watching carefully to make sure the garlic does not burn. Just as it looks like the garlic is about to turn color, pour in both cans of the chick peas, juice and all. Add some salt and pepper and stir. Bring this mixture back to a boil, lower flame, and cover. Cook this for about 15 minutes, stirring occasionally.

Meanwhile, check the pasta for doneness (should be very al dente, as it is going to cook the rest of the way in the soup). Drain the pasta through a strainer into a heat-safe bowl or another pot, reserving ALL of the pasta water. Stir the pasta into the chick peas. Add just enough pasta water to make it a little soupy. Add the parsley. Simmer with the pasta and pasta water for another 10 minutes. Shut off the gas and allow to rest before serving. Taste and add more salt and/or pepper, if needed.

If it looks like the liquid has absorbed, and you want it a little soupier, add a little more of the pasta water. Serve in individual bowls and sprinkle on some of the reserved fresh parsley as a garnish.

Serves 6 (if serving as a soup before a meal);
Serves 4 (if eating as your meal).

Sauté the garlic and celery.

Add the chick peas with juice.

Strain pasta, reserving the water.

Add strained pasta to the chick peas and gradually add some of the pasta water. Add parsley.

ESCAROLE AND BEANS

One level up from *Pasta e Fagioli*, on our family hierarchy of staple soups, is *Escarole and Beans*. One thing to note about this dish is that it really is not a soup, even though we used to eat it during that time of the meal where one would normally eat a soup course. And, as you will see in a later recipe, we also have an actual soup that contains escarole as one of the main ingredients (*Stuffed Escarole Soup*). Escarole and beans is mostly eaten with a fork, but it is served in a soup dish. I'm not even sure you would classify it as a stew, as stews are something that cook long and slow. It's more along the lines of a sauté. It can be used as an appetizer, a side dish, or even the main meal. In our family, we have used this for all these purposes.

Like the *Pasta e Fagioli*, the beans in this recipe are not drained and the entire contents of the can are used. The difference here is that there are no mass amounts of liquid added that will make it soupy. When explaining this dish to people, I like to explain it as kind of an Italian version of the southern dish "Collard Greens and Black Eyed Peas." Of course, escarole is a more tender green than the collard type and does not require spine/stem removal, nor does it have to be cooked as long.

For the last 9 years of my mother's life, she and my father lived in Florida. We used to travel from NJ and visit them at least twice a year. While there, we could always count on having *Escarole and Beans* at least once during the visit. No matter when we went, no matter what time we got off the plane, day or night, we'd arrive at the house and she'd say, "Are you hungry? I have *Escarole and Beans*." Granted, I do love this dish. However, I don't like it at 11:00 at night.

Not only is this dish tasty, it quite possibly possesses miracle healing properties. (**Note:** If there are any doctors reading this right now, you may want to sit up and take notice. There may be a great medical discovery looming in what I am about to tell you.) Now, I'm sure this is not medically proven, nor documented in any medical journals, nor have I ever personally tested this theory. My Uncle Tony

(Mom's brother) is diabetic. He swears that whenever his blood sugar spikes, all he has to do is eat a bowl of *Escarole and Beans* to make it come back under control. Hey, who am I to say, right? All I know is if any doctor takes this information, proves it is true, and obtains some sort of Nobel Peace Prize or goes down in medical history, please give some credit to my Uncle Tony, who made the amazing discovery. It's the least you can do.

When cooking with escarole, you have to make sure you wash the leaves thoroughly, as it can tend to be sandy. I usually separate the leaves from the head and soak them in a big pot of cold water, allowing the sand to drop to the bottom of the pot (similar to what is done with a leek). Then I transfer the washed leaves to a colander, dump the water, rinse the pot, and repeat that process once more for good measure (trust me, there is nothing worse than chewing on sand).

I think if you like greens that have been cooked, you will definitely enjoy this recipe. It's a good, healthy, economical dish. As with any Italian dish, you can kick up the volume with some crushed red pepper flakes, if that's your preference. Good Italian bread makes a great complement and is perfect for soaking up the juices. Mmmmmm. . . good!

Mom, Dad, and me in front of her new Florida kitchen (c. 1998).

ESCAROLE AND BEANS

3 large heads of escarole

2 cloves garlic, minced (can do whole or crushed if you just want flavor and don't like to eat)

1 can of cannellini beans (white kidney beans) + juice + ½ can of water

Olive oil

Salt and pepper to taste

OPTIONAL: Crushed red pepper flakes

Cut off the bottoms of the escarole heads and separate the leaves. In a large pot of cold water, soak the escarole leaves well and allow the sand/dirt to sink to the bottom of the pot. Rinse the leaves very well, as you don't want any sandy grit. Repeat, if necessary. Transfer the escarole leaves to a colander and wash the pot. Using the same pot, add enough water to fill the pot about ¼ of the way. Bring this to a boil. Add some salt to the water and add all the escarole to the pot. Cover and allow the boiling water to steam and cook the escarole down, stirring occasionally, until it is totally wilted.

Strain the wilted escarole and remove all the water from the pot. Dry out the pot and return it to the stove. Over a medium flame, add enough olive oil to coat the bottom of the pot. Heat the oil and add garlic. Cook the garlic, but DO NOT BURN!! (watch it carefully). Once it looks like the garlic is just about to turn brown, throw the wilted escarole back into the pot and sauté in the oil and garlic for about 5 minutes.

Open the can of beans, but do not drain. Pour the entire contents of the beans, juice and all, into the pot and carefully stir in the beans, being careful not to crush them. Take the bean can and fill it ½ of the way with water (swirling around to clean out the remaining juices) and add the water to the pot. Add salt and pepper to taste. Let this mixture simmer on a low flame for about 10 minutes.

Let stand about 15 minutes before serving. Serve in a soup bowl with crusty Italian bread (as a meal) or serve in a smaller side bowl (as a side dish).

Makes enough escarole and beans for about 4 soup-sized bowls.

Cut the bottom off and separate the leaves.

Place into a large pot with some boiling water.

Rinse in a pot of cold water and repeat, if necessary.

Add the strained escarole to the hot oil and garlic.

Boil down until the escarole is totally wilted.

Fry the escarole and add the beans, juice and all.

Escarole and Beans.

BASIC CHICKEN STOCK

I know that making chicken stock is not rocket science. Most people already know how to make stock. . . you throw a bunch of stuff in some water with a chicken and let it boil. There are a lot of recipes in this book that call for chicken stock and/or boiled chicken. I am including this recipe so that it is handy for anyone who wants to use the fresh stock and is not sure how to make it. You won't have to search out a recipe or directions elsewhere. It's all right here for you.

Point of fact, my mother never used canned stock (that I can remember). Perhaps she did in her later years, when it was just my mother and father alone. If so, I was not around to notice, but she did not use canned stock when I was living at home, anyway. I'm not as fussy as my mother, especially if I am using stock as part of another recipe. If I need just a little, I might even make some quickly using chicken bullion powder or cubes. I have even used canned stock as a base for different types of cream or puréed soups. However, I find it is true that when you are making an actual chicken soup dish, with the main ingredient being the broth itself (as you will see in the soup recipes that follow), the homemade stock is the best tasting.

I put on a pot of chicken stock earlier so I could measure out the ingredients for the recipe that follows. I am writing this as it is cooking. I have to tell you, right now, the house smells phenomenal. This aroma always brings me back to one of my pre-school days when, one afternoon, my mother and I made a call on my grandmother at her house in Montclair, NJ. Remembering as if it were yesterday, we entered the back stairway and I could smell something wonderful cooking. Sometimes, we'd pass the first floor tenant as she was coming out of her door. Mom and she would chat and she'd say to my mother, "Oh, he's so cute," and give me the customary *"coochie-coochie-coo,"* before we continued to the second floor, where my grandparents lived. The kitchen was the first room you encountered upon entering. It then became apparent where that wonderful aroma was coming from. I can still see my mother, the first thing she did before anything else, walking over to the stove, lifting the cover off of the pot of simmering stock, and picking up a wooden spoon to steal a taste. Good memories!

My grandparents owned this Montclair, NJ, multi-family house and lived on the 2nd floor. The property had vegetable and rose gardens that my grandfather impeccably kept.

Besides flavor, probably the best thing about using a homemade stock is you can control the ingredients that are going into it (thus, into you). Today's canned stocks, and even the bullions, contain an unbelievable amount of sodium. If I do use canned stocks, I always opt for the low sodium variety. If you are concerned that your homemade stock is too fatty, allow the stock to get cold and the fat will harden on the surface. You can remove all the fat, if you like, but be wary that you are also removing a lot of flavor, as well. I always meet it halfway and remove half of the surface fat, as a compromise between healthy and tasty.

If you have a turkey carcass available after your Thanksgiving dinner, you can make a nice stock with that, as well, and turkey stock is a very nice substitute for recipes that call for chicken stock. Nothing goes to waste in our house, so I always make stock with a leftover turkey carcass. However, because it is just a carcass, and not a whole bird, it produces a less flavorful broth. I usually give it a "boost" with some bullion, whereas the stock made with a whole chicken is flavored enough by the meat, skin, and gizzards. You can use any greens you want for your stock, even the pre-portioned soup greens mix sold in the produce section. The results will be parallel. I am providing a recipe that uses, what I feel is, a standard mix that creates a nice tasting broth with flavors that work well together.

One more thing I would like to mention (while I am on the subject of chicken soup). When my friend Ilene heard that I was writing this book, and including a chicken soup recipe, she asked if I would come over to show her how to make it. We set aside a Sunday in November and she hosted, along with her husband Scott, the first "Chicken Soup Party" (which just goes to show you that you can make a party out of anything). I have to say, we had a lovely time. She and I started the soup at about 1:30 in the afternoon. She invited other friends and we sipped cocktails and had appetizers all afternoon. At about 4:00, I strained the soup and Ilene made matzo balls. We reused the carrots, celery, and chicken that we made the soup with, and we all sat down to a Sunday dinner of matzo ball soup (which was a light and perfect meal after all those appetizers). I took some photos and I promised Ilene I would include them in my book. So, Ilene, here is your 15 minutes of fame. . . .

BASIC CHICKEN STOCK

4 quarts of water (16 cups)

1 whole chicken, about 4 - 4 ½ pounds (Using the neck and gizzards is optional)

4 large carrots, washed and ends trimmed off

3 stalks of celery, washed and cut crosswise into thirds, retaining leaves

2 onions, peeled and quartered

1 large handful fresh parsley

2 tablespoons salt

1 teaspoon pepper

½ teaspoon poultry seasoning

Friend Ilene, serving up Chicken Matzo Ball Soup at her "Chicken Soup Party."

Add water to a pot large enough so that the 4 quarts of water comes halfway up. Turn the heat up high under the water and add the salt, pepper, and poultry seasoning. Remove the chicken from its package and take the neck/gizzards out of the cavity. Rinse the chicken and place into the water. Remove the neck and the gizzards out of their package and add to the pot. Add the onion quarters, carrots, and celery. With the parsley leaves still on their stems, crumple the leaves in your palm (as if to crumple a piece of paper) to release the parsley aroma and place the greens into a pot. Stir this all together. Bring to a boil, cover, and cook over a medium-low heat for about 1 ½ to 2 hours. Stir about halfway through the cook time (chicken will begin to float as it is cooking through).

After the cooking cycle, shut off the heat and carefully remove the chicken, carrots, and celery from the pot and set aside. Allow the stock to substantially cool in the pot before the next step. (**Note:** Do not place hot pot in the refrigerator, as it will heat up the inside of the refrigerator and possibly spoil your other food.)

Place a strainer on top of another pot or a large bowl. Carefully pour the stock from the cooking pot through the strainer. If not using all of the stock right away, transfer the stock into plastic containers suitable for freezing. Repeat this process until the whole batch is strained and portioned out. Use a combination of large and small containers for convenience. Discard the strained sediment.

Cover the chicken and vegetables and refrigerate until used. Some quick applications: Use the boiled chicken to create a quick chicken salad. Use the broth, chicken, carrots, and celery to make a quick chicken soup, adding some pre-cooked pasta pearls, noodles, or rice. Use the chicken and the stock to make *Chicken Chow Mein* (see page 135).

Add the chicken and vegetables to the water.

Cook about 2 hours for a deep, golden stock.

Carefully remove the body of the chicken.

Remove other parts that become dislodged.

Remove the vegetables.

Strain off the debris and portion out to freeze.

ITALIAN CHICKEN VEGETABLE SOUP (WITH MEATBALLS)

Let's face it. Mothers like to feed their children food that is nutritious and economical. Kids, on the other hand, want food that tastes good and is fun to eat. My mother covered all the bases with this soup. Always made with her homemade stock (i.e., nutritious/economical), she would put in little meatballs (i.e., tastes good) and pastina or alphabets (i.e., fun) to make it kid-friendly for us. I remember learning how to spell from eating a bowl of my mother's chicken alphabet soup. I suppose, nowadays, if the soup doesn't come with a *spellchecker*, the kids wouldn't be interested.

Seeing as kids grow up into adults (sometimes), she made a "grown up" version of this soup, which I present to you here. This soup, made with stock that is created from the recipe in this book, tastes so fresh and good. The addition of meatballs, pasta pearls, and fresh parsley garnish gives the plain old chicken stock a nice Italian twist. I remember having this soup as a starter to many a family meal. It was always served with parmesan cheese at the table, for those so inclined to sprinkle some on top. The little shavings of parmesan cheese melted together in the hot soup takes it to a whole new level.

This recipe is just one of my many favorite ways to enjoy the homemade stock. My second favorite is with white rice and chicken pieces. There were so many ways my mother prepared soup, and she made it good, and she made it often, at our house. As for my father, well, he was not such a fan of the chicken soup. Of course, he liked the *Stuffed Escarole Soup*, but basically the chicken soup scene wasn't where it was at for him. I can remember many a dirty look and a belch coming from that end of the table. I believe the phrase *"damn hospital food"* also comes to mind. He definitely likes his food with a little kick, and my mother liked her food bland (the proverbial *"Jack Sprat ate no fat, his*

Dad, in his younger days, shown here with his "not chicken soup, again" face.

wife would eat no lean. . ."). Of course, later in life, she credited her chicken soup, and other healthy cooking, for keeping him alive.

I can remember, on occasion, having this exact soup at a large family gathering around our dining room table. It brings to mind my Uncle Mike (who was the husband of Mary, my mother's sister) and how he ate his soup. Soup that had anything in the broth that was chunky or coarse, he would always eat using a fork. He would take a forkful of these soup "solids" and pull some up out of the broth, allowing the liquid to run off through the tines of the fork. Then he would later eat the liquid part using the spoon. As a small child, I was amused and fascinated by this. . . "Uncle Mike, you're not supposed to eat soup with a fork. You're supposed to use a spoon," I would say. He would then begin reasoning with a small child, justifying why it made more sense to eat the soup with a fork. Even as a child, I wasn't buying it. You use a spoon to eat a little soup and solid together. At the very least, you should eat all the broth first, so you have that nice pasta and meatballs left over to eat by themselves. Now THAT is the way a kid should eat this soup! Uncle Mike has recently passed on and he is dearly missed.

Later in my life, I discovered that Campbell's started somewhat of a public debate about the "Uncle Mike approach" to eating soup, as brought to light by their Chunky Soup commercials: "Soup so chunky you can eat it with a fork . . ." With my *Italian Chicken Vegetable Soup (with Meatballs),* you can eat it any way you like. However, I still stand behind Campbell's other side of the argument, ". . . but use a spoon. You'll want to get every drop."

Uncle Mike (1980s).

Italian Chicken Vegetable Soup (with Meatballs).

ITALIAN CHICKEN VEGETABLE SOUP (WITH MEATBALLS)

TINY MEATBALLS:

(½ of the Basic Meatball Recipe, made tiny, eliminating the parsley, and no browning):

- ½ lb. of ground beef/pork/veal blend (sually sold as "meatloaf mix")
- ½ teaspoon of garlic powder
- 1 tablespoons grated parmesan cheese
- 1 egg
- ¼ teaspoon salt
- Dash of pepper
- ¼ cup plain bread crumbs

Combine all the above ingredients. Using a level teaspoon of meat, roll into little meatballs no bigger than ¾ of an inch. Do this until all the meat is rolled into meatballs and set aside.

SOUP:

- 4 cups of chicken stock, as prepared in the Basic Chicken Stock recipe (or pre-packaged/canned)
- 1 large carrot, diced
- 1 large stalk of celery, sliced ½ inch crosswise
- ½ cup fresh parsley leaves, chopped coarsely
- ½ cup peas (either canned or frozen/thawed)
- ½ cup kernel corn (either canned or frozen/thawed)
- ¼ cup (dry) acini pepe (pearl pasta), cooked and drained
- Parmesan cheese (served separately as an additional garnish)

In a 5-quart pot, simmer the carrots and the celery in the chicken stock. Meanwhile, cook the pearl pasta in a separate pot until cooked. When the carrots are cooked, raise the heat to bring the broth to a rolling boil and drop the tiny meatballs into the boiling broth (if there is a little foamy residue that floats on the top from the meat, skim off using a small strainer or a slotted spoon).

When the meatballs float to the top, they are cooked (this should happen fairly quickly). Stir in the peas, corn, cooked pearl pasta, and chopped parsley. Stir around, cover, and shut off the heat.

Allow the soup to rest for about 5 minutes before serving. Sprinkle on a little parmesan cheese as an individual garnish, if desired. Makes 4 servings.

All the ingredients.

Mix the Basic Meatball recipe and make into tiny meatballs.

Cook pasta separately.

Add raw meatballs.

Cook them in the boiling soup.

Meatballs float when cooked.

Add the strained, cooked pasta.

STUFFED ESCAROLE SOUP

This is another wonderful soup that Nana handed down to us. It is one of many recipes in this book that I would deem a "family classic." Other than coming from my father's side of the family, I'm not sure of the true origins of this particular recipe, or how far back it goes past Nana. I just know one thing. . . it's good!

We would mostly eat this soup during a holiday meal, usually on Easter and/or Christmas, just after the antipasto course, but prior to the main course. Because we saved it for special occasions, it was usually served in a nice rimmed soup bowl, making it what I would call "rustic elegance." The soup is reminiscent of a basic Italian wedding soup, with the broth, greens, and meat, but it does not contain pasta pearls (or any type of pasta, for that matter), nor does it contain the little tiny meatballs. Using chicken stock as the base, when all is said and done, it is exactly what the title implies. . . escarole, which is stuffed with meat concoction, in a soup. This meat "concoction," and its contents, will be unveiled in the recipe. But first I'd like to make some comments about this dish.

Every time I serve this soup to people for the first time, they are not only in awe of the flavor, but also the concept. Nowhere else have I ever seen soup done like this. Not in any recipe book, not at any restaurant, nowhere, no how. My grandmother Nana and her foremothers, if you will, were culinary geniuses in that they were so innovative in the kitchen. They never used their innovations for financial gain. They did it for their own satisfaction and for enjoyment by their families. If you decide to make this soup, you will then understand my motivation and the premise of this book. . . to share these unique recipes with others before they are lost forever.

Especially on Easter, my mother would make a sweet bread to eat with this soup, called ruzzelle (pronounced roots-sel). To make it, she basically used dough that was similar to the biscotti dough. A funny thing, you have to understand that she made these in small loaves that were shaped into four, little round sections. Because the dough was soft, it would form a peak. When they came out of the oven, they resembled the upper portion of the female anatomy. Without getting too graphic about the "peaks," it will suffice to say that we would always tease my mother by calling her the "Erotic Baker." Not a year would go by where someone would forget to mention this oddity and we would always get a good laugh out of it. Yes, traditions do hold true, no matter what shape or form they come in.

Ruzzelle (Easter 2010).

Mom and "Ruzzelle" (c. 1980s).

The way this dish is really meant to be made is that the escarole leaves are to be wilted first, rolled around the raw meat filling, and then each one tied (thus the name *Stuffed Escarole Soup*). These stuffed "bundles" should then be plopped into the soup to cook. Each person is served one escarole/meat bundle in broth. Nana always went the whole route. . . wilt, stuff, tie, plop! On the other hand, my mother never resisted the urge for a good shortcut and would skip the "stuff" and "tie" steps completely. She just added the escarole and the meat separately to the soup (she would form the filling mixture into an oblong shaped meatball, reminiscent of the stuffed version). I usually don't like shortcutting traditional recipes, but I hate to admit it. Being a busy guy living in the 21st century, I think I need to side with Mom and go with the shortcut on this one. With the tied method, the escarole always falls away into the soup anyway after it is untied. Done either way, I think you will find this soup to be very special and delicious.

STUFFED ESCAROLE SOUP

3 medium heads escarole

3 quarts of chicken stock (home made or canned)

MEAT FILLING:

1 ½ lbs. ground beef + ½ lb. of ground pork
(or use a 2 pounds of all ground beef, if desired)

2 eggs

2 cloves garlic, minced fine

½ cup plain bread crumbs

¼ cup grated parmesan cheese

¼ cup pignoli nuts

8 slices of prosciutto, coarsely chopped

4 ounces mozzarella cheese, cubed small (use the mozzarella from the dairy case, not the deli fresh)

½ teaspoon salt

½ teaspoon black pepper

Fill a large pot with cold water. Separate the leaves of the escarole and wash well by soaking in the cold water. Repeat if really sandy. Drain the washed escarole in a colander. Dump the dirty water, rinse the pot, and fill about ¼ the way up with water. Salt the water, bring to a boil, and add the escarole. Cover, wilt down, and strain when done.

Return the pot to the stove and add the chicken stock. While heating, mix all of the meat-filling ingredients together well. Form into an oblong shaped meatball, pushing any mozzarella cubes into the center the best you can (some will melt out when cooked, but that is okay). When the stock is at a rapid boil, drop the meat into the stock one at a time. Follow by adding back the wilted escarole and cook at medium to high heat for about 20 minutes. The meat will begin to float to the top as it is cooked. Shut off and allow it to rest for a long time. Reheat, if necessary, just prior to serving. Serve hot. Each serving gets one meatball, stock, and some escarole. It is better (and easier) to prepare each serving from the kitchen and serve individually, instead of family style.

Note: This recipe makes an amount large enough to serve 12 people in a soup course. You may want to halve the recipe if not cooking for that many people. It also freezes well for future meals. It is better to make this hours before you plan to serve it, as the flavors have a chance to meld together.

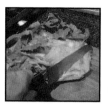 

Separate leaves and wash well by soaking in cold water Wilt the escarole in salted, boiling water.

Cut the prosciutto and mozzarella. Blend in with the meat mixture. Form into large, oblong meatballs and drop into rapid boiling chicken stock.

Add the wilted escarole and stir all in together. Bring back to rapid boil. Meat will float when done.

Stuffed Escarole Soup.

ITALIAN-STYLE BEEF STEW

Here is another *"just throw everything into a pot, bread dunking"* favorite of mine. . . beef stew, in which my mother put an Italian twist on the great American classic. Everyone knows beef stew as a hearty dish of beef surrounded by potatoes and vegetables, all swimming in rich, brown gravy. Basically, it's a whole balanced meal in a bowl. My mother's stew was made the same way, but the gravy is slightly reddened with tomato, with hints of green bell pepper and garlic flavor that make it unmistakably Italian. Of course, the recipe can be simply modified to produce a traditional brown stew, if you like.

Whether made red or brown, there are a few things that makes this stew special for me, the main thing being the potatoes, which are cut big. I love those especially big, chunky potatoes. They are my favorite part. When this stew is eaten the first day, all the vegetables are big and chunky like that. However, something happens overnight when you store away the leftovers. On the next day, you will find that the potatoes have broken down in size, and the gravy thickened by the additional starch. What you have is a wonderful, chunky style soup for lunch the next day.

Right out of college, when I was still living at home, I remember eating this stew for dinner, and my mother packing up some for me in a microwavable container to take to work the next day. She would include a couple of pieces of Italian bread for dunking. My-coworkers would be sitting around the break room eating their dry ham and cheese sandwiches, *Lean Cuisines,* or expensive take-out orders. Eventually, the smell would waft over to them and

they would look up from their newspaper or magazine and say, "Bob, what are you eating over there that smells so good?" As a matter of fact, now that I think of it, I found them saying that about most of the things I would bring in for lunch.

A few years later, I moved out on my own and I did not have the luxury of Mom packing me a lunch anymore. Like all 20-somethings, I was lazy in doing that stuff for myself, plus I had something even way cooler than my mother packing my lunchbox. I was now working for large companies, with gourmet cafeterias, and that is where it was at for me. On many an occasion, I would go out to lunch with my work buddies. You see, it was the prosperous 1980s, the Reagan era, and I was fast becoming a "YUP-pie" (Young Upwardly [mobile] Professional). I did not "brown bag" it anymore. I was making the best money I had ever made in my life, and I intended to spend some of it.

Now, for anyone that has not lived through that era, or is too young to remember, I can only explain it as a time in which you would sell out your own grandmother to move up the ladder and make a buck (ah, the good times). Surely, you know I jest. I would not have sold my grandmother for a BILLION dollars! However, I don't kid you when I say that it was a time when you could have been optimistic about your future and making your dreams a reality. In that regard, it was a very good time and one I do not think we will see again for a long, long time.

Well, those days are over now. I came back down to earth long before the economy went south, and I have always been happy living a simpler life, doing what I love, cooking my favorite foods (and writing about them), eating more meals at home, and making my own lunch. If you are feeling that the world has gotten way too complicated, have a bowl of good old fashioned, homemade beef stew to bring the whole thing back into perspective. Try this dish on a cold, dreary day, when you need some comfort food. This stew will just throw out its arms and hug you to pieces. Try it and you will understand what I am saying.

Italian-style Beef Stew.

ITALIAN STYLE BEEF STEW

1 to 1 ½ pounds lean beef chuck, cubed for stew

4 potatoes, peeled and cut into eighths

1 onion, cut into eighths

15 oz. can of peas, drained

3 large carrots cut into ¾-inch pieces, crosswise

½ lb. fresh green beans,
tips trimmed off and cut in half crosswise

½ green bell pepper
(seeded and left whole, just for flavor)

15 oz. can of beef broth

1 garlic clove crushed

8 oz. can of tomato sauce

Salt and pepper to taste

1 tablespoon olive oil

2 tablespoons of flour,
whisked with ½ cup of water (for thickening)

OPTIONAL: Leave out the tomato sauce and green pepper, and add 1 can of drained kernel corn, for a traditional American style brown stew.

If your beef is already purchased cubed, cut some of the larger pieces in half (against the grain) so that they are about 1-inch cubes. Be sure to remove any fat or gristle. Dry them and sprinkle with some salt and pepper.

Heat olive oil in a large pot. Sear the cubed meat in the oil until all sides are browned (about 5 minutes). Add the onion slices and the crushed garlic clove to the pot and cook with the meat cubes until the onion starts to wilt (about another 5 minutes).

In the pot, add the cut carrots, green beans, potatoes, and green pepper (do not add peas yet). Add the can of beef broth and fill the rest of the pot with warm water (about 3 – 4 cups) so that the liquids just come to the top of the vegetable pile. Stir in the tomato sauce. Cover the pot over medium/high heat until it comes to a bubbling boil. Then reduce the heat to medium/low and simmer with the cover tilted for about 30 minutes.

Whisk the flour/water together in a separate bowl until smooth. When the potatoes are cooked, add the flour mixture to the pot along with the peas (and kernel corn, if using). Stir in with the rest of the stew, and cook for about another 10 minutes. Turn off the heat and allow the stew to rest for about 15 minutes before serving. Serve with bread for dunking in the gravy.

Makes 6 to 8 servings of stew.

Trim fat from beef and cut the beans. Brown meat with the onions. Add all vegetables, except peas.

Add the can of tomato sauce and water, cover, & cook until the potatoes are done.

MIXED VEGETABLE STEW (GIAMBOTTO)

My grandfather (Carmine, my mother's father) was a landscape gardener, by trade. Every summer, he grew an immense vegetable garden in his back yard. So, it only stands to reason that Grandma (His wife, Victoria) would have many methods for cooking all types of vegetables that were harvested from this bountiful source. One of those methods used was stewing. My mother continued this tradition of stewing, where she created tasty vegetable medleys in a pot of liquid.

There is a word in Italian that was used for vegetables cooked in this fashion: *Giambotto* (which I always heard pronounced as "jam-bawt"). Inquisitive at its true meaning, I looked in an Italian-English dictionary, but I found no such word. I was dissatisfied with this, as there had to be some Italian word out there that is the origin of *Giambotto*. I'm sure this word did not appear from just anywhere. Baffled, I called my key technical resource (i.e., my father) to ask about this. He said, with utmost certainty, that the term meant *"mixture,"* as in a *"mixture of vegetables in a stew."* Now, mixture is one word I hadn't tried, and it made sense. I hung up and plugged *"mixture"* into the Italian-English dictionary. To my dismay, it still did not come up with an Italian word that resembled the word *Giambotto* in any way. It finally occurred to me that it may not even be a proper Italian term, as my mother's Italian was an extreme dialect picked up from her Italian-born parents, and I should just move on, take my father's word for it, and just continue writing. Turns out, I was right. I conferred with a friend who is of Italian descent and she verified that *Giambotto* is, in fact, dialect for "mixture" (ah! I feel better now).

Mixed Vegetable Stew can be made with any combination of vegetables using the same base ingredients of olive oil, onion, tomato sauce, basil, salt, pepper, and water. Two of my mother's favorite versions of vegetable stew were *Stewed Zucchini* and *Stewed String Beans with Potatoes* (both included in this book). It is worth noting that you are not limited to these versions and can add any additional vegetables of your choice. We would always eat *Giambotto* as a side dish to a main meal, but I don't see any reason why one couldn't eat a large bowl of this as a vegetarian main dish, especially when potatoes are included to add bulk.

Now, referring back to my introduction and the concept of *"your taste buds don't expire,"* here is a perfect example of what I meant by that. When I first got the instructions for making this, a number of years back, my mother told me to put some green pepper in for some flavor. I like the taste of green pepper. However, sometimes it gives me *acida* (a-chee-da), which is a common Italian term used for "acid reflux," or basically, it just plain old *"repeats."* Since it is not a primary ingredient, I decided it would not hurt to leave out the green pepper. . . Bad decision! I remember it tasting okay, but it just did not taste like my mother's. I came to the conclusion that the missing green pepper was the reason, and I was correct. My taste buds told me that it needs the green pepper just to *make it taste right.* I now add the green pepper and we persevere. Moral of the story: "Flavor trumps all, and antacids are cheap."

These stews taste best when made a couple of hours in advance of serving them. The longer it rests after cooking, the better it tastes. At the very least, don't serve it too hot. I love it the next day, after it has done some time in the refrigerator. You can even blend the cold *Giambotto* into a refreshing gazpacho-like soup (that's my own idea).

Zucchini Giambotto.

ZUCCHINI GIAMBOTTO

3 large zucchini, sliced crosswise
into rounds no less than ½-inch wide

1 large onion, cut into quarters and
then sliced thin into quarter-rounds

⅓ cup olive oil

8 oz. can of tomato sauce

½ green bell pepper —
cut further into 2 halves (2 quarter pieces)

4 leaves of fresh basil, chopped coarsely
(or ½ teaspoon of dried basil)

1 teaspoon salt

½ teaspoon pepper

½ teaspoon garlic powder

Step 1: In a large pot with a cover, sauté the onion until clear. Add the whole can of tomato sauce, salt, pepper, garlic powder, basil, and green pepper slices.

Step 2: Add all of the zucchini slices to the pot.

Step 3: Add the can of tomato sauce and enough water to just cover the top of the vegetables. Stir.

Step 4: Bring to a boil, tilted cover, reduce heat to low and simmer until cooked. When the zucchini is cooked well, it is done.

Step 5: Cool down before serving (serve hot, but not boiling hot).

Cut Zucchini thick, crosswise.

Sauté the onion.

Add other ingredients, plus water.

POTATOES AND STRING BEANS GIAMBOTTO

Same ingredients as the Zucchini Giambotto, but replace the sliced zucchini with:

1 lb. of fresh green beans,
tips trimmed, and cut in half crosswise

4 medium potatoes, peeled and cut into quarters

Step 1: Same as Step 1 on left, as written.

Step 2: Add the cut potatoes and the green beans to the pot.

Steps 3 through 5: Same as on left, as written. When potatoes are cooked through, it is done.

Cut the potatoes and beans. Sauté the onions.
Throw in potatoes, beans, tomato sauce,
and water and cook until the potatoes are done.

Potatoes and String Beans Giambotto.

LENTILS AND RICE

In our house, lentils were usually prepared one of two ways: The first way was as a soup, made by boiling the lentils in salted water with garlic, onion, and other chopped vegetables (a method that most people are familiar with). The second way was by cooking them in a tomato base, then finishing the soup by mixing in cooked white rice. It is this second recipe that I am showing you here. One would never think of lentils as "comfort food," but this preparation definitely qualifies it as such.

Lentils and Rice is similar to *Pasta e Fagioli,* in that it starts out somewhat soupy, but thickens as it absorbs the liquid. It is in this "thickened" state that I love it the best. By the second day, out of the refrigerator, it is sometimes thick enough to serve as a side dish, right on the plate next to the main course, without it running into the other food. It complements any meat, poultry, or fish. At our house, we usually ate it out of a soup bowl as a first course, especially when it preceded a lighter meal. Sometimes, we just ate it alone as the meal.

As a meal, all by itself, this dish is a good source of protein and fiber, for those interested in that sort of thing. Looking at a package of lentils, they have 8g fiber and 9g protein, along with only 0g fat, 0g cholesterol, 0g sugar, and 5mg sodium. It makes for only 70 calories in a ¼ cup (dry) serving, with 0 calories from fat. Heck, even if you eat twice (or thrice) this amount, that is one low calorie meal that packs a healthy punch. The little bit of added rice provides just enough starch and carbohydrates to allow you to get up from the table satisfied.

Speaking of nutrition, I finally discovered the secret to keeping weight off, for good. . . *by eating. . . and eating a lot!* (Seriously.) I dropped 20 pounds, and have kept it off. How? Never skip breakfast. Always eat a high fiber or high protein breakfast to get your metabolism started in the morning (just the digestion process alone burns calories). Then, keep the metabolism going by eating a mid-morning snack (something light, like a piece of fruit, a handful of almonds, a yogurt, or cheese on a wheat crisp).

Then, by the time lunch comes, you won't have to stuff yourself because you will not be ravenous. At lunch, again, eat something with protein and fiber and allow yourself a dessert (e.g., a tuna or turkey sandwich on whole wheat, spread with guacamole instead of mayo, eaten with some carrots or celery, and followed by a piece of dark chocolate). For a mid-afternoon snack, curb your dinner with another snack (something like plain popcorn, string cheese, or an apple). Finally, by dinnertime, you will be able to cut your usual portions down, but should still eat a square meal (a protein, starch, and a vegetable). I cheat sometimes, but when I do, I get back on track right away.

I bet you feel stuffed just reading all of that. It doesn't sound like a diet at all, does it? Additionally, throw in routine muscle toning to burn fat, as it takes more calories to maintain muscle than fat. (Yes, you can actually increase the number of calories you burn by just standing still!) This is just what works for me. I am really not a diet expert and this is not a diet book, by any means. It is just good information I picked up along the way.

If you need to know more about diet and lifestyle changes, there is a ton of information around on this subject. Earlier, I promised a book that would offer economical and nutritious home-cooked dishes and, as a matter of fact, *Lentils and Rice* is a perfect example of what I meant by that.

Lentils and Rice.

LENTILS AND RICE

32 oz. package of lentils

8 cups of water

8 oz. can of tomato sauce

1 tablespoon olive oil

3-4 garlic cloves (whole/smashed, if you want to remove; chopped fine, if you want to leave in)

2 teaspoons salt

¼ teaspoon pepper

2 cups cooked white rice (i.e., 1 cup dry, cooked separately according to package directions)

Place lentils into a strainer and move around with your finger to look for any irregular pieces, such as lentils dark in color or stone like (remove any of those). Rinse the lentils thoroughly. Set aside.

In a large pot with a cover (at least 5-quart size), cook the garlic pieces in the hot oil to infuse the flavor. When the garlic is just ready to turn brown, remove the garlic (or leave it in if you want additional garlic flavor cooked into the lentils*). Add the water, salt, and pepper to the pot. Stir in tomato sauce and the lentils.

Bring all of this to a boil. Reduce heat and tilt the cover on the pot, allowing some steam to escape. Simmer on medium/low heat, stirring occasionally, for about 45 minutes, or until the lentils are cooked and tender.

Meanwhile, cook the rice separately, per the cooking directions. Strain off any unabsorbed rice water.

When the lentils are cooked, shut off the heat and stir in the rice. Cover the pot completely and allow the *Lentils and Rice* to stand for at least 15 minutes before serving.

The number of servings may vary depending on whether you serve as a meal in a larger soup bowl, or as an appetizer/side in a smaller bowl. This recipe makes family-size quantity of lentils. It refrigerates and freezes well. (If you cut the recipe in half, it is okay to still use the whole can of tomato sauce. The results will not be that different.)

(* *Note:* If you decide to leave the garlic in to cook with the lentils, but want to remove it before serving, it is suggested that you remove the garlic BEFORE adding the rice, otherwise the garlic will be very difficult to locate.)

Add all the ingredients to the pot.

Lentils are tender in about 30 minutes.

Add cooked and drained rice.

Allow rice to sit in lentils for 15 minutes.

3

SAUCES AND SUCH

BASIC MARINARA SAUCE

In our household, you were always sure to find a can of tomato sauce and a box of linguini in our kitchen cupboard. With *marinara* sauce being such a staple in our house, we were never at a loss for something to eat. We always had the simple ingredients for this basic sauce on hand. It is not only used as a pasta sauce, but also serves as a quick sauce for chicken or eggplant parmesan. The canned sauce, by itself, is used in many recipes as a "reddener," as you have seen with *Lentils and Rice*, *Giambotto*, and will see with later recipes. We also religiously abided by what I will call our "general pasta rule." The rule is:

> *Meatless marinara sauce for pasta should never touch any pasta type other than linguini, AND, no grated parmesan allowed atop any marinara-sauced pasta. If you are making a meat sauce for pasta, any pasta type other than linguini should be used, and grated parmesan cheese is allowed.*

(Later, I will further explain meat sauce and discuss the topic, *"Is it sauce or is it gravy?"*) If you are going to use the marinara sauce for any other application, like a chicken or eggplant parm, add cheese to your hearts content (you see, the "cheese/no cheese" rule only seemed to apply when topping pasta). You are probably saying, "Who gives a flying batooty what I use cheese on." Well, you go right ahead and cheese up your marinara. If thunder rolls across the skies, all I can say is that, "I warned you."

Not only is *Basic Marinara Sauce* quick and easy to make, is also makes for a good disciplinary tool. One of my earliest childhood memories is a scene where my mother, father, brother, and I were sitting down at supper. I could not have been more than four at the time. This would have made my brother approximately nine and, as a typical nine year old, he was acting up at the table. I don't remember much else about that day other than we were eating linguini marinara and my father, repeatedly, telling my brother to stop his deplorable behavior. Finally, my father warned him to sit and eat his macaroni or he was "going to wear it." My father, mind you, was

never one to hit us kids, but my brother must have raised my father's ire to the boiling point that day. The next thing I know, my father took my brother's dish of macaroni and threw the entire contents in his face. Picture this: Marinara-laden linguini dripping from face to floor, my brother wailing, my mother screaming, and I (chin dropped and eyes wide) in total astonishment. It was great!! (tee-hee).

Of course, this is another recipe that is pre-loaded into my memory banks and no formal written recipe exists. I make it with my eyes closed. For the sake of the book, I measured out the ingredients for you. The measurements in the recipe that follows will accurately help you recreate a *Basic Marinara Sauce*.

Please note that I will be referring to this basic recipe for other recipes that follow. I think, once you make it a few times, you will be able to adjust the flavors to your own liking by increasing or decreasing various ingredients. What is nice about this sauce is that it is easily adaptable to other dishes. Add some onion and oregano and you can create a delicious pizza topping. Add seafood, and you have a nice red seafood sauce. Add vegetables, such as peas and mushrooms, and you have a nutritious vegetarian meal. Used on linguini, it can be paired with a salad for a main meal, or eaten as a side dish. Have fun with it.

Linguini Marinara.

BASIC MARINARA SAUCE

15 oz. can of tomato sauce

¼ cup olive oil

1 to 2 cloves of garlic (depending on size)

3 fresh basil leaves

¼ cup water

½ teaspoon salt

¼ teaspoon pepper

OPTIONAL : ½ green pepper, cut into 4 large slices

In a saucepan, heat the olive oil (open up the tomato sauce can to have it ready). Remove skin from the garlic clove(s) and crush to release the garlic flavor (you can also chop the garlic fine, if you want). Cook the garlic in the hot oil, but do not burn. When the garlic is just getting ready to brown, and being wary of splatter, add the tomato sauce and stir into the garlic-flavored oil. Add the water to the can and swirl around to gather any tomato sauce left behind on the sides and bottom of the can. Then, add the water to the pot from the can.

Coarsely chop the basil leaves and stir into the pot. Stir in salt and pepper. Add the green pepper slices (for flavor), if using. Cover, and when sauce is at a bubbling boil, slightly tilt the lid (this will allow steam to escape and help the sauce to thicken a bit) and lower the heat. Simmer on low heat for at least 20 minutes, stirring occasionally. Sauce will turn from a bright red to a darker red when cooked.

Serve over linguini-style pasta, or use as a sauce for other "parmesan" style dishes, such as chicken or eggplant. This recipe makes make enough sauce for about 1 pound of linguini.

Linguini Marinara.
(It may not look like anything special, but it smells wonderful when it is cooking!)

PIZZA SAUCE AND SICILIAN STYLE PIZZA

The *Basic Marinara Sauce* recipe is easily modified for other applications, where by changing up just a few of the ingredients you can create a quick pizza sauce. My mother made pizza, which we always called "tomato pie," on many occasions. However, the pizza recipe I attempt to recreate here is inspired by a Sicilian-style pizza that I remember eating as a young boy. The recipe I am trying to emulate is not my mother's tomato pie. My favorite pizza was made by her good friend, and our long-time neighbor, Angie. Growing up next door, Angie's children (Diane, Laure, and Larry) were my childhood friends. For her kids' birthday parties, Angie would always make her delicious pizza. It was for us kids, without a doubt, like "Forget the cake. . . more pizza please!"

To best describe it, Angie's pizza crust was on the thick side, but not gooey. The edges and bottom had a nice crispy crust. The sauce was light and somewhat chunky, with a spattering of clear onions, all topped with melted mozzarella cheese and cut into little squares. Even my mother admitted that she could not make pizza as good as this. Recently, I asked Angie about the secret to her pizza dough and she replied, "I buy it from the pizzeria." Well, then,. . . okay! Even though my vision of Angie in her kitchen, mixing and kneading dough, was just shattered to smithereens, that answer was good enough for me. Off I went to the neighborhood pizzeria, where four bucks got me a hunk of dough, enough for one pizza (one might say that it was a lot of "dough" for a little dough).

Laure and me (1963).

Angie with daughter Diane and "Puggy" (mid 1950s).

Laure, Larry, and Me (1965-ish).

Angie, Mom, Laure, Larry, Nana, & Dad (late 1960s).

I also love a New York City-influenced thin-crust pizza, however, the best thin-crust, old-world-style pizza I ever had was not in NYC. When I was in college, my dorm mates and I took a road trip to Boston, MA. I was told that I was about to eat, hands-down, the best pizza I ever had. Being a cocky New Jerseyite, I said, "No way, NYC pizza rules." We ventured into an area called Boston's Italian North End. I was shown the door into a tavern-like restaurant. There was a crowd eagerly awaiting their take-out orders, or to be seated. We waited a fair amount of time for a table. When the pizzas finally arrived, I must say, it did look quite good. When I tasted it, all I can think to myself was "Mmmmmm, oh my God!" When asked what I thought, I replied smugly, "Yeah, its okay" (fingers crossed). Of course, later, I admitted that it WAS the best pizza I had ever eaten. In that regard, the pizza was easier to swallow than my pride.

Folding pizza in a Boston Marketplace (1983).

This reminds me of another college story that involves pizza, oddly enough. One night, a few of us were in downtown Manchester, NH and went into a place for some pizza. The place was not crowded, except for a table of giggly school girls, a scattering of other patrons, and us. When our pizza arrived, we dove into it like a bunch of hungry vultures. My friends, who were all from the New England area, used their knives and forks to cut their pizza in a civilized manner. As for me, Mr. New Jersey, I instinctively picked up my slice and folded it. Just as I was getting ready to bite into it, all you could hear was one girl from the "giggly" table exclaiming, "Ewww! That guy folds his pizza!" Needless to say, I

froze for a moment, pizza hovering in front of my face. I dropped the pizza back onto my plate (unbitten), my friends were hysterical, her friends were hysterical, I was mortified, and her face was redder than her pizza. My friends got a lot of mileage out of that story. It actually was quite funny.

Sicilian Pizza (left) Thin Crust Pesto Pizza (right).

I often make thin-crust pizza at home using a pizza stone. I've been making my own dough, but truth be told, my crust has been hit or miss (sometimes crispy, sometimes chewy). The pizza crust with the purchased dough turns out nicer than any dough I've ever made. I think I am definitely going to use the "Angie Dough Method" and buy it, as the crust came out really good when I tested this recipe. I was impressed, but I should have known it would be successful, coming from the "master" herself.

As for Angie, the pizza lady, she is living in Florida near her daughters, Diane and Laure. Laure, who is only one year apart from me in age, stayed close to my mother over the years and visits my father now, keeping him busy since my mother's passing in 2006. She does not realize how grateful I am for this.

Mom, pictured with Laure & Angie on New Year's Eve in Florida (2005).

PIZZA SAUCE

28 oz. can crushed tomatoes

1 small onion

¼ cup olive oil

2 to 3 cloves of garlic (depending on size)

½ teaspoon salt (use 1 teaspoon if the tomatoes are salt free)

¼ teaspoon pepper

1 teaspoon of dry oregano

In a covered pot, heat the ¼ cup of olive oil. Remove skin from the garlic cloves and crush to release the garlic flavor (you can also chop the garlic fine, if you want). Chop the onion medium fine. Cook the onion in the hot oil until clear. Add the garlic and allow it to cook for a couple of minutes with the onion. Add the crushed tomatoes, oregano, salt, and pepper. Stir, bring to a boil, then cover and lower the heat. Simmer for at least 15 minutes, stirring occasionally. When done, allow the sauce to cool somewhat before applying it to the pizza dough. Sauce can be made well ahead of the pizza. Remove the garlic cloves before topping the pizza dough. Makes enough for two pizzas (leftover sauce can be frozen for later use).

SICILIAN STYLE PIZZA

1 *Pizza Sauce* recipe, prepared (on left)

1 tablespoon olive oil

Grated parmesan cheese

4 oz. of shredded mozzarella or shredded Italian Blend cheese

Pizza dough — purchased from the local pizzeria

Preheat oven to 400 degrees. Grease a 12 x 18 shallow baking pan with the olive oil. Flour a piece of waxed paper and roll the dough out flat and oblong to almost match the size of the pan. Turn the waxed paper over so the dough falls into the pan. Work the dough from the center into the sides and corners. Spoon the sauce evenly onto the dough, leaving about ½ inch of the dough exposed around the edges to make a crust. Brush the exposed edges with a little olive oil. Sprinkle evenly with some grated parmesan cheese (do not add the mozzarella cheese yet).

Bake for 10 minutes. Remove from the oven and sprinkle evenly with the shredded mozzarella cheese. Bake for another 10 minutes or until the cheese bubbles. Watch it carefully. If the cheese starts to brown, remove from the oven immediately, as you do not want it to burn. Cool in the pan for 5 minutes. Pizza should slide easily about the pan. With a pizza cutter on a large cutting board (or just using kitchen shears), cut equal size squares in the size of your choice. Cut larger squares for individual servings, or smaller for a party platter.

Sicilian Style Pizza.

Purchased pizza dough.

Roll to size of pan on a floured surface.

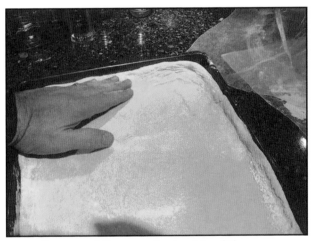

Form crust from center to side of the pan.

Spoon sauce on evenly.

Top with cheeses and bake as directed.

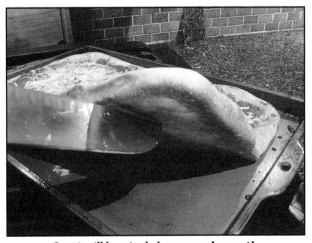

Crust will be nicely brown underneath.

MEAT SAUCE FOR PASTA
(WITH MEATBALLS AND OTHER MEAT ADDITIONS)

One of my fondest memories is of Sunday afternoons at home. We would always have Sunday dinner, a ritual that took place around 2:00 PM, and would almost always involve some type of pasta dressed with my mother's homemade gravy. Mid-afternoon seemed like the perfect time to eat a large meal, seeing as we would usually have a late breakfast on Sundays (I'm not going to lie and say we got up to go to church). It gave us the afternoon to fully digest. We would lounge around the rest of the day, receive visitors, or go visiting ourselves afterward. Our late day meal, supper so to speak, would be a sandwich or leftovers.

I remember, right after breakfast, my mother would make up a shopping list. I would ride up to Market Street on my Schwinn Varsity bicycle to get the bread and the cold cuts for later. Now, this was a very specific list and needed to be strictly adhered to. The rolls were always pre-ordered and waiting for pickup at the Allwood Bakery. The cold cuts needed to be sliced thin, but never from the end piece, and had to be purchased at Wayne's Deli because he had the best Virginia ham. The salads,

I rode my Schwinn Varsity everywhere, which included numerous trips to Market Street on Sundays.

however, had to be purchased up the street at Joe's Deli, as he made the best potato salad and coleslaw (which, incidentally, was the inspiration for my *Classic Coleslaw* recipe included in this book). When I finally maneuvered through that maze, I would walk into the house with the goods and could smell the gravy cooking on the stove. I performed this weekly routine from early childhood, right into my late teens.

I think one question that every Italian-American has come across in their lives. . . Is it "gravy" or is it "sauce?" Here is the rule, as I always understood it to be:

> *"Gravy" is tomato sauce made with various meats and used on most pastas like spaghetti, rigatoni, ziti, etc. It is also used on fresh pasta dishes like cavatelli, ravioli, manicotti, and lasagna.*
> *"Sauce" is meatless, as in marinara sauce, and is used on linguini and in other non-pasta dishes such as pizza, eggplant, and chicken parmesan.*

Since this "gravy vs. sauce" concept may be hard to grasp for some, I went ahead and just called it *Meat Sauce for Pasta*. Okay, that's settled.

Before I continue, you must understand one thing, if nothing else. My mother never used store-bought, jarred sauce in her entire life. She made it all from scratch. Of course, she used canned tomatoes and did not go as far as putting up her own (that would be ludicrous even by my mother's standards). But she did add her own meat. What type of meat are we talking about?. . . Meatballs, homemade of course, and sausage, for sure. Other meats would vary, depending on what looked good that week. Sometimes she would use a pork roast or beef eye round. Sometimes, she would use pork neck bones, spare ribs, or make braciole. She was very versatile in the meats that she used, but one thing to be certain about is that she did NOT use anything that involved any sort of ground up beef "sawdust," swimming in a sea of tomato. I got enough of that in my high school cafeteria. Just for the record, there are no onions used anywhere in this sauce.

You might notice that I include two recipes in this book for meatballs. One is a basic recipe using plain bread crumbs and is the one I have always used. The other is my attempt to recreate Nana's meatballs, which I have never seen or tasted anything like since her passing. My basic recipe is a good one, and great for making the tiny meatballs used for a few other recipes. However, since this is a book about reviving lost recipes, I only saw it fit to include an attempt at Nana's recipe. I'll explain a bit more about the magic of *Meatballs, Nana Style* later when you read about that recipe.

No doubt, making meat sauce from scratch can be an ordeal, especially for those that do not have the sauce-making gene. Yes, it can be a big deal, but it is worth it. If not only for the flavor of the sauce, but for the nice variety of meats accompanying your pasta meal. Since it is a time-consuming task, I usually make enough to freeze portions of sauce and meat for future meals. I use those plastic wonton soup or deli containers (the ones that everyone has floating around). I write on the lids using a wide-tip marker, "Sauce, 4 MB, 4 Sausage," or "Sauce only," or something like that.

To make the task go faster, I usually multi-task. I get the tomato base simmering first in a large, heavy pot. Then I mix the meat and form the meatballs while the sausage is browning. If making braciole, I make those first and have them ready to brown before starting anything else. Once the sausage is browned, I start to brown the braciole (or pork roast, if I am including that). I brown the meatballs last. Once everything is in the pot, I set the burner to simmer, tilt the lid, clean up a little, and then go do something else for about 2 to 3 hours.

The key to any good meat sauce is letting it simmer in the pot for a long time. This will totally exchange the flavors between the meats and the tomato and help thicken the sauce into rich tasting gravy.

Browning the meat prior to simmering also is necessary for adding flavor to the sauce and sealing flavor into the meat. I have seen people just throw meatballs into tomato sauce, raw, without browning. Don't do this, please. If you prefer not to fry, sear the meatballs in a hot oven before tossing them into the sauce. That pre-browning makes a world of difference in flavor.

Now that I have discussed the meats, I would like to discuss tomatoes you can use as the base for your sauce. It's not crucial, but using tomato paste (in addition to your tomato base) will act as a thickening agent and give the sauce the richness it needs. The main tomato base can be tomato puree, crushed tomato, or (sit down for this one), *tomato juice.* Yes, you read that correctly. . . tomato juice. I like using the tomato juice, best of all, because it makes gravy that is not acidy, as is the case with some of the other tomato choices.

My mother started using the tomato juice method after my Aunt Mary (her sister) introduced the idea. Where Aunt Mary got the idea from, I do not know, but I have been using the tomato juice method ever since I started making meat sauce on my own. It always gets raves from my pasta-eating guests. People that I have given this tip to over the years still say that they use *"that tomato juice recipe"* for their sauce. I know it sounds odd, but try this recipe once with the tomato juice and you can be the judge.

For those looking to shun store-bought sauce for the first time, and dive head first into making a pot of red gravy, I am going to present a recipe for meat sauce that is made with just meatballs and sausage only (for the ease of it). Afterward, I include alternative meat additions that can be included in the same way, such as pork roast. I also include recipes for the even more advanced meat components you can add, such as braciole and *Meatballs, Nana Style,* a recipe that I am still in the process of mastering for myself. So, for now, the *Basic Meatball Recipe* follows.

BASIC MEATBALL RECIPE

When it came to meatballs, my mother made very good ones So good, in fact, that my sister-in-law, Judie, told me that my mother's meatball always cured her headache. (Honestly, that is what she told me.) Whenever she had a headache, my mother's meatballs made her feel better. So now, we have two foods of my mother's that can be used for medicinal purposes: *Escarole and Beans* for lowering blood sugar, and meatballs for curing headaches. I can just hear the doctors now. . . *"Take two meatballs and call me in the morning."*

I call this my *Basic Meatball Recipe* because it is referred to in many other recipes in this book. It is made from a list of ingredients that my mother gave to me over the phone, many years ago, when I first moved out of the house and was an aspiring Italian gravy maker. I have been using it ever since. Although I get great results by just throwing the ingredients into a bowl haphazardly, I though it best to come up with measurements for you. Once you do this enough, then I think the "eyeballing" method of measurement will yield you the results you are looking for. As long as the flavors are there, and you use the right mix of meat, they will be good.

My mother and grandmother always browned their meatballs by frying them in a pan before adding them to the sauce. If you're not crazy about frying, place them on a sheet pan and sear them in the oven at a very high temperature (about 450 – 475 degrees).

Hint: Use this recipe when also making the little meatballs for *Lasagna Margherite* (page 88), *Risotto* (page 96), and *Italian Chicken Vegetable Soup* (page 53).

BASIC MEATBALL RECIPE

1 lb. (+ or -) of ground beef/pork/veal blend (usually sold as meatloaf mix)

1 clove garlic, chopped fine
— or —
1 teaspoon of garlic powder

3 tablespoons fresh, finely chopped parsley

2 tablespoons grated parmesan cheese

1 egg

½ teaspoon salt

½ teaspoon pepper

½ cup plain bread crumbs + 3 tablespoons milk

Combine the bread crumbs with the milk and mix in evenly to moisten the bread crumbs. Add the meat, garlic, parsley, parmesan cheese, egg, salt, and pepper to the bread crumbs. Mix the entire contents thoroughly, but do not overwork it (use your hands). Set aside for 15 minutes.

Take enough meat out of the mixture to form a meatball that is about 1½ - 2 inches in diameter (an ice cream scoop makes a good measure). Set aside on a plate. Continue to roll the meat in this fashion until all the mixture is used up. (If making tiny meatballs needed for some recipes, use a level teaspoon as a measure. Level the teaspoon by sliding the spoon up the side of the bowl, then roll into tiny balls.)

Heat a large, non-stick skillet. Place the meatballs into the skillet and brown on all sides. Use tongs or a spoon to move them directly from the pan to the simmering tomato base (see the *Meat Sauce for Pasta* recipe that follows).

MEAT SAUCE FOR PASTA
(WITH MEATBALLS AND SAUSAGE ONLY)

46 oz. can of tomato juice

6 oz. can of tomato paste

4 fresh basil leaves, cut up coarsely

1 teaspoon garlic powder

1 teaspoon salt

½ teaspoon pepper

1 six-count package of sweet Italian sausage

1 meatball recipe, as made per the
Basic Meatball Recipe, Meatballs, Nana Style,
or any meatball recipe of your own liking

Note: If adding other meats besides sausage and meatballs, double the amount of tomato juice, tomato paste, and seasonings so meats can be adequately immersed in the sauce while simmering. Sausage and/or meatballs may also be doubled, if desired. Additional sauce/meat can be frozen.)

Using an adequately-sized pot, allowing room for displacement, pour in the tomato juice. Turn the burner to medium heat. Mix in the salt, pepper, garlic powder, and basil. Cover and bring to a boil. Meanwhile, heat up a non-stick skillet and brown the sausage on all sides. Transfer the browned sausages to the big pot and cover again (do not be concerned if sausages are cooked, as they will continue to cook in the sauce). In the same hot skillet used for the sausage, brown the meatballs on all sides. Use tongs, a spatula, or spoon to turn the meatballs, and not a fork, as you do not want to pierce or break them. The meatballs will also continue cooking in the sauce.

The reason you want to brown the meatballs last is because they will render the most fat, which is needed for the next step. In the same skillet, add the tomato paste from the can. Using a wooden spoon, stir the tomato paste in with the beef renderings generated from the meatballs (cook over medium heat for about 3 minutes). When the tomato paste looks nice and loose, transfer it to the big pot. Gently incorporate the tomato paste mixture with the tomato juice.

Stir the pot contents by sliding the wooden spoon down the side of the pot. Move it around the sides, gently agitating the spoon and the sauce contents (instead of jamming the spoon into the center and stirring vigorously, running the risk of breaking the meatballs). Tilt the lid to allow steam to escape and to promote thickening. Lower the heat and simmer for at least 2 hours, stirring occasionally. Taste the sauce about 1 hour into the simmer time. Increase salt if needed. When the simmer time is complete, the sauce should take on a deep, red color. Remove the cover and allow the sauce to rest and cool down significantly. Remove all meat using tongs or a spoon. Divide the meat and sauce into containers as desired. Freeze if not using all the sauce at once.

Meatballs and sausage.

Pictures represent a DOUBLED recipe:

Make meatballs and set aside. Begin heating the tomato juice with basil. Brown the sausage first.

Transfer the browned sausage to the big pot. Brown the meatballs. Transfer the browned meatballs to the pot.

Add tomato paste to the fat from the meatballs and fry until the paste loosens up.

Gently stir the paste into the pot with the rest of the tomato base. Tilt the lid and simmer for at least 2 hours.

Separate and freeze for future use.

BRACIOLE IN MEAT SAUCE

There are many kinds of braciole (pronounced (brä-chē-ˈō–lə) recipes out there. Braciole is basically a flat cut of meat rolled up with some type of filling. Sometimes braciole is made with an actual stuffing and braised in the oven. The braciole of my family was mostly a roll up of herbs, spices, parmesan cheese, pignoli nuts, and prosciutto, and not a stuffing, per say. It is typically secured by toothpicks, or string, and cooked by searing first, then simmering in a pot of tomato sauce. Served sliced on a platter, it makes an interesting addition to the other gravy meats from your sauce that you are serving.

Most times, braciole is made with beef, either a thin-sliced top round or flank steak (which can always be found in the supermarket meat case). My grandmother, Nana, put her own twist on braciole and made hers with veal. That veal braciole, let me tell you, was something very special. When you had a pasta meal at Nana's house, it came right along with her fabulous meatballs and veal braciole. This was eating at its best. Because veal can be a bit expensive, I am going to suggest going the beef route with this recipe. The beef cut will also be easier to find without going to a butcher. I suppose, if one wanted to, the veal could be rolled up inside of the beef, sort of tur-duck-in style. Mmm. . . I may try that some time and call it "beal braciole" (or "veef", perhaps?).

BRACIOLE IN MEAT SAUCE

3 beef top round, cut thin — or — 3 thin flank steaks, cut thin (about 1 ½ to 1 ¾ pounds total)

3 garlic cloves, chopped fine

½ - ¾ cup whole fresh parsley leaves, chopped

¼ cup pignoli nuts

3 teaspoons parmesan cheese

9 slices of thinly sliced prosciutto (will provide enough saltiness, so no salt needed)

Fresh ground pepper

Preparing one braciole at a time, use a meat pounder and pound the entire surface of the meat. Take ⅓ of the chopped garlic, parsley, and pignoli nuts and arrange evenly on the meat surface. Add a little fresh ground pepper. Lay 3 slices of the prosciutto evenly, covering the meat.

Roll the meat around the toppings. Continue rolling until all rolled up, pushing any protruding filling back into the sides of the rolled meat. Secure the flap by interweaving a toothpick through it, lengthwise along the rollette. Secure both sides of the roll up with additional toothpicks, or tie with a white string, if desired.

Repeat this process for the next two steaks. When making as part of the pasta sauce (see *Meat Sauce for Pasta* recipe), sear off all sides of the braciole and transfer to the pot to simmer with the other meat.

Carefully remove toothpicks. Slice diagonally and arrange on a platter to serve with the other meat.

Makes 3 braciole, sliced into about 15 slices.

Braciole in Meat Sauce.

Tenderize the meat first.

Add the seasonings and the cheese.

Layer the sliced prosciutto over top.

Form a rollette.

Secure with toothpicks.

Brown all sides.

Brown and add to the pot with other meat.

Slice thick when serving.

PORK ROAST IN MEAT SAUCE
(ITALIAN "PULLED PORK")

The first time I made a pork roast like this for Chris, he knew he was not going to let me get away easily. Many years have passed, and I've cooked a lot of things since that time, but to this day, this pork roast remains his favorite. Think about how pork barbeque is so tender that it falls apart when you slice it. The same is true for this pork loin, which has been simmering for hours in a pot of tomato sauce. It's what I like to call my Italian version of pulled pork.

My mother cooked pork roasts in her meat sauce often. Even more often than that, she used the same method for cooking beef eye round roast. I liked the beef roast just fine, but sometimes it tended to be a bit dryer than the pork. For this reason I would like to try doing this with a different cut of beef, such as a chuck roast or a brisket, to see if I can achieve those same tender shreds of meat you get with the pork. . . interesting thought.

This is, by far, the easiest meat to put in your sauce, as it does not require any special preparation, like braciole or meatballs do. Just the three S's. . . Season, Sear, and Sauce! Set it and forget it. If I am including a roast in the sauce with other meats, I will sear it off first and add it to the big pot before cooking the sausage, braciole, or meatballs (I would recommend doubling up on the tomato juice, tomato paste, and other seasonings in the *Meat Sauce for Pasta* recipe, otherwise the roast is going to crowd out the other meats).

If you have never made a roast this way, try it. It is not only delicious as a companion to your pasta dish, but it also makes a terrific sandwich the next day.

PORK ROAST IN MEAT SAUCE

Pork loin roast, about 3 ½ to 4 pounds

Salt

Pepper

Garlic powder

OPTIONAL: Use the same technique, but use spare ribs, neck bones, or beef roast instead.

Season all sides of the meat by sprinkling on some salt, pepper, and garlic powder. In a hot, non-stick skillet, sear all sides of the meat to provide flavor and hold the juices in. Use tongs to turn the meat and not a fork, as you do not want to pierce the meat and allow juices to escape.

When the searing process is complete, transfer the pork roast to the big pot and immerse completely in the tomato base, along with the other meat.

To serve, slice and arrange on a platter with the other meat. If pork does not slice easily and shreds instead, that is okay. Mound the shredded pork on the platter and drizzle some meat sauce on top. Serves about 6 to 8 people, depending on how many other meats are being served alongside.

Pork Roast in Meat Sauce.

Put meat into the hot pan.

Brown on all sides.

Add the seared pork roast to the big pot.

Pork will raise to the top as it cooks.

Can slice or shred.

Pork, shown with braciole, meatballs, & sausage.

MEATBALLS, NANA STYLE

Nana.

Everyone has a special recipe for meatballs. There are so many of them that use different ingredients, preparation techniques, and cooking methods. And, of course, everyone has a reason for loving their mama's or grandma's meatballs, and rightly so. I am no exception. My mother's meatballs were very good and I liked them just fine. However, the moistest and most consistently delicious meatballs I ever ate were made by Nana. Since her passing, I have yet to experience a meatball that tastes like hers. Even the ones I created using this recipe are close but, I have to admit, are no match. That is why I call them *Meatballs, Nana Style* because I could never call them "Nana's Meatballs."

So what was it about Nana's meatballs that I loved so much? If I could explain them in one word, that would be "complex." Yes, that's it. They not only had a complexity to them visually when you cut into them, but also when you bit into them. The texture was like velvet on your tongue. And the flavor of her meatballs was unique, as well. I don't know if it was the mix of meat that she used, an unusual seasoning, or just the technique she used to make them. All I know is, if ever I needed to collaborate with anyone on a recipe, she would be the one, and this would be the recipe.

Unfortunately, I did not ask her when she was around, so all I can do is close my eyes and conjure up a recipe from the one fact I do know. . . they contained large amounts of moistened bread, almost like a stuffing. When you cut into one, you saw the swirls of bread intertwined with the meat. The breading exchanged flavors with the meat and provided a distinct density and moistness. The meat was not "saw-dusty," like many other meatballs I've had.

I had to try this recipe out more than once to get to a point where I felt it was an acceptable duplicate. I used the same ingredients and seasonings I used in the *Basic Meatball Recipe* (page 72). However, one main difference being that I replaced the bread crumbs with cubed, day old Italian bread, which had been soaked with milk (a technique that I know for sure she used). I also changed the meat from a standard, pre-packaged meatloaf mix to separate packages of ground meats that I mixed together myself (seeing as Nana had a neighborhood butcher to get her meat, and not a supermarket, this seemed to make more sense in recreating her recipe). I changed the percentages of the various meats in the mix, using a larger percentage of ground beef, to a lesser amount of pork. I omitted the ground veal. If desired, you can use all ground beef, but it cannot be too lean, otherwise the meatballs will be dry. I would say no more lean than an 80/20 meat to fat ratio.

To demonstrate how to make these meatballs, I am using the same basic *Meat Sauce for Pasta* recipe seen just prior, but I pick it up from the meatball step using this recipe instead. You can add another meat to the sauce besides the meatballs, if desired. Use what you like the best.

Note: Please refer to the basic *Meat Sauce for Pasta* recipe on page 73 for the sauce-making technique.

Spaghetti with "Meatballs, Nana Style."

MEATBALLS, NANA STYLE

1 ¼ pounds ground beef (about 80/20 lean)

¾ lb. ground pork

2 eggs

1 teaspoon salt

½ teaspoon black pepper

2 cups day-old Italian or French bread, cubed (about ½ loaf)

1 cup milk

¼ cup grated parmesan cheese

2 cloves garlic, minced fine

2 tablespoon chopped fresh parsley

Add the milk, ½ cup at a time, to the bread cubes. Using your hands, incorporate the milk in to moisten. (Add the other ½ cup of milk gradually, if needed, and stop when it has the consistency of a stuffing: Moist, but not too drenched.) Mix the parmesan cheese, parsley, and garlic into the bread mixture.

In a larger bowl, mix the beef and pork together with the eggs, salt, and pepper. Then, mix the bread mixture in with the meat mixture, again using your hands. (**Note:** Do not use an electric mixer for any of this, as you want the bread to be incorporated with the meat, but to retain some of its original structure.) The meat and the bread mixture should have a "marbled" effect to it.

Form into larger-sized meatballs (or medium-sized using an ice cream scoop as a measure). When forming the meatballs, try to push any bread pieces from the surface into the center of the meatball, and have mostly meat on the outer surface. This will help seal the breaded part in better. (If some of the meat breaks away from the meatball in the sauce, that's okay. The beauty of Nana's sauce was always the rich gravy with these lovely particles of meat floating about.)

Brown the meatballs on all sides before adding to the sauce pot. Simmer in the tomato base for 1 to 1 ½ hours, until the sauce is deep red in color and has thickened. Makes 1 dozen large meatballs or 1 ½ dozen medium-sized meatballs.

Add milk to the bread cubes and moisten. Add herbs and cheese to the bread.
Add the eggs, salt, and pepper to the beef/pork mixture. The bread should have the consistency of a stuffing.

Mix bread mixture in with the meat. Do not overwork. Form into meatballs and brown on all sides.

Transfer to a pot with the tomato base that has already come to a boil. Gently stir so meatballs are immersed.
Add the tomato paste to the pot. Tilt the cover and simmer for about 1 to 1 ½ hours.

Meatballs, Nana Style.

TWICE-FRIED MEATBALLS

So now that we've made all of these meatballs, there are bound to be some left over. If you have left over meatballs from your meat sauce, and are sick of boring meatball sandwiches, you should try doing this.

Everyone, at some point in their life, has had (or heard of) "Twice Baked Potatoes." If not, that is when you take a baked potato, scoop out the inside, mash it all up with some herbs, butter, and cheese, stuff it back into the skins, and bake them again. This is the same concept. Meatballs that have been cooked the first time, but we are taking them and using them as an ingredient to cook something totally different.

It was inspired from a quick little trick I learned as a kid from my father. It's a crazy little recipe. . . So simple, but so good. I sometimes like to describe it as an "Italian Sloppy Joe." It can be made into a sandwich, or just eaten by itself, paired off with a salad and a piece of bread. All I can really say about this is if you like the flavor of lasagna, you'll love this.

We've always made it using leftover meatballs, but I suppose you can even do the same with leftover sausage and get similar results. You can even mix meatballs and sausage together. If you have some mozzarella cheese, add some of that into the mix for some stretchy deliciousness.

TWICE-FRIED MEATBALLS

2 to 3 leftover meatballs, covered with a little meat sauce

2 eggs

1 teaspoon of olive oil

An Italian roll (or other hard roll, such as a Kaiser roll)

Parmesan cheese (optional)

Shredded mozzarella cheese (optional)

Heat the olive oil in a hot, non-stick pan. Beat the eggs in a bowl. Mash the meatballs and break them up, somewhat finely, and mix in with the beaten eggs. Pour the egg/meatball mixture into the hot pan. With a spatula, scramble as you would with scrambled eggs. Sprinkle with some parmesan cheese (if using). Press the mixture flat in the hot pan and allow it to brown a little (hash style). When the egg is sufficiently cooked, turn off the heat and let it cool slightly. Serve on a hard roll or alone on a plate. Top with some shredded mozzarella, if desired.

Makes 1 larger sandwich or 2 smaller ones.

Add eggs to bowl and smash the meatballs.

Mix the smashed meatball in with the eggs.

Fry, hash style, until egg cooks and begins to brown. Add parmesan. Turn and cook other side.

Top with shredded mozzarella, if desired. . . Enjoy!

4

PASTAS

MANICOTTI

If you want to make the lightest, most delicious manicotti you have ever tasted, please try this recipe. My mother got the recipe for the manicotti shells from a family friend and has been making them ever since. It is one of the recipes that I made sure to include in this collection. I've made them so often myself, I can almost do it with my eyes closed.

They have the look, texture, and taste of homemade pasta, but without the fuss of kneading and rolling. They are much lighter than any manicotti made with boxed pasta shells that you need to pre-boil. The manicotti is made using crepes made from a flour/water/egg mixture (which, when you think of it, is essentially the ingredients used in basic pasta dough) and finished with homemade meat sauce. They puff up as they are baked and are so light, you just can't stop eating them.

Just as a forewarning, like fresh pasta, you would not want to eat the manicotti shells if they are not cooked to completion. This means that, even though it is cooked in a hot pan as a "crepe," they still have a raw, rubbery texture until they are filled, dressed with sauce, and baked. The baking process cooks the egg/flour elements, just as boiling does for fresh pasta.

MANICOTTI

SHELL BATTER:

4 eggs

2 cups water

2 cups flour

These proportions will yield about 2 dozen shells, give or take, depending on the surface size of the pan and/or the size of your spoon. As pictured, these proportions fill an 11 x 15 baking pan. Of course, the recipe can be halved using a smaller baking pan.

SHELL PREP:

Before you start this step, prepare yourself little squares of waxed paper to put in between the crepes. It will make it easier to separate them. Make about as many squares as the estimated shells you plan to yield from the recipe.

In a bowl, mix eggs, water, and flour. Whisk together into a smooth, light batter.

Season a small, non-stick omelet pan with oil.

Using a serving spoon or small ladle, pour some batter into a HOT pan, just enough to cover the flat, bottom surface of the pan (spoon it into the center and roll the pan to work the batter to the edges). When the batter dries out, use a spatula to loosen and shake the pan until the shell slides freely. Flip to the other side for just a few seconds. Stack each between waxed paper.

Repeat the above step until all the batter is used up.

Manicotti.

FILLING:

2 lb. ricotta cheese

¼ cup parmesan cheese

½ cup shredded mozzarella (optional)

⅓ cup fresh chopped parsley

1 egg

1 teaspoon garlic powder

1 teaspoon salt

¼ teaspoon black pepper

FILLING PREP:

In a large bowl, mix all the filling ingredients together well using a large spoon (do not do this in a mixer or food processor, as you don't want the filling to get too loose).

MANICOTTI PREP:

Preheat oven to 350 degrees. Grease a large baking pan. Spoon some tomato sauce into the bottom of the baking pan, enough to coat the bottom completely.

Take one of the shells and spoon some of the filling into the center. Roll the shell around the mixture, overlapping the edges of the shell. Place into a glass or stainless steel baking pan (do not use an aluminum pan*), overlapped side down.

Repeat with remaining shells and place them in the baking pan, butting the sides up against each other until the pan is full.

Top the manicotti with meat sauce. Sprinkle with parmesan cheese and bake, uncovered, for about 20 - 30 minutes, or until the manicotti "puffs up" and the sauce is bubbling. Let stand about 5 - 10 minutes before serving. Serve carefully using a spatula, keeping the manicotti in tact. The manicotti can be made ahead of time and baked prior to serving.

Do not cover with aluminum foil (or use an aluminum pan), as the aluminum will react with the egg component and may cause "gray-spotting" on the manicotti.

Prepare the waxed paper, mix the batter, and season a hot non-stick pan with oil.

Spoon in the batter and roll the pan around to spread. When it "dries" out, work the crepe loose and flip.

Stack between waxed paper and repeat until batter is finished. Mix all filling ingredients by hand.

One at a time, spoon some filling into the center of the shell and bring both flaps together.

Prepare a baking pan with sauce and arrange in rows, opening down. Add a light layer of sauce and parmesan cheese prior to baking (stop here and refrigerate if preparing ahead of time).

Bake 20 - 30 minutes until they "puff up."

LASAGNA MARGHERITE

Everyone Loves Lasagna. . . I am positive that's what my mother's TV show would have been called, if she starred in one. Unfortunately, *Raymond* got the idea before she had the chance. (Of course, I am referring to the sitcom *Everybody Loves Raymond,* a show that, incidentally, my mother was a fanatic over.) I only mention this because, if ever a TV family situation hit so close to home, that family was it. . . the two sons (one married and one single), the obstinate father, and the strong-willed Italian mother, who cooked her way into her sons' hearts with her lasagna.

If you have ever seen the episode of *Raymond* where they give Marie a gift membership to the "Fruit of the Month Club," you would know she got really nervous about having "too much fruit" around the house. "What am I going to do with all of this fruit!" she exclaimed. Well, that was my mother to a "T." She was always nervous about having too many cans of food on hand, or too much stuff in the refrigerator or freezer. Although we ate really well in our house, if you ever came in and looked in our cupboards, you would have thought, "Oh, these poor people." But, that was not the case at all. My mother just liked buying food and using it right away. She definitely would not have been a fan of the "Fruit of the Month" club.

One dish that my mother made very well was her own version of lasagna. I have successfully recreated a knock-off of this lasagna, as I remember it. Before I did, I had not had this type of lasagna since I was a kid. Truthfully, I don't think my mother even made it for quite some time herself, as the actual pasta she used was discontinued by the manufacturer a long time ago.

Normally, lasagna is made with the wide strips of pasta especially made for this purpose. It is usually layered in a pan with ground beef, meat sauce, ricotta cheese, and various other cheeses. It is then baked and served up in nice square portions. My mother put her own spin on lasagna in that she used a short, curly pasta that was made by The Ronzoni Company. I believe they used to call it

Margherite (or something like that), so my father told me. I looked in stores, and on the Ronzoni website, and I did not see any pasta resembling that name. I also searched the web, in general, but no pasta with the name *Margherite* could be found. The closest I came was *Pizza Margherita,* described as a pizza where the three colors of the Italian flag are represented by red tomatoes, green basil, and white cheese. The pizza was named after its creator, *Margherita,* which means *daisy* in Italian.

Not to be foiled by this obstacle, I thought, "What current day pasta best resembles this *Margherite?*" I settled on a basic, medium-width egg noodle. This can certainly be found easily in any supermarket. Now, what to call this dish. . . the English-Italian dictionary translates "noodles" as "tagliatelle." I suppose that I could have called it *Tagliatelle Lasagna.* Instead, I opted in keeping with tradition and called my recipe *Lasagna Margherite.*

Lasagna Margherite contains all of the key elements of traditional lasagna, but some elements take on a different form. We already discussed how the pasta is different. For the meat component, we use tiny meatballs instead of loose ground beef. By interspersing them throughout the casserole, each portion allows for a number of meatballs so, as you are eating, you suddenly get a hit of a meatball, which carries flavors of its own. I use homemade meat sauce for this, as my mother always did. You can use your favorite store-bought meat sauce, which has been doctored up with the little meat balls. (I will do this on occasion, in a pinch, but I find that lasagna made with the homemade sauce has an extra special deliciousness.) Point is, if having to make your own meat sauce from scratch is going to deter you from making this, by all means, please use your favorite jarred sauce. You will find that simmering with your own meatballs actually makes a jarred sauce tastier. I just personally find that jarred meat sauces are generally too sweet.

This lasagna makes an excellent buffet item. It is lighter than traditional lasagna and is an inspiring alternative to its wearisome relative, baked ziti.

LASAGNA MARGHERITE

1 lb. package of medium-width, curly egg noodles

16 oz. of meat sauce

(2) 15 oz. containers of ricotta cheese

1 egg

3 tablespoons fresh, finely chopped parsley

2 teaspoons garlic powder

1 tablespoon grated parmesan cheese
(+ more on hand for sprinkling)

¼ teaspoon salt

¼ teaspoon pepper

4 oz. shredded mozzarella or Italian Blend cheese

Tiny meatballs, made using the *Basic Meatball Recipe* in this book (**Note:** For this recipe, cutting the meatball recipe in half will suffice. However, if you are doubling this recipe for a larger party size pan of lasagna, then make the whole meatball recipe).

Begin by making your meat sauce with the tiny meatballs.

Prepare the meatballs as directed in the *Basic Meatball Recipe,* but instead of making the meatballs with an ice cream scoop, you are going to make them tiny. Using a teaspoon measure as a guide, scrape some meat up against the side of the bowl making a level teaspoon full. Roll the small amount of meat in between your fingers, forming a tiny meatball. Continue to do this until all the meat mixture is completed. Add the meatballs to a hot, non-stick skillet and brown completely. Transfer the browned meatballs to the simmering tomato base. Stir in and continue to simmer the sauce for at least 1 hour, or enough time to allow the meat to cook and the sauce to thicken.

Start up a large pot of salted water and bring to a boil for the noodles.

Ricotta filling: Add the ricotta cheese, egg, parsley, garlic powder, salt, pepper, and teaspoon of parmesan to a bowl and stir until all these ingredients are incorporated well together. Set aside.

When the sauce is done, cook the noodles in the boiling water until they are just "al dente." Do not overcook them. When ready, strain the noodles in a colander and rinse thoroughly with cold water to stop the cooking process. Allow all the water to drain off completely before assembling.

Preheat oven to 350 degrees. Using a 9x13 pan, you should have enough of everything to assemble four layers of sauce/meatballs, three layers of noodles, and two layers of ricotta cheese. Begin layering as follows:

Layer 1: Sauce and meatballs, enough sauce to coat the bottom of the pan, with meatballs evenly spaced. Sprinkle with some parmesan cheese.

Layer 2: Enough noodles to cover the first layer of sauce/meatballs.

Layer 3: Spoon dabs of the ricotta mixture in rows evenly across the layer of noodles.

Layer 4: Sauce and meatballs, again, meatballs evenly spaced. Intersperse sauce somewhat with the ricotta, generous enough on sauce, as no white noodle should be showing. Sprinkle with parmesan cheese.

Layer 5: Add another layer of noodles, same as in Layer 2.

Layer 6: Repeat ricotta mixture, as in Layer 3.

Layer 7: Repeat sauce/meatballs/cheese, as in Layer 4.

Layer 8: Add final layer of noodles.

On top: Finish with one layer of sauce only (no meatballs) and sprinkle with parmesan cheese. Top generously with the shredded mozzarella (or Italian cheese blend).

Using aluminum foil, make a dome-like cover for the baking pan (shiny side in). What you want is for the foil to not touch the cheese and to create an air space for the heat, which will melt the mozzarella cheese nice and evenly without burning. Bake on the center rack for about 1 hour.

Allow the lasagna to rest for about 15 minutes prior to serving. Cut into squares and serve with a spatula. The 9x13 pan will feed about 6 to 8 people a lasagna dinner. If being served with other foods on a buffet, count on feeding about 10 to 12 people.

Note: If preparing ahead of time, cover the lasagna with **plastic wrap** (storing overnight with aluminum may cause the egg product to turn gray), and refrigerate without baking. On the day you plan to cook the lasagna, bring it to room temperature. Remove the plastic wrap and tent with foil, as directed above. Begin to bake about 2 hours before you plan on serving it.

Make meatball mix according to the *Basic Meatball Recipe*, but use a teaspoon to size the meatball. Brown on all sides and simmer in tomato base (see *Basic Meatball Recipe / Meat Sauce for Pasta*, pages 72-73).

Coat the bottom of the pan with sauce. Add the layer of noodles, ricotta, and parmesan, and repeat.

Top with a final layer of sauce and shredded mozzarella and tent with foil, forming an air pocket.

Bake, and allow to rest before serving.

CHEESE RAVIOLI

Homemade pastas are a common thing to see nowadays. My first exposure to homemade pasta occurred somewhere around my later childhood, quite possibly into my early teens. My Nana introduced me to a fettuccini type noodle, made through a hand-cranked contraption. I'll never forget how my father would pick Nana up on a Sunday afternoon and bring her back to our house for dinner. As she entered the house, shopping bag in hand, I knew its contents. . . homemade pasta. Oh boy!

At a time when I thought macaroni only came from a box (and a *blue* box, at that), this whole "make it yourself" concept was awe inspiring for me. Compared to boxed pasta, homemade noodles are so light, you cannot stop eating them. To a kid like me, it seemed like such an advanced cooking endeavor (and one only to be embarked upon by grandmothers) that I could never see myself doing it. Low and behold, I have conquered the great pasta divide and I now make it with ease.

My mother picked up on Nana's craft and began making pasta on many occasions. She had a pasta machine and a drying rack. In the early days, the machine had a crank (later to be retrofitted with a motor) and was clamped to the edge of the table. The pasta was made and cut in the kitchen but, because space was limited there, the dining room table became the drying department. Picture strands of pasta hanging from rack of wooden dowels, very similar to a folding clothes drying rack (I've never actually done this, but I would imagine that anyone hard pressed for space could effectively use numerous wooden garment hangers for drying pasta). After mastering pasta making, my mother moved to the more advanced craft of making ravioli, and she did it very well, I might add.

From what you have read so far, you can just imagine how spoiled I was, especially when it came to ravioli. Just how spoiled?. . . In 1974 my friends and I went on a backpacking trip on the Suffern-Bear Mountain Trail in Harriman State Park, NY. It was for a few days, so we needed individual servings of food that could be easily heated on a one-burner propane stove. Now, mind you, we had no coolers, so Mom packing something for me to

Backpacking the SBM trail, NY State (1974).

Me (far left), with friends at a trail vista point.

reheat was not an option. Dried and canned foods were it, so off we went to the local A&P and shopped the aisles for our rations. Interestingly, canned *Spaghetti-Os, Beef Stew,* and *Chunky Soup* were a favorite amongst the others.

Being a teenager, needing to parallel his peers, but at the same time not accustomed to eating factory-prepared foods, I halfheartedly went along. Knowing I would not be a fan of *Spaghetti-Os,* I opted for the more upscale meat ravioli. At that point in my life, I had never eaten canned ravioli, let alone meat filled (our ravioli at home was always cheese), but I figured how bad can it be? Well, upon first taste I found out, but I was so hungry that I ate it. And that, my friends, is the story of the first (and last) time I ate canned ravioli. What was I thinking?

People, at the very least, you can find better ravioli in the frozen food section that can be paired with a decent jarred sauce. Opting for canned ravioli over frozen is like saying, "Hey, I'm so lazy, I don't even want to boil water." It reminds me of an episode of *Will & Grace,* when Will said to Grace, as she proudly served boxed macaroni and cheese to her dinner guests. . . "Ah yes, a cuisine of *Chef-Boy-Are-You-Lazy*" (I do love that line).

No special tools are needed to make ravioli, although there are gadgets available out there that can speed up some of the processes (cutters and such). All you need is flour, eggs, salt, a knife (or pizza cutter), and a fork. A pasta-making contraption does make the job easier, but don't run out for one just yet. Try it using a rolling pin. I tested the recipe using both, and it can be done. As a matter of fact, I recently learned from Aunts Mary and Dolly about how my grandmother Victoria used to roll her pasta dough for ravioli. She would roll it with a pin on a big board and then take the rolled dough and "snap" it out like a big sheet, just prior to dabbing on the filling. This I found fascinating and further proves the amazing cooking abilities of these women. Now, you don't need to "snap" pasta dough. If you can bake cookies, you can do this, honestly. It is definitely worth a try. The ravioli can be made ahead of time and refrigerated or frozen until ready to be cooked.

CHEESE RAVIOLI

PASTA DOUGH FOR RAVIOLI:

2 ½ cups of all purpose flour

1 teaspoon salt

2 eggs

1 tablespoon olive oil

Warm water, as needed

Corn meal (needed to keep ravioli from sticking to drying surface)

FILLING:

15 oz. container of ricotta cheese

1 tablespoon parsley, finely chopped

2 tablespoons of parmesan cheese

½ teaspoon garlic powder

¼ teaspoon salt

Pinch of fresh ground pepper

Since the dough has to rest for about 20 minutes before rolling, make the dough first.

BY HAND: Mix the flour with the salt. Put the flour/salt mixture into a pile on a board and make a well in the center. Beat the eggs with the olive oil and pour into the well. Using a fork, gradually incorporate the flour from the inner wall of the well, all the way around, working toward the outer wall until the egg and flour becomes soft dough. If it appears dry, add a little warm water gradually. Scrape any dough from the board. Continue with the kneading process (below).

BY STAND MIXER: Using the dough hook attachment at a low speed, mix the flour and the salt first. Add each egg separately and then the olive oil. Add a little warm water if it looks too dry. Mix until a smooth dough is formed. Remove dough from the mixer bowl and continue with the kneading process (below).

KNEADING: Spread a little flour on a large board. Knead the dough by pressing and folding the edges into the center. Do this kneading process for about 5 minutes until elastic and smooth.

Brush the dough with a little olive oil, cover with plastic, and let it stand for at least 20 minutes before rolling.

Meanwhile, mix all of the filling ingredients together in a bowl, BY HAND, and set in the refrigerator until needed (do not use an electric mixer for the filling, as you do not want it to become to loose).

ROLLING OUT THE DOUGH

Take the ball of dough, cut into quarters, then cut each quarter in half so you have 8 identical pieces (re-cover the pieces you are not currently working with to keep them from drying out).

ROLL BY HAND: When rolling by hand, roll all sheets out before you start assembling. Take one of the dough pieces, roll into a ball, and press flat onto a floured board. Use a rolling pin to roll flat and oblong. Continue to roll until very thin, and no more than $\frac{1}{16}$ of an inch thick. Set aside on a floured surface. Repeat until all pieces are rolled out in identically shaped flats of dough.

ROLL BY MACHINE: When using a rolling machine, it is easier to roll the pasta sheets out as you need them. Take one of the dough pieces, roll into a ball, flatten with your hands, and pass it twice through the widest setting on the roller. Notch it down one setting and run it through that setting twice. Keep repeating, notching down one setting, until rolled through the narrowest setting. Set one rolled sheet of pasta aside on a floured surface for preparation.

ASSEMBLING THE RAVIOLI

Lay some wax or parchment paper on a sheet pan, liberally spread with some cornmeal (to place the finished ravioli on), and set aside. Take one of the pasta sheets and lay it flat on a floured board. With a teaspoon or a small scoop, dab some ricotta cheese mixture 4 inches apart. Brush pasta around the cheese mounds with some warm water (this is a key step to make sure the edges adhere and seal in the filling). Take an identical sheet, position it, and lay it carefully over the top of the cheese mounds. With your fingers, gently press the top layer around the cheese, allowing the dough surrounding the

cheese to just touch the bottom layer, forming bumps in the top layer of dough. Be careful and do not allow the cheese filling to come between the edges of the top and the lower pasta.

Note: When making the ravioli, consider that they will grow in size once they are boiled.

To make round ravioli, use a metal ⅓ cup dry measure (or a can, jar, or anything with about a 2½ inch opening) and press down to form a pattern around the cheese mound. Use the tip of a sharp knife to score the dough further. *To make square ravioli,* use a pizza cutter or a knife to score the dough in a square pattern around the mounds.

After you have cut around each mound, remove the surrounding dough, roll back into a ball, and cover (for later use). Use the tines of a fork to crimp the top and bottom edges of the ravioli and seal in the filling. Move the ravioli to the wax or parchment paper that has been prepared with the cornmeal.

Repeat the rolling and assembling process with the next two sheets of pasta. Roll all of the leftover dough into a ball and repeat from the rolling out/ assembling processes until it is no longer feasible to make any more ravioli with the dough that is left. Refrigerate the ravioli if not cooking right away.

TO COOK: Carefully drop ravioli, individually, into a large pot of boiling, salted water. Gently stir ravioli while cooking using a wooded spoon. Cook for about 5 to 7 minutes, or until the ravioli float to the top. Do not pour out of the pot (they may break). Remove each from the water separately, using a slotted spoon, and put into a colander to drain further.

TO SERVE: To fix family style, layer ravioli, tomato sauce, and parmesan cheese in a large pasta bowl. To serve individual portions, place a few ravioli on the plate and spoon on some of your favorite sauce. Makes about 2 dozen ravioli.

Make a well in the flour. Add beaten eggs, oil, and water. Knead dough, brush with oil, and rest.

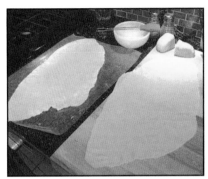

Section out and roll out 2 sheets, either by hand or machine (one for the bottom and the top).

Spoon on the filling, leaving space in between. Brush water around the filling
and carefully cover with the other sheet of dough.

Form shape with something round. Afterward, shore up the cut with a sharp knife (if necessary).

Reuse excess dough
(Ball up, divide, roll out, etc.).

Seal the cheese in the well
by using a fork.

Set aside on a cornmeal surface.

Remove boiled ravioli from water
(make sure they are drained well)
and layer in the serving bowl
with a little meat sauce
and parmesan cheese.

Homemade Cheese Ravioli.

RISOTTO

Okay folks. Now we are really cooking. If you thought that the *Manicotti* and *Ravioli* looked good, this definitely ups the ante. This rice dish is a family classic that came from Nana's repertoire of unique recipes. I cannot think of a single time that risotto was served up to someone for the first time without them taking the first taste and rolling their eyes back, saying, "Mmm. . . Oh, that's good!," only to be followed up later in the meal with a moan and an, "Oh, God. I ate so much."

When you first saw that this was a risotto recipe, it may have conjured up a picture in your mind of what this dish might be. Before I continue telling you about this recipe, it is important to make a major distinction between this risotto recipe and the risotto you may be familiar with. Almost always, people think of risotto as made with Arborio rice, cooked in a pot, using large quantities of liquid, and served loosely in a shallow bowl, mostly as a side dish, but sometimes as an entrée.

This *Risotto* recipe (always pronounced in our family as "riz-zawt") is an adaptation using regular long grain white rice and is baked *en casserole*. Think of this risotto as sort of "rice lasagna," but it does not use any ricotta cheese. Similarly to the *Lasagna Margherite* recipe, tiny meatballs are used and layered throughout rice and egg, along with mozza-rella cheese, parmesan cheese, and meat sauce. The mozzarella is the prevailing cheese, as it stretches from plate to mouth with each forkful of rice and meatball. All topped with a buttery, bread crumb topping, baked, and served by cutting square portions from the deep pan.

If anywhere a good pasta sauce is key to the success of a dish, this is it. You'll need more of it, as well, because the rice is very absorbent. You might want to double my meat sauce recipe (with regard to the tomato juice and tomato paste) just to make sure you do not run short. Another thing I learned is to not skimp on the mozzarella cheese. One time, I used the small package and I should have used a large package. It makes a big difference. And, finally (as my mother will turn over in her grave if I do not tell you this), do not use instant rice for this. Boiled rice on top of the stove and it MUST be the brand that comes in a brown, white, and orangey-red package, its name starting with "C." (**Hint:** There are two U.S. states containing this name in their names, one "North" and one "South.")* Mom says it is the ONLY rice for this. Using any other brand of rice could affect the success of this dish, and she was right, so. . . Oop, tut, tut. . . shh!. . . No questions. Just do as Mom said and use this brand of rice.

*Carolina

My nephew, Jonathan (c. 1983).

Judie, Jon, and brother, Randy (c. 2005).

I can probably count the times on one hand that I made risotto. Actually, there are three Christmases that I can recollect where I served risotto. Each time, my sister-in-law, Judie, told how it always reminded her of the first time she had eaten it. My mother made it when Judie was expecting with my nephew Jonathan. She said that all she could do was keep eating it and that mine tasted just like my mother's (the greatest compliment I could get).

For this book, I perfected my recipe and tested it out on some friends that gave it their "thumbs up." The number of risotto fans is growing outside of our family boundaries, and to them I'd like to say, "This recipe is for you." A word of advice, limit the salt to what is needed for cooking the rice. The meatballs, mozzarella, and buttered crumb topping will provide a lot of the salt flavoring.

It is actually better the next day and microwaves nicely. I found that this risotto does not freeze well, as freezing seems to separate the moisture out of the rice, giving it a mealy texture. The flavors are still there, but it's just better if you do not freeze it. You won't need to worry about this anyway, as it will disappear very quickly. Plan on eating any leftovers until it is gone.

Risotto.

RISOTTO

16 oz. (uncooked) extra long grain white rice

16 oz. mozzarella cheese
(use the packaged type from the dairy case and not the wet mozzarella), cut into ½ inch cubes

2 eggs

¼ cup grated parmesan cheese,
plus a little more for sprinkling

¼ teaspoon black pepper

¼ cup garlic powder

1 ½ to 2 quarts of meat sauce (for this, make a double recipe of *Basic Meat Sauce for Pasta*)

1 lb. of tiny meatballs, made by using the *Basic Meatball* recipe in this book

1 tablespoon melted butter

1 tablespoon fresh parsley, chopped

¼ cup plain bread crumbs

To make the tiny meatballs, follow the *Basic Meatball* recipe found in this book. Do a quick sear on them before simmering in the meat sauce, preferably homemade sauce, but you can also use your favorite jarred meat sauce too (**Hint:** This step can be done in advance of assembling the casserole).

Cook the rice according to the directions. When done, rinse under cold water to cool and stop the cooking process. Drain well. Add to a large bowl. In a separate bowl, beat together eggs, pepper, and garlic powder. Stir the egg evenly in with the rice, along with the parmesan cheese and 2 cups of meat sauce. In another bowl, mix the melted butter with the bread crumbs and parsley using your fingers.

Preheat oven to 325 degrees. Using a 9x13 pan, begin layering as follows:

Layer 1: Sauce and meatballs, enough to coat the bottom of the pan, meatballs evenly spaced.

Layer 2: ½ of the rice mixture spread evenly over Layer 1.

Layer 3: A layer sauce, meatballs, and ½ of the mozzarella cubes evenly spaced. Sprinkle with some parmesan cheese.

Layers 4 & 5: Repeat layers 2 and 3, but push the meatballs and cheese in so they are at least part way buried in the top layer of rice.

On top: Sprinkle the buttered crumbs evenly on top before baking (**Note:** If assembling the casserole ahead of time, do not top with bread crumbs until just before baking).

Bake for one hour (First ½ hour covered loosely and last ½ hour uncovered), or until a fair amount of bubbling is seen from the center. Allow to stand for at least 15 minutes before serving. Serve individual square portions using a spatula to cut into it (lasagna style). Makes 8 servings of risotto.

Cube the mozzarella cheese.

Cook the rice, as per package directions. Strain and rinse to cool.

Add the egg to the cooled rice. Add the sauce and other ingredients, as directed.

Coat the bottom of the pan with sauce. Add first layer of rice, sauce, meatballs, mozzarella, and parmesan.
Then repeat with second layer.

Prepare the bread crumbs with butter and seasoning.
Sprinkle over the top before baking.

Cover loosely for first ½ hour
of baking, uncovered last ½ hour.

Our Family "Risotto."

LINGUINI AGLIO E OLIO
(LINGUINI WITH GARLIC AND OIL)

Whoever said that the simplest things in life are the best things in life was right (well, if nobody actually said this, for the record, I am saying it now). *Simplicity* is one way to describe this wonderful pasta dish. . . simple ingredients. . . simple to make. . . simply delicious!

For as many recipes in this book that I try to mimic my mother's, this is one dish that I think I actually make better than she did. To her credit, the toasted bread crumbs came from her version. They add a nice third dimension to it, so the bread crumbs have to stay. However, my mother, for as much as she used it, was always afraid of garlic. Whenever there was a recipe that called for garlic, she always opted to just cook the cloves whole/crushed for the flavor and remove them before serving. I perfected this recipe by using finely chopped garlic and toasting it along with the bread crumbs. The people who have taste-tested this recipe agree that the garlic should stay in.

We always had this as a side dish, but paired with a salad, it can be a main course. Either way, you will want to make sure your mate eats this along with you, because nobody will want to kiss you any time soon after. For a quick and easy clam sauce, you can add a can of chopped clams (with the juice, and all). The added moisture from the clam juice allows the bread crumbs to take on the role of a sauce thickener.

LINGUINI AGLIO E OLIO
(LINGUINI WITH GARLIC AND OIL)

½ lb. (uncooked) linguini, or thin spaghetti

½ cup of olive oil

3 fresh garlic cloves, chopped fine (whole or crushed if you only want the flavor and then remove it)

¼ teaspoon salt

Dash of pepper

¼ cup plain bread crumbs

2 tablespoons fresh parsley, chopped (for garnish)

OPTIONAL: 1 tablespoon of pignoli nuts

Bring a pot of salted water to a boil and cook the pasta, as per directions on the box. Meanwhile, in a sauce pan, heat the olive oil until it shimmers. Add the salt, pepper, chopped garlic and the bread crumbs (also, add the pignoli nuts now, if using). Cook this until the garlic turns brown. What you want is the garlic and the bread crumbs to be toasted, but not burnt. As soon as this happens, remove from the burner immediately and set aside.

Meanwhile, drain the cooked pasta well and add to a serving bowl. Pour all of the garlic/bread crumb sauce over the top. Add the fresh chopped parsley and toss so all of the garlic, oil, and bread crumbs are evenly coating the pasta. Serve immediately. Makes 4 side servings or 2 dinner portions.

Linguini Aglio e Olio.

Cook the garlic and bread crumbs in hot olive oil.

Shut off the heat when garlic is toasted, but not burnt.

LINGUINI WITH SHRIMP, SCALLOPS, AND STUFFED CALAMARI

Christmas Eve (c. 1971)
At left: Mom, Me, shrimp, scallop,
& Calamari Linguini,
and Stuffed Vinegar Peppers.

Thinking back on this dish, it reminds me of a childhood Christmas tradition. On Christmas Eve, we would eat at home (usually Mom's "Shrimp, Scallops, and Calamari Sauce over Linguini") and then later on we would glom onto someone else (or be glommed upon ourselves). Often, we congregated at Dolores and Bill's house, with other neighbors, for an evening of fun. "Dori," as we called her (who is my Nana's niece, my father's cousin), and her husband Bill also happened to be our neighbors on Brighton Road in Clifton. The adults would have cocktails, coffee, dessert, and play cards until after midnight. The kids would pair off and play, anticipating Christmas day. I remember, one time, we kids all went out caroling to other neighbors' houses. All this was going on while Christmas songs played and the *Yule Log* blazed on WPIX-TV (These were the pre-*Christmas Story* days, where there was no movie to repeat endlessly for 24 hours). When the night was over, we would descend to the street and walk home, just four houses down. Good times, for sure.

Me (right), later that evening with 2nd cousins
Eileen (left) and Billy (right) and his now wife, Nancy.

Stuffed Calamari with Linguini
and Shrimp & Scallop Sauce.

LINGUINI WITH SHRIMP, SCALLOPS, AND STUFFED CALAMARI

1 lb. (uncooked) of linguini pasta

FOR SAUCE:

8 calamari tubes, cleaned, cartilage removed, and stuffed (save tentacles, if they have them)

1 dozen large (or extra large) shrimp, peeled and deveined (tails removed)

8 medium to large scallops

15 oz. can of tomato sauce + ½ can of water

2 garlic cloves chopped fine

2 tablespoons of olive oil

3 basil leaves, chopped (or ½ teaspoon dry basil)

Salt and pepper to taste

CALAMARI STUFFING:

1 ½ cups plain bread crumbs

1 tablespoon fresh parsley, chopped

½ teaspoon dry oregano

1 tablespoon pignoli nuts

½ cup olive oil

½ teaspoon garlic powder

Mix all the stuffing ingredients together well in a bowl. Pack the calamari tubes with the stuffing mixture, pressing it in tightly with your finger. Pinch the open end together and weave a toothpick through, securing the stuffing inside. Set aside on a plate.

To make the sauce, heat the 2 tablespoons of olive oil in a pot that is large enough to accommodate the stuffed calamari and the rest of the seafood. Cook the chopped garlic in the oil, but do not burn. When the garlic is just starting to brown, add the canned tomato sauce, plus ½ can of water. Add the basil, plus some salt and pepper. Cook the sauce for about 5 minutes, and when it reaches a rapid boil, add all of the stuffed calamari tubes. Bring back to a boil, lower heat, and simmer for about 10 minutes with just the stuffed calamari tubes in there.

After the 10 minutes, add the scallops and shrimp (and calamari tentacles, if using) to the pot. Stir in gently and allow all to cook for another 3 minutes. Shut off the heat, cover, and allow to rest while cooking the pasta. Cook the linguini pasta according to the package directions.

Strain the cooked pasta well and put into a large pasta bowl. Move the stuffed calamari to a separate platter and top the linguini with the sauce, shrimp, and scallops. Serve family style.

Serves 4.

A Christmas Eve dinner.

Mix all the stuffing ingredients together, stuff the calamari tubes, and close securely with a toothpick.

Make the sauce and cook the stuffed calamari first before the other seafood ingredients.

When the calamari is just about cooked, add the other seafood.

Cook the pasta and dress with the sauce.

5

VEGETABLES

HOT POTATO SALAD

If you like mayonnaise-free style potato salads, and can stand a little heat, you may like this recipe. Although it is called *Hot Potato Salad,* the "hot" refers to the spiciness and not the temperature. Like most potato salads, it is meant to be served cold. Even if you don't like hot, spicy foods, you may develop a liking to this. I remember loving this salad as a kid, so how hot can it be? My mother, who could not stand anything spicy, even ate this. This salad will be a hit at summertime barbeques as an alternative for anyone tired of the same old picnic fare and mayonnaise-dressed salads. It makes a nice buffet addition and pairs up well with a burger and a beer. Just remember to warn people that it is, in fact, hot. It is very easy to make, too. Summer immediately came to mind when I smelled this cooking for the first time in over 30 years, in my own kitchen.

Where this recipe originated, I don't know for sure, but it was inspired by a recipe obtained from my father's cousin Dolores (the same Dori I introduced previously; see *Linguini with Shrimp, Scallops, & Stuffed Calamari*). I remember eating this potato salad for the first time at a graduation party over at their house. My mother obtained the recipe and made *Hot Potato Salad* many times that summer. Thinking back, it was nice having relatives living on the block. Billy, Eileen, my brother, and I (all second cousins to each other) were part of the entire clan of neighborhood kids that I now like to call *The Brighton Brigade.*

Here are a few tips I discovered that were not explained in my mother's recipe box version of this. It called for "parboiling" the potatoes. That's all it said. I had to come up with my own definition of what that meant for this recipe. I found out that "parboiling" means "actually cooking," but still firm enough to handle without turning to mush. The written recipe also called for 6 hot cherry peppers, but I remember my mother using peppers that were already sliced, from a small jar (called *"So Hot"*). I found these

exact peppers in an 8 oz. jar (**Hint:** *Victoria*), but only after I tested the recipe using a different, 12 ounce jar, pre-sliced substitute (**Hint:** *B&G*). The pre-sliced hot peppers gave the results I remember, but the salad was much hotter than I recollect, but still very good. After baking my first test batch, I tasted them at room temperature and I said, "WOW! That is Hot!!!" However, when I had them the next day (cold), it was more the level of heat I expected, but still way hotter than I remembered.

I came to the conclusion that the 12 oz. jar was too big for the recipe. I made them again using the 8 oz. jar of the sliced peppers packed in oil (the "So Hot") and the taste was more in line with what I remembered it to be. Either way, my advice would be to make the potato salad one day in advance of when you plan to serve it, and definitely serve it cold, as you would a regular potato salad. Use the 8 oz. jar of the "So Hot" sliced peppers, if they are available in your area. If not, adjust the heat by using less of the hot cherry peppers.

Front: Beverly, Larry, Robert (Me), Laure, Peter
Back: Billy (2nd Cousin), Diane, Joanne, Kenny, Nancy,
Julie, Eileen (2nd Cousin), Randy (my brother)
Far back: Neighbor Dolly (peeking over).

HOT POTATO SALAD

6 potatoes

1 large onion

8 oz. jar of sliced "So Hot" cherry peppers in oil, plus all of the oil

½ teaspoon salt

2 tablespoons of olive oil, plus additional, if needed

OPTIONAL: Use 6 whole hot cherry peppers, seeded and sliced, instead of the "So Hot" sliced. Use ¼ cup of the jar liquid mixed with ½ cup of olive oil (as a replacement for the "So Hot" jar oil)

Boil the potatoes until they are cooked, but not too soft. Transfer the potatoes to a colander and run under cold water until the potatoes are cool enough to handle. Peel the skin off of each potato (should be able to easily do this with your fingers once they are cooked). Cut each peeled potato into quarters, lengthwise, and then cross cut into small slices. Add to a large mixing bowl.

Preheat oven to 350 degrees.

Meanwhile, cut the onion into quarters, and then each quarter into small slices. Add to the potatoes in the bowl.

Pour the entire contents of the jar of peppers, oil included, into the bowl. Add the salt. (**Note:** if you are using peppers that are not packaged in oil, mix some juice and oil, as specified in "optional" above, and use that instead.) Gently stir all of the ingredients in with the potato slices. Turn into a non-stick baking pan. Drizzle with the 2 tablespoons of olive oil.

Bake for 1 hour, stirring and turning the mixture every 20 minutes. When done, the potatoes should still be somewhat white, and NOT browned or crispy. The onions will be cooked and wilted.

Cool the potatoes completely. Mound the potatoes into a serving bowl. Cover and place into the refrigerator at least a few hours. Before serving, stir in a little more olive oil if it looks dry.

Makes 10 to 12 side servings of potatoes.

Boil the potatoes until just about done. Cool and slice.

Mix with other ingredients in a baking pan.

Hot Potato Salad.

EGGPLANT PARMESAN

Eggplant Parmesan.

The one thing I like most about my mother's eggplant parmesan is the fact that it is not heavy or oily. Most eggplant parmesan recipes out there call for coating the slices with flower, egg, and bread crumbs which, when fried, holds a lot of grease. This one is made with a light and loose marinara type sauce. The slices are floured up first, then egged (no bread crumbs) before frying. There is no mozzarella cheese used in this recipe either. Just parmesan cheese is used. So, if you love eggplant parm, but don't want the extra calories and fat contained in the typical versions that you see out there, you may be interested in this recipe.

As long as we are on the subject of light cooking, this is a perfect example of how my mother cooked in a light and healthy way. Because she cooked in a healthy way, and ate her meals very slowly, she remained thin for her entire adult life. I remember when I was away at college, I would tell my friends about what a great cook my mother was and how I missed her cooking (heck, that is why I took a job in the campus kitchen, so I could make myself something decent to eat). She would send care packages and my friends found lots to like in there. I guess because she was an Italian mother and such a good cook, they somehow pictured her as a fat lady, with

a mustache, in a house dress! The opposite couldn't be truer—my mother was a very slender woman. When my college friends finally met her on graduation day, they asked, "Wow, that's your mother?" I said, "Yes, it is, and you should have been there when I was growing up and my school friends used to come over and see her sunning herself in our backyard. . . in short shorts. How mortifying was that for a young boy?!" Well, let's get back to the subject of eggplant parmesan before I need a therapist. . . .

Mom, enjoying the sun in our yard (mid-1960s).

Another difference from typical eggplant casserole recipes is that this one is meant to eat cold. You probably would not want to serve this hot, let's say, on a buffet where people normally cut out a square portion for themselves. This version is better when you peel off the slices individually and stack them on a Kaiser roll or sliced Italian bread as a sandwich. That is the way we always ate it.

One key tip when making this—Mom always peeled the skin off of the eggplant. I have made it with and without the skin. It's up to you, whatever you like. Not peeling is always easier and I find that the skin adds another dimension to the dish without altering the flavor.

Frying up the slices is the worse part of making this dish. My mother even dreaded this step, so much that every time she bought an eggplant she would say, "Uh, why did I every buy that stupid eggplant?" Yes, she'd say it, EVERY time. It's become such a tradition that now I have to say it too, every time I buy one. I have to, just because.

At this point, I need to say, on a somber note, that this is the last thing my mother cooked for me when I saw her for the last time before she died. I was visiting my folks in Florida over the New Year's holiday in January 2006. We were out shopping and we stopped at one of her favorite farm stands. I saw these beautiful eggplants there. I looked at the eggplants, then looked at her, back at the eggplants, and finally back at her. "No. Don't make me buy and fry this stupid eggplant," she said. I pleaded with sad eyes, "Oh, please mommy, please?" (Mind you, this was a 47-year-old man begging his mother like a child, but I knew that would get to her.) Well, we bought that eggplant and I watched her make it and it's a good thing I did. She passed away 3 months later, the ultimate result of a fall.

Mom & Dad – Her last picture taken at my brother's home in Florida, 12/31/2005.

EGGPLANT PARMESAN

1 medium eggplant

½ cup flour

3 eggs, beaten with ⅓ cup water

½ cup oil (peanut, vegetable, or canola), plus additional (as needed)

8 oz. can of tomato sauce, plus 1 can of water

1 garlic clove, chopped

4 leaves of fresh basil, chopped (or teaspoon of dry)

¼ cup olive oil

Parmesan cheese

1 teaspoon Salt

½ teaspoon Pepper

Start by making the sauce: Heat the olive oil in a small pot. Add the chopped garlic to the hot oil and cook for a short time, watching to make sure it does not burn. When the garlic is just about to turn brown, add the tomato sauce. Fill the tomato sauce can with water, stirring it to loosen up the sauce left behind, and add that water to the pot (sauce should be on the thinner side). Add salt, pepper, and basil. Stir, and simmer on a low flame for about 20 minutes, stirring occasionally.

Meanwhile, cut the stem off of the eggplant. With a potato peeler, remove the purple skin (or you can keep the skin on if you like). With a long, sharp knife, slice the eggplant lengthwise so the slices are oblong in shape. Try to make the slices as thin as you can, about 1/16 to 1/8 of an inch. In a large, non-stick skillet, heat the ½ cup oil (or enough to generously cover the bottom of the skillet). Put flour onto a plate. Beat the eggs in a shallow bowl. Take each eggplant slice and flour first, then egg, then put into the hot oil, placing just enough pieces in to cover the pan surface without overlapping. Cook on each side until just golden in color. Drain on paper towels. Repeat this process until all the eggplant is fried (add a little more oil to the pan, as needed).

By this time, your sauce is done and you can begin to assemble your casserole.

Preheat the oven to 350 degrees.

In a small glass baking dish (about 8x8 will do), coat the bottom with a small amount of sauce. Make a layer of eggplant, slightly overlapping the slices, laying them in the same direction. Add another light layer of sauce and sprinkle with some parmesan cheese. Prepare the next layer by laying the eggplant pieces across the previous slices in the other direction. Add another layer of sauce and parmesan cheese.

Keep repeating this procedure until all the eggplant and sauce is used. Add a final layer of sauce and parmesan cheese on top and place into the oven, uncovered, for about 30 – 35 minutes. When the eggplant is bubbling, remove it from the oven and cool completely. This eggplant is best when eaten cool or even cold, right out of the refrigerator. Serve by peeling the slices off from the layers and making a sandwich on sliced Italian bread or a hard roll.

Make sauce, as directed. Slice the whole eggplant thin. Flour first, then egg.

  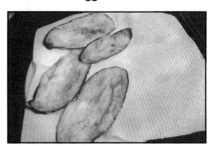

Fry in hot oil, turning when lightly brown. Drain between paper towels.

When all the slices are fried, assemble with the first layer of sauce, then one layer of eggplant.

Add a light layer of sauce and lightly sprinkle with parmesan cheese.
Repeat with similar layers until all the eggplant is used up. Bake for 30 minutes.

TOMATO AND CUCUMBER SALAD

One of our family's simple summer staples was the *Tomato and Cucumber Salad.* It's such a basic recipe, but since this book is about the lost foods of my family, I feel inclined to mention it. I have made this salad so many times, but it never tastes the same to me as it did back then, having supper at our wooden picnic table on a balmy summer evening. I found that, by using the right ingredients, you can come very close to what I am talking about. What is needed to make this salad great is a garden-grown, vine-ripened tomato (preferably a Jersey tomato). This is the star of the show. Any cucumbers will do, as they are a mere co-star. You can even leave them out if you have the right tomatoes. I like them for the additional "crunch" they provide. **Warning:** If you plan to make this with a supermarket tomato, I'm going to tell you before you start. . . don't even bother. It's not going to be the salad I intended here.

There is no doubt that "summertime" meant fresh vegetables for me and my family. My mother's father, Carmine, was a gardener by trade. The one thing that Grandpa always had every summer, no matter where he was living, was a full garden of fresh vegetables and herbs. I'll always remember my grandparents coming to visit and walking in with fresh tomatoes, cucumbers, peppers, lettuce, arugula, basil, parsley, and figs. . . yes, even figs. . . from a tree in their backyard in Montclair, NJ. (My grandfather would wrap the fig tree in canvas for the winter to keep it from freezing.) Even more interesting than that, in his younger years, he grew his own grapes and pressed them to make his own wine and vinegar (I believe that my cousin still has the actual grape press he used). Grandpa was amazing that way. Oh, please. . . I can write a book just about him.

Grandpa lived with us for a short time after my grandmother had passed away and before he remarried. The plan was that both he and my grandmother were to live with us. You see, my grandmother had been suffering from heart ailments and

Tomato and Cucumber Salad.

Grandpa & Grandma in their Montclair yard (Garden can be seen on the right, back behind the tree).

Grandma died in Oct '63. Pictured here with Aunt Mary and Uncle Mike, the date stamp on photo indicates that this was taken one month prior to her death (JFK was still the president when taken).

my mother was going to help her. My parents had an in-law apartment built especially for them on the second floor of our house. I'm sad to say that grandma passed away in her sleep that very October morning of the day they were supposed to move in. That was back in 1963. It was a devastating time for my mother. Ironically, one month later, we lost our president at the hand of an assassin. That topped off 1963 as a bad year for us, and the entire country.

The following spring, my grandfather (now living with us) staked his claim in our backyard and planted his traditional summer garden. He shared his garden space and let me plant carrots and radishes in one small corner of the garden. I remember being very excited about watching them grow and eating something I had grown myself. It was fun. Of course, his tomato plants towered over my head. That is a time I like to call *the summer of endless tomatoes.* We had them all kinds of ways, many more ways than just in salad form. One of my favorite snacks was fresh picked Jersey garden tomato, sliced between two pieces of bread, with mayonnaise. Sometimes I would also add a slice of American cheese. Sometimes I'd even eat them alone, with a little salt.

This is the type of tomato needed for a great tomato salad. Even better than the tomato itself, is the juice that collects in the bottom of the bowl. You will definitely want a piece of Italian bread handy to dunk and sop up all that juicy deliciousness. I always clean the plate dry, pressing the bits of onion into the bread. What a terrific summertime flavor.

TOMATO AND CUCUMBER SALAD

3 ripened tomatoes (preferably vine ripened, fresh from the garden)

1 cucumber

¼ of an onion

4 fresh basil leaves

¼ cup olive oil

1 tablespoon red wine vinegar

Salt and pepper, to taste

OPTIONAL: Use a tablespoon of dried oregano, in place of the basil, as another complementary flavor

Wash and remove the stems from the tomatoes. Cut into ⅛ size wedges. Peel the cucumber, cut in half lengthwise, and slice each half crosswise into ¼-inch slices. Chop the onion and basil leaves fairly fine.

Put all the above ingredients into a suitable sized bowl. Toss gently with the olive oil, vinegar, salt, and pepper. Allow to stand in the refrigerator for about ½ hour. Before serving, gently toss again to reincorporate the juices from the bottom. Serve as an appetizer or a side dish with your favorite summer meal. Serve with Italian bread (for gathering up the juices).

Makes about 4 servings.

Grandpa and the summer of endless tomatoes (Pictured, from right: me, Laure, Larry, Beverly, & Peter).

(1964) Mom, sunning in our yard near Grandpa's garden.

Dormer apartment under construction (1963).

EASY SUMMER GREEN BEAN SALAD WITH FRESH MINT

This simple salad is nice during the summer because of the availability of fresh mint. Do you find you have a ton of mint in the summer that you don't know what to do with? Besides making mint iced tea and mojitos, fresh mint is also a nice complement to vegetables. I mean, how many mojitos can one possibly drink anyway? (Oh, I'm seeing a lot of hands going up, so apparently for some people, a lot.) It grows so wild. To this day, I'm afraid to plant mint, because of how invasive it can get. However, there are times I think it would come in handy and I wish we had it. We have something called lemon mint, but it is just not the same.

Growing up, we didn't have mint growing in our yard either. We didn't have to. Our next door neighbor, Angie (yes, the pizza recipe lady) had loads of fresh mint growing alongside of her garage. We were welcome to it any time we needed it. When my mother wanted to make this salad, she would say, "Go next door and get me some fresh mint." Thinking back, that path past our neighbor's garage was a well known

"cut through" to the street behind ours. During my teenage years, I would often go out after supper to meet up with my friends. I remember taking this shortcut often. Without fail, I would grab a couple of mint leaves on the way and chew on them.

To this day, whenever I see fresh mint, I think of this time in my life. The timeframe was 1972 to 1975, or what I call my "hanging out" years. . . Those rebellious, coming of age years where I declared independence and built strong bonds with kids my own age. We were a core group of friends, with a revolving cast of wacky characters that came and went over this three-year timeframe. We did some crazy and bad things back then, but we were still good kids in spite of it. On a given day, you would find us hanging down at the local park. If we were chased away, we would go down behind a warehouse building. There was this little wooden bridge back there (that we aptly named "the bridge"). It crossed a little brook and it was next to an industrial railroad. We'd spend hours sitting there, our

Me, as a hippy at age 14 (1973).

And, at age 15, with my dog, springer (1974).

feet hanging off of that bridge, and talking and laughing about the things that 15 year olds talk about. It was our own little refuge away from the rest of the world. We were rarely bothered back there. On more than one occasion, we would befriend an 18-year old and con them into buying us beer. We hid it and kept it cold in the brook. We'd meet back there later to drink it.

During the summer months, we occasionally had "sleep out" nights. We'd just party all night. Eventually, we would venture over to the local commercial zone. We were very elusive, as we hid to ditch cars that were driving by in the wee, dark hours of the morning. We knew it was almost time for the supermarket to receive a bakery delivery. Oh yes, we had it all figured out. We'd hide until the truck came to drop off the delivery. They'd leave and we would run over and grab packs of baked goods from the plastic bins. Sometimes, we'd go over to the bakery. They'd give us day-old baked goodies (yes, we were that ballsy, some of us more than others). Of course, we were not poor, and did not need to beg for food. It was the early 70s and we were just teenagers pushing the envelope and having fun. We had a lot of laughs, and we really didn't hurt anyone. I would not trade those times for anything.

It's so funny, the path that thinking of fresh mint can take you down. Anyway, try these green beans, with the mint and just a hint of lemon and garlic flavor. They go great with lamb, a meat usually eaten with mint jelly. . . even better if you don't like eating green slime from a jar with your lamb!

EASY SUMMER GREEN BEAN SALAD WITH FRESH MINT

1 lb. fresh green beans, stems trimmed off

3 tablespoons fresh mint leaves, chopped very coarse or torn in pieces

¼ teaspoon salt

¼ teaspoon garlic powder

Fresh ground pepper, to taste

Juice of ½ lemon (can substitute with ¼ cup white wine vinegar, if desired)

1 tablespoon olive oil

Steam or boil the green beans until cooked, but still firm. Rinse the cooked beans under very cold water to stop them from cooking further. Refrigerate the beans get them thoroughly cold (or you can shock them directly in ice water). Place cold beans in a bowl. Coarsely chop or tear the mint leaves. Whisk together the oil, lemon juice, garlic powder, salt, and pepper and pour over the beans. Add the chopped mint leaves and toss together until the beans are evenly coated with the dressing and the mint nicely distributed.

Allow to sit for about 15 minutes to let all the flavors converge. Taste and adjust seasonings to your liking. Transfer to a serving platter. Makes 4 side servings of green beans.

Steam the beans and shock with cold water to stop the cooking process, then toss with the other ingredients.

Easy Summer Green Bean Salad with Fresh Mint.

(Shown here paired with grilled lamb chops).

EARLY PEAS AND CARAMELIZED ONIONS

This recipe is so easy, and such a no brainer, that I almost opted to leave it out of the book. Here is why I decided to include it. I was reading the cookbook *Paula Deen Celebrates* by the illustrious Paula Deen herself. I came across her recipe for "Green Peas" (page 70). It occurred to me, right then and there, that no recipe is too inconsequential to publish. I will not reproduce her recipe here, but let's just suffice to say that it is basically pouring a drained can of peas into ½ stick of melted butter. Maybe it's me, but you can be the judge. I mean, here is a notorious cook. Who doesn't already know how to make buttered, canned peas? Kudos to her for making the diet version, as she only uses ½ stick of butter, instead of the usual whole stick. And, she knows it is funny, as she qualifies the "recipe" with a comment that starts out by saying, "Don't laugh . . ." In all seriousness, I love you, Paula. Sorry I had to call you out on this. I am great fan of yours and have tried many of your recipes. My copy of "Paula Deen Celebrates!" is even autographed by you and your husband, and was a gift to me from my dear friend Laure. Keep spreading the joy that you do.

My mother's version of *Early Peas and Caramelized Onions* was always a fallback when she needed a quick side dish. I follow her lead on this practice to this day. There is always an onion in the fridge and a can of peas in the pantry. You can even jazz it up with other ingredients like crumbled bacon or sliced mushrooms.

Since we are on the topic of "no brainer" recipes, I'll give you another quick side dish recipe (sort of unofficially, off the cuff) that my mother always fell back on in a pinch. . .

Pickled Beet Salad:
Take a can of whole beets. Drain and quarter the beets. Take a few dill pickles and slice them, crosswise. In a bowl, mix the cut beets and the sliced pickles with a little minced onion, salt, and pepper. Add some fresh chopped parsley, if available. Drizzle with a little olive oil and a couple of teaspoons of the juice from the pickle jar. Voila!. . . Quick, healthy beet salad. If you want to make it a little more substantial, add a drained can of chick peas or white kidney beans to the mix.

It's nice to have an arsenal of these quick recipes in your back pocket. I have many of them that I either picked up from Mom, or developed myself along the way. Make sure you always have your pantry stocked with these canned veggies. Use your imagination. I think, once you try the following recipe for the peas and onions, it will become a standard of yours, as it did for me.

EARLY PEAS AND CARAMELIZED ONIONS

15 oz. can of very young, small, sweet peas

¼ of an onion, chopped medium fine

1 tablespoon of olive oil

Pinch of salt

Dash of pepper

OPTIONAL: Lessen the salt and crumble in a couple of slices of cooked, crisp bacon. Or, add some sliced mushrooms.

Drain the peas completely. Heat the oil in a non-stick pan and sauté the chopped onion until it starts to brown and is somewhat caramelized. Add the peas, salt, and pepper.

Turn the peas gently with a spatula from underneath, mixing them in with the onion and being careful not to mash them. Heat the peas until they are just hot (This will only take a couple of minutes, as the peas are already cooked and just need to be heated).

Serve immediately as a side dish with your favorite meat, chicken, or fish.

Makes 2 to 3 side portions of peas.

Note: If you do not like canned peas, use a 10 oz. package of frozen peas that have been steamed prior to putting them in the pan with the onions.

CLASSIC COLESLAW

Earlier, when you read my story about *Meat Sauce for Pasta,* I told you how my mother prepared it for Sunday dinner while she sent me to the deli on my bike. I explained how she strictly instructed me to go to one deli for the meats and to a second deli for the salads, as they had the best potato salad and coleslaw. It is that coleslaw we purchased there that became the inspiration for this recipe.

Purchased coleslaw. . . I know this may seem like a break away from my theme of reviving actual family recipes, but after experiencing many slaws over my lifetime, I have only come across a few that I actually like. Occasionally, a good one will pop up, some-where, by surprise. Others, more often, I have found to be too sweet, too overdressed, too chopped, or just too yuck! That is the reason I wanted to devise a slaw of my own. In doing so, I needed to dig deep into my mind and actually think about the flavors and textures that I liked most about the coleslaw that my family enjoyed from Joe's Deli years ago.

The main thing about their slaw was that the cabbage was sliced into long, thin strands. I remember being in that deli once and seeing them cutting up the cabbage on the meat slicer. It was these thinner strands, I concluded, that allow the cabbage to wilt (in a good way) as it absorbed the moisture and the flavors of the dressing. Also, I found that the flavor of the cabbage prevailed, with only mild hints of flavor introduced by the other ingredients. The dressing was tangy, with just a hint of sweetness. A light onion flavor was also present, with some finely shredded carrot providing alternate texture, flavor, and color.

I remember my mother's attempt at making cole-slaw. I might add that it was also one of the few things my mother made that I never cared for. She used a popular, purchased *miracle* product as the dressing. That dressing made her coleslaw way too sweet and it just had this distinct, odd flavor (almost nauseating, now that I think of it). With such good coleslaw available right up the street, I don't know why she even bothered to make it herself. Perhaps for economical reasons, who knows?

Rest assured in that you will find no *miracle* dressings here. The dressing that I devised is mayonnaise-based (and who doesn't like mayo?). The mild sweetness it needs comes from adding just a little sugar, which is automatically counter-balanced by the tang of a little white vinegar. I obtained the stringiness of the cabbage by slicing on a mandolin. Of course, if you don't own a mandolin, you can al-ways slice the cabbage thin using a "Santoku" style knife, or any longer kitchen knife you may have (Just resist the urge to chop it).

To obtain the best taste and optimal texture, you will need to make this coleslaw at least one day in advance of serving it. I found that the longer it is al-lowed to sit to absorb the flavors, the better it is. As a matter of fact, I just had a taste of the sample batch I made five days ago. It was still at its best and tasted delicious. You will find that the dressing gets milky from the moisture of the cabbage. It may help to let the cabbage drain after you slice it, but before you dress it. I didn't, though. As it was resting, I took it out of the fridge occasionally and stirred up the dressing from the bottom. Just prior to serving for the first time, I gave it one last stir and then drained off some, but not all, of the dressing from the bottom. Remember to mix the dressing up from the bottom each time you serve it for the best taste, and serve it in a little side bowl to keep it from making your sandwich soggy.

CLASSIC COLESLAW

1 head of green cabbage

1 small onion (or ½ of a larger one)

2 carrots

¼ cup chopped fresh parsley

1 teaspoon salt

½ teaspoon pepper

1 teaspoon garlic powder

1 ½ cups of mayonnaise

1 teaspoon sugar

2 tablespoons white vinegar

Use a very large bowl, one deep enough that you will be able to freely stir the contents around easily.

Cut the cabbage head into quarters and remove the core. Using an electric slicer, mandolin, or large knife, slice the cabbage into very thin shreds. Slice the onion thinly, in the same fashion. Shred or chop the carrots very fine. Add the cabbage, onion, carrots, parsley, salt, pepper, and garlic powder into the big bowl and toss to distribute the contents evenly.

In a smaller bowl, whisk together the mayonnaise, sugar, and vinegar into a nice, smooth dressing. Add the dressing to the cabbage mix (use a rubber bowl scraper to get all of the dressing from the small bowl). Mix the dressing thoroughly with the cabbage mixture. Cover, or transfer to a storage container, and refrigerate overnight or longer (this will allow the cabbage to relax and absorb all the other flavors).

The next day, remove from the refrigerator and stir. If the dressing has become milky, drain about half of it off prior to returning to the refrigerator or serving. Transfer the coleslaw to a serving bowl. (Use a smaller bowl than the original bowl you mixed it in. This will allow the coleslaw to pile high and look nice and bountiful.) Sprinkle the top with a little paprika, for color, if desired.

The coleslaw will last in the refrigerator for days. Each time you serve it, redistribute it with any dressing that may have settled to the bottom.

This recipe will make enough coleslaw for a small party. The recipe can be halved to serve about 6 to 8 side servings of coleslaw.

Add all vegetables in a large bowl and dress.

Classic Coleslaw.

BROCCOLI RABE

Broccoli rabe, most times referred to as "ripini" (what we called "broccoli di rape" in our house), is leafier than traditional broccoli. The stems are much thinner, but tougher, with smaller, more delicate flowerets that resemble little broccoli heads. The flavor is quite different too. Broccoli rabe, even after cooked, can have a somewhat bitter flavor. If you are not familiar with it, I would be lying if I told you that you will love it straight away and needn't acquire a taste for it. If prepared correctly, with the right counterbalancing flavors, broccoli rabe can be a nice complement to strong main courses like grilled steak or chicken. I found that boiling the broccoli rabe down in water that has been generously salted counteracts a lot of the natural bitterness.

The recipe that follows is for a sautéed *Broccoli Rabe*, to be used as a side dish. The final result mimics that of leafy, sautéed spinach, but it can easily be cut up smaller and tossed in with the pasta of your choice (like shells, penne, twists, or bow ties). Used in this way, it holds up really well for a buffet item and can be made days in advance of your party. It is also delicious in this form served as a cold pasta salad. If you have ever seen broccoli rabe used anywhere at all, it would have most likely been mixed in with cavatelli. When roughly chopped, in conjunction with the garlic and oil flavors, it is reminiscent of a pesto sauce when used in this fashion.

When I was a young lad, I loved when the broccoli rabe was leftover from the previous night's supper. American cheese and broccoli rabe make a great sandwich. Now that I think of it, you can probably grill that same sandwich for a special panini-like grilled cheese. That would bring a sandwich like that to a whole new level. Bet on me trying it the first chance I get.

If you are adventurous and trying broccoli rabe for the first time, don't be turned off if your first bite is not Shangri-La. Give it another try, perhaps in a restaurant, or with this same recipe again at home. Try mixing it with your favorite pasta. Chris is living proof that a seasoned palate can emerge out of the gastronomically cautious. Before he met me, he had not experienced many of the less common foods that I was used to eating my entire life, but now he eats them all. Broccoli rabe was not one of his favorites, initially. However, he was willing to keep trying it because he knew that, somewhere in there, there was something he liked. He now gets elated when I tell him that I am making broccoli rabe with our dinner.

Some variations I have tried that you might enjoy:

- Adding a sprinkle of crushed red pepper flakes
- Adding some toasted pignoli nuts
- Mixing in with your favorite pasta
- All of the above

Broccoli Rabe.

BROCCOLI RABE

1 bunch broccoli rabe
(as tied and sold in the produce section).

3 garlic cloves, sliced thin (can do whole or crushed if you just want the flavor and don't like to eat it)

⅓ cup extra virgin olive oil (Use ½ cup of oil if you are planning to toss in with pasta)

1 tablespoon salt

Additional salt and pepper to taste

OPTIONAL:
• Add crushed red pepper flakes and/or pignoli nuts
• Mix in as a dressing for ½ lb. (dry) pasta, cooked

Cut off the fatter, bottom stems of the broccoli rabe and separate the leaves somewhat. In a colander, rinse under cold water to wash the leaves/stems thoroughly. Drain well.

In a large pot with a cover (at least 5-quart size), add enough water to fill the pot about ¼ of the way up. Bring this to a boil and add the tablespoon of salt to the water. Add the broccoli rabe to the pot. Cover and allow the boiling water and steam to cook the leaves and stems down, stirring occasionally until it is totally wilted in the boiling water. Boil in this wilted state for about 10 - 15 minutes.

Strain the cooked broccoli rabe in the colander and remove all the water from the pot. Dry out the pot and return it to the stove. Over a medium flame, add the olive oil and allow the oil to cover the entire bottom of the pot. Heat the oil and add the garlic. Cook the garlic, BUT DO NOT BURN!! (Add the pignoli nuts at this time, if using.) Before the garlic turns brown, throw the parboiled, drained broccoli rabe back into the pot and sauté in the oil and garlic, incorporating all the garlic and oil around the leaves in a stir-fry fashion.

Add some pepper and some additional salt (also add the crushed red pepper flakes, if using). Lower the heat, cover, and simmer for another 5 – 10 minutes, allowing all the additional flavors to meld in.

Rest for about 5 minutes and serve alone as a side dish, or toss in with cooked pasta (if you are going to add it to pasta, start a separate pot of boiling water for that purpose).

Makes enough for two, large-sized side portions.

Boil the broccoli rabe down before sautéing in garlic and oil.

SPINACH, ITALIAN STYLE

A hero. . . every child has one. I had one too, but it was not your typical superhero or sports star. While other boys were flying around like Superman, or up at bat pretending to be Mickey Mantle, I had a somewhat stranger celebrated hero. . . *Popeye, the Sailor Man.* I am not quite sure exactly what my attraction was to that cartoon, but I just loved it. I had Popeye 45 RPM records, toys, books, Colorforms, pajamas, you name it. I would fantasize about obtaining instant strength and beating up big bullies. Another effect of this curious infatuation with Popeye was a love of boats, sailor suits, corn cob pipes, and, of course, SPINACH!

Little did I know, back then, the intent of *Popeye* was to encourage little children to eat spinach. I figured that out long after I had learned to love it. One thing for certain, Popeye never had spinach the way my mother made it. His was either eaten raw, as he was brutally flung into the farmer's spinach patch, or by squeezing it out of a can by popping off the lid. At the very least, if Popeye did have home-cooked spinach, it would have been boiled in water and not *Olive Oyl* (ha, get it?).

One thing for certain, this is a fast recipe to make. The spinach will wilt within a few minutes. Once it does, you will not want to cook it for too much longer after that. It is so fast and easy. When you get

Dressed as Popeye for Halloween.

Birthday Surprise (pictured with Nana, Brother Randy, and cousin, Ronnie).

Playing Popeye (1964).

right down to it, it is just putting raw spinach into a pot. I would classify it more as a cooking method, rather than a recipe. A method in which no water is used, but the spinach is wilted directly in garlic infused oil instead of water. In fact, with most boiled-down spinaches, you would strain the water off before adding other flavors (usually butter). The flavor here comes from olive oil, garlic, salt, and pepper, so no butter is used or required.

Flavorful juices are rendered from steam moisture and the spinach itself. I think that the juice is one of the best byproducts of this dish. Do not dump the juice. It is full of nutrients. When serving this as a side dish, include some of the juice. Use individual-size serving bowls instead of serving it on a plate (to keep the juices from running into the main course). Then, once you've eaten all the spinach, say to the others, "Hey, is that a $20 bill I see on the floor over there?" When they all turn and look, pick up your bowl and slurp down the delicious spinach juice, *Popeye style.* If you need a more dignified way to get to those juices, just soak them up with a nice piece of Italian bread.

Speaking of bread and spinach, when I was a kid, my favorite thing to do with spinach was to make a pocket sandwich. I would cut an Italian roll in half, crosswise. I'd remove the inner white part of the bread, leaving only the crust, and replace it with cooked spinach. So you can see, even at that early age, I was always experimenting with food, changing its form right at the supper table. Of course, I did this the whole time remembering one thing, and you should remember too, as Popeye always sang at the end of each episode. . .

> *"You'll be strong to the finish,*
>   *When you eat(s?) your spinach,*
>   *Like Popeye the sailor man (Toot! Toot!)"*

SPINACH, ITALIAN STYLE

10 oz. package of spinach

3 garlic cloves, peeled and crushed

3 tablespoons olive oil

¼ teaspoon salt

Pinch of pepper

Remove the spinach from the package and rinse well using a colander. Drain thoroughly. Heat the olive oil in a large pot (one with a cover, at least 5-quart size). Cook the crushed garlic cloves in the hot oil. When it looks like it is just starting to get a little brown, remove all of the garlic from the oil (do not let it burn). Add the salt and pepper to the oil. Put the raw spinach leaves into the pot and cover. After a minute, gently stir up the already wilting leaves from the bottom, allowing the non-wilted leaves to fall to the bottom. Cover again. Check again in another minute. Once all the spinach is wilted, gently stir around in the pot. Cover again and let it cook for only another minute or so. The spinach will be cooked and tender very fast. When this cooking process is done, shut the heat off completely. It is done. Keep covered until ready to serve. Makes 2 to 3 side servings of spinach.

Spinach, Italian Style.

CANDIED SWEET POTATOES

Wow! It is already the first week of October. There was a bit of a chill in the air this morning. I woke to the sound of the furnace pushing warm air through the vents for the first time since April. Not only was this a subtle reminder to me that winter is approaching (sigh), but also that *holiday* feeling suddenly came upon me. You know the feeling, don't you?. . . Turkey, stuffing, pumpkin pie, and a whole plethora of foods. I suddenly felt energized and motivated to jump out of bed and begin writing about autumn foods.

One of those foods is *Candied Sweet Potatoes*, like the ones that my mother contributed yearly to our Thanksgiving feast. Whether enjoyed at home or brought *over the river and through the woods* style to our host, Mom made the best. They weren't roasted, mashed, or baked into a pie, and there was nary a marshmallow within miles of her kitchen. The sweet potatoes were peeled, cut crosswise into thick round disks, and cooked slowly on top of the stove, in a covered skillet with butter and caramelized brown sugar. In my mind, I used to call them *hockey pucks from heaven* (Okay, okay. . . I know that I'm taking a healthy food, such as sweet potatoes, and loading them up with fat and sugar. Hey, Thanksgiving only comes once a year. Hit the gym on Black Friday, while everyone else is breaking down doors at the local mall, and you'll get back on track).

I remember the crazy "food fests" we used to have at Thanksgiving. Actually, thinking back, just sick is what it was. Picture this, if you can. . . We started eating at about 2:00 PM. We would have antipasto first. Then we would have soup, followed by manicotti, and then turkey with all the trimmings and sides, including these delicious *Candied Sweet Potatoes.* After that, we would have a "pre-dessert" of fruit and nuts. And, finally, we'd wrap it up with coffee and dessert (apple pie, pumpkin pie, cookies, etc.). Quite frankly, I don't know where we found room inside us for all of that food, but we sure put it away (keep in mind that we were not a family of big people to start with).

Uncle Mike carving the turkey.

Candied Sweet Potatoes.

From left: Cousins Gary, Ronnie, and Me at the "kids" table.

When all was said and done, the whole meal ended at around 6:00, or. . . *did it?* About an hour later, some idiot (not to offend anyone, but it could have even been me, for as much as I can remember) would come in and say, "I'm hungry. I think I'm going to have a Turkey sandwich." "What, are you crazy?" the masses would respond in agony. "That's okay," replied the idiot. "You all don't have to have any. I'll just eat." (I think you know where this story is going.) Before you could say "gobble, gobble," all of the leftovers ended up back out on the table. As the "hungry one" ate, you'd hear from the other end of that table, "Hey, give me some of that stuffing, down here. . ." "I'll take that turkey leg over here. . ." "Heat up those manicotti. . ." "Pass me those, sweet potatoes, will ya. . ." Well, you get the picture. It only takes one person to pull a pebble from a stone wall, causing it to come down in a pile of rocks. This time it was one massive avalanche of food. Who ever said idiocy is not contagious?

Of course, now that we are older, eating like that is out of the question. Things have been toned down to a sensible four-course meal: antipasto, the turkey main event, the pre-dessert, and then dessert. The number of people has also dwindled down, as relatives moved away to other states (or passed on). All that is left are those crazy, wonderful Thanksgiving memories. I cannot bring those days (or people) back, but I can certainly keep the flavors alive forever. That is what recreating this recipe means to me.

CANDIED SWEET POTATOES

4 sweet potatoes, peeled and sliced crosswise into ¾ inch disks
¼ lb. of butter (1 stick)
1 cup of dark brown sugar
¼ cup water
Black pepper

In a large non-stick frying pan with a lid (if you don't have a lid, cover with some aluminum foil), arrange the potatoes so that they are side by side, lying flat on the pan surface and not overlapping. Add the water into the pan. Sprinkle evenly with a little black pepper. Place a pat of butter on top of each sweet potato. Sprinkle them evenly with the brown sugar.

Place the cover on the pan and turn the heat up under the skillet to medium-low. Cook for about 30 minutes covered. The butter and the sugar will begin to caramelize with the water as the potatoes cook. Check it often to make sure that it is not cooking too rapidly, as you do not want them to burn. Lower the heat under the pan, if necessary.

Remove the cover and cook for another 10 minutes. This will allow the liquid to reduce and thicken the syrup. The potatoes are cooked when a knife inserts very easily. Allow to stand for 10 minutes. Transfer to a serving dish and spoon some of the syrup over the potatoes before serving.

Makes 4 side servings of sweet potatoes.

Slice into thick chunky disks, and place in a pan with butter, brown sugar, and water.

Allow the liquid to reduce and become syrupy.

POTATOES, PEPPERS, AND EGGS

This is one classic Italian sandwich. If you can handle the extra time it takes (and a few extra carbs), the potatoes add a nice complement to the eggs. If you want, you can leave out the green pepper, but the peppers add another level of flavor and texture to the mix. Often, my mother would just make peppers and eggs (without the potatoes) in a pinch. Either version is delicious served up as a sandwich on an Italian-style roll, or alone with toasted, sliced Italian bread. This is also a great way to cook the potatoes alone, without any peppers and eggs, and serve them as a crunchy side dish to fish, hamburgers, or any food you would normally pair up with French fries. Just let the potatoes cook to your desired level of crunchiness. Peanut oil is the best oil for this.

POTATOES, PEPPERS, AND EGGS

4 eggs

2 medium potatoes

1 medium green pepper

2 tablespoons chopped onion

½ cup peanut oil

Salt and pepper, to taste

Peel and slice potatoes fairly thin (about 1/8 inch). In a large, non-stick skillet, heat the peanut oil. When hot, test the oil temperature with one potato slice (there should be a slight sizzle around the potato). When that occurs, add the potato slices, arranging them so that most of the surface of the potato is touching hot oil and they only overlap slightly, if at all.

Meanwhile, chop up your onion fine and the green pepper in chunks. When the undersides of the potatoes are somewhat brown, flip them over to cook on the other side. Move the potatoes around, if necessary, separating them and exposing uncooked potatoes to the hot oil. When they are a mostly brown in color and soft, they are done. (For *Potatoes, Peppers, and Eggs,* you want some of the potatoes slightly browned, some crispy, and some just cooked soft.)

With a spatula or slotted spoon, remove the potatoes to a bowl lined with a paper towel. Add the onion and green pepper into the same skillet and cook over low heat until the peppers are soft. Toss the potatoes back into the pan, arranging evenly. Break the eggs into the potatoes and peppers. Move the egg around with the spatula, breaking the yolks while scrambling with the egg whites evenly throughout the mixture. Add a good dose of salt and pepper at this time. When the eggs are done, move to a plate and allow to rest and cool slightly before serving. Makes 2 - 3 sandwiches.

Slice the potatoes thin, chop the onion and green pepper, and add sliced potatoes to hot oil.

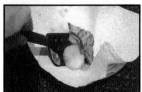

Turn the potatoes. When somewhat brown and soft, drain. Cook the onion and green pepper.

Add potatoes back to the pan, break in the eggs, and mix in evenly with the rest of the mixture.

Turn the mixture over to cook the egg on the other side. Rest on a plate before serving.

6

MEAT, POULTRY, AND FISH

CHICKEN PARMESAN

Remember the story about my childhood friend that stayed for dinner and was terrified of the stuffed artichoke? Well, thank goodness, for his sake, my mother was serving *Chicken Parmesan* as a main course that night. He gobbled up that chicken and I can't blame him. This chicken parm was nothing like anything he had ever eaten at home. You can imagine my delight when it was broadcasted to the rest of our friends what a great cook my mother was, and the great meal he had at our house (aside from the artichoke, of course).

Thinking back, and knowing my mother, she most likely paired that chicken parm with her mashed potatoes, which were also the best, as they were fluffy, smooth, and never a lump to be found. My favorite dinner was *Chicken Parmesan,* mashed potatoes, and *Early Peas and Caramelized Onions.* I loved the way the sauce and the stretchy cheese merged with the potatoes on the plate, and the way you were able to pick up the peas using a forkful of the potatoes. Just the best, but this chicken parm pairs well with any pasta side. Leftover chicken parm is also great the next day, right out of the refrigerator. A sandwich of cold chicken parmesan on a roll or sliced Italian bread is delicious.

If you want, you can skip the sauce and cheese for the makings of a quick *Chicken Milanese. Chicken Milanese* is such a blank canvass that you can top it with any sauce. Try a lemony hollandaise or a caper sauce. You can also spice up the dish with some hot sauce. I usually top it with some thinly sliced lemon which adds flavor, in addition to color.

As with any chicken recipe, I have to mention (and I will say this only once, people) to be careful when handling chicken (or any raw meat) to avoid cross-contamination. Use a non-porous surface for preparation and wash all surfaces, utensils, and hands before touching any other foods or surfaces.

As long as we are on the subject of washing hands, this makes a perfect place to tell you about this: I am the son of a mother that washed her hands constantly. We used to joke and say to her, "Oh, I'm not eating that. You touched it." Where she would seriously reply, "Yea, well, then you are going to starve because I touched everything on this table." We would eat it, of course. But we would always tease her about her hand-washing obsession and say that

Chicken Parmesan.

Chicken Milanese
(Chicken Parm without the sauce).

"Army Dad" (mid-1940s).

she washed her hands "50 times a day," and "You're going to wash the skin right off of your hands." She had built in sonar, too. No matter where she was in the house, if she heard my father, brother, or me in the kitchen, she'd shout, "DID YOU WASH YOUR HANDS?" "Yessssssss, mother."

My father, on the other hand, was just the opposite. Dad, you see, served in combat in Europe during WWII. Somewhere, along the way, we got the notion that he used to eat his meals out of his army helmet (or, perhaps, cook food in his helmet, or some such thing like that). When anything was questionable "food wise," as to the wholesomeness, cleanliness, or even its level of attraction, we would joke and

say, "Give it to dad. He used to eat out of his helmet." We'd all laugh (well, I guess you had to be there).

Anyway, the key thing to remember when making sauce for chicken parm is that it is better when it has a thin consistency. It will absorb nicely into the chicken and make it moist without being over laden with heavy tomato. Also, use a marinara (meatless) sauce instead of meat (or meat-flavored) sauce, where the rich flavor of the meat is going to fight with the chicken. That is the one important point I needed to make. In the meantime, enjoy this recipe and read on to learn about the other "million and one" ways my mother prepared chicken.

CHICKEN PARMESAN

12 medium chicken cutlets, pounded flat

2 cups plain bread crumbs

¼ cup fresh chopped parsley

1 teaspoon garlic powder

¼ teaspoon salt

¼ teaspoon pepper

1 egg

¼ cup milk

½ cup peanut oil (vegetable or canola will also do)

8 oz. mozzarella cheese (use the packaged type from the dairy case and not the wet mozzarella)

parmesan cheese

Ingredients for the *Basic Marinara Sauce* recipe (as found in this book)

Prepare *Basic Marinara Sauce,* as shown in this book.

In a shallow dish, season the bread crumbs with the parsley, salt, pepper, and garlic powder. In a medium bowl, beat the egg and milk together. Add cutlets to the egg mixture and let bathe for a few minutes. Dredge each cutlet in the seasoned bread crumbs, covering both sides well. Arrange all breaded pieces on waxed paper and refrigerate for at least 30 minutes (this will allow for flavors to absorb, plus will provide better adhesion of crumbs when browning). Discard unused bread crumbs.

Heat the oil in a non-stick skillet. Cook the chicken cutlets in hot oil on both sides until golden in color. Drain on a paper towel and continue until all the pieces are brown. Set aside.

Note: Stop here if making *Chicken Milanese* without the marinara sauce and the mozzarella. Garnish with lemon slices.

Using a baking pan, coat the bottom with a small amount of marinara sauce first. Place the cutlets side by side into the pan on top of the sauce. Spoon the rest of the sauce over the chicken until all pieces are covered (if running short, stretch it with a little water). Sprinkle with parmesan cheese.

Slice mozzarella into ⅛-inch-thick slices and place one slice on top of each piece of chicken. Cover with aluminum foil (shiny side down) being careful not to let the foil rest on top of the mozzarella cheese. Bake on the center rack for about 30 to 40 minutes at 350 degrees, until the cheese is fully melted and bubbling around the chicken. (**Note:** Keep the foil on while cooking to keep the cheese from burning.)

This will make about 4 to 5 servings, depending on your appetite.

Dip chicken in egg, dredge in bread crumbs, brown, and move to a pan that has been coated with sauce. Sprinkle with parmesan cheese and top with mozzarella slices. Cover and bake.

CHICKEN CORDON BLEU

My mother always went on, what I would call, "food kicks." She was the type of person that, once she cooked something she liked, you just kept on seeing that food pop up over and over and over again. That is exactly what happened when she discovered how to make *Chicken Cordon Bleu*. Don't get me wrong, I *love* this dish, especially the way my mother made it. However, when it started to seem like she was making it all too often, I would secretly find myself calling it "Chicken Cordon *Blah*." Well, a lot of years have passed since then, I've matured (I think), and I now have a renewed hankering for these bundles of deliciousness.

I remember the last time my mother made this for us. It was in back in 1997. Chris and I had gone up to North Jersey to pick up my mother's car and to scavenger hunt for treasures out of my parents' basement. You see, they were getting ready to move to Florida and they were only taking one car with them. The other car, my mother's 1985 Ford LTD, was given to me. My mother made dinner for us that night. When we walked in, I asked, "What are you cooking, ma?"

She replied, "Chicken Cordon Bleu." Well, the fear of God began to show on Chris' face. I looked at him and assured him, "It'll be fine, honest. This is *good* Chicken Cordon Bleu. You will like it."

Now, the reader must understand that, before I met Chris, he and his family once ate a bad batch of Chicken Cordon Bleu at a wedding reception. At this point in time, just the words *Chicken Cordon Bleu* made him a little blue (in the face). Well, needless to say, he was polite and ate it that night. And, you know what? He really liked it. However, Chicken Cordon Bleu was never mentioned again in our house until recently, when I tested the recipe for this book.

Once again, there was no written recipe for my mother's version of this chicken dish. She is now gone, so I cannot ask her. I had to recreate the recipe completely from the memory of eating it. Since she made it often, I do have some recollection of watching my mother make this, which definitely helped, but that was a long time ago. I made a test sample so I could properly apportion the ingredients and the chicken turned out just as I had remembered. I must say, I definitely nailed it the first time out of the gate. A little too salty, but I tweaked the salt for my recipe, as needed.

Our house, built in 1955, as it looked when sold in 1997.

Chicken Cordon Bleu.

Having this again, after so many years, I now understand why my mother went on her Chicken Cordon Bleu "kick." As Chris, the reformed Chicken Cordon Bleu skeptic, gobbled the samples up, it was right then and there that I decided to serve this dish to some guests that were coming for dinner later that week. Which meant I would be eating Chicken Cordon Bleu twice in a 4-day timeframe and that, yes, I had officially turned into my mother. Needless to say, our guests raved about it and urged me to do more "recipe testing" on them in the future.

One key note of interest, with the many other Chicken Cordon Bleu recipes you will find out there, Swiss cheese is used. This recipe calls for mozzarella cheese, which gives it an Italian twist. One hint when making this, limit the salt because the ham, cheese, and chicken broth add enough saltiness to the chicken. I learned this the first time I tried to recreate it and I want to give you the benefit of my experience before you over salt it.

Incidentally, that 1985 Ford I acquired was 12 years old in 1997, loaded, with 32,000 original miles, white with a blue canvas roof, very comfortable, but similar to what an *Avon* lady would drive. I took four years of ribbing from various people for it, "Here comes Bob in the *Avon* car. . . very funny, people. Let's eat some CCB!

My "Avon Lady" car –
Mom's 1985 Ford LTD at 12 years old

CHICKEN CORDON BLEU

8 chicken cutlets, pounded flat

1 cup plain bread crumbs

2 tablespoons fresh chopped parsley

1 teaspoon garlic powder

¼ teaspoon salt

¼ teaspoon pepper

1 egg

2 tablespoons milk

½ cup light olive oil (vegetable or canola will also do)

8 slices of deli sliced ham (fairly thin)

4 oz. mozzarella cheese (use the packaged type from the dairy case and not the wet mozzarella)

¼ cup dry white wine

1 cup chicken stock

In a shallow dish, season the bread crumbs with the parsley, salt, pepper, and garlic powder. In another bowl, beat the egg and milk together well. Slice the mozzarella into eight 1" x ½" rectangles.

On a board or a plate, lay one chicken cutlet out flat. Take one slice of ham and cover the entire surface of the cutlet. Place one piece of mozzarella at one end of the cutlet, crosswise, on top of the ham. Roll the chicken/ham around the cheese. Continue rolling until all rolled up, pushing any protruding ham back into the sides of the rolled chicken. (If your chicken cutlet is small, you may want to first roll the ham around the cheese, then roll the chicken around that.) Secure the flap by interweaving a toothpick through it, lengthwise along the rollette. Repeat until all the cutlets are rolled and picked.

Coat each rollette in the egg bath and roll in the seasoned bread crumbs, covering all sides well. Arrange all breaded pieces on a plate and refrigerate for at least 30 minutes (this will allow for flavors to absorb, plus will provide better adhesion of crumbs when browning).

Heat the olive oil in a non-stick skillet (with cover), big enough to fit all the chicken. Remove the chicken from the refrigerator and place the pieces into the hot oil, turning occasionally to brown on all sides. When uniformly golden all around, remove them to a clean plate and set aside. Dump the oil from the pan, and return the hot pan to the stove.

Over medium heat, deglaze the pan with the white wine and add the chicken broth. Return all the chicken back into the broth, cover, and simmer for 30 minutes, checking and carefully rolling around about halfway through the cooking time. When done, allow the chicken to rest for about 10 minutes before serving. Arrange each piece on a platter and pour all the pan juices on top. Serve with your favorite potato or pasta.

This dish makes 4 servings at 2 pieces per serving.

Roll the mozzarella inside the ham, rolled into the chicken cutlet. Secure with toothpick.

Dip in egg and seasoned bread crumbs. Brown on all sides and simmer in white wine/stock.

CHICKEN CACCIATORE

Thus far, I have presented a marinara (meatless) sauce, a meat sauce, and a seafood sauce. I now present to you yet another sauce that is the result of cooking an Italian chicken dish called *Chicken Cacciatore*. With this, we are not making a sauce, per se, but more of a saucy dish where the renderings serve as a delicious topping to any starch served with the chicken. Sides of rice, pasta, noodles, or even mashed potatoes, topped with the sauce, are perfect examples of starches that the chicken can be served upon.

Chicken Cacciatore is a rustic Italian dish, as the Italian word "cacciatore" itself means "hunter" in English. The recipe originated in Italy, when hunters caught rabbit, and prepared them *hunter style.* It was a recipe that adapted very well to poultry (and, of course, this makes perfect sense because anyone that has eaten rabbit will tell you, *"it tastes like chicken"*). I'm not sure if Elmer Fudd had this recipe in mind when he was *"being vwery qwuiet. . .shh"* and hunting for Bugs Bunny, but I'm sure he would have "woved" it, had he finally gotten the chance to cook that hare.

The basic components of food prepared *cacciatore style* are tomatoes, onion, mushrooms, bell pepper, and herbs. I remember my mother using these ingredients to a "T" when she made her Chicken Cacciatore. Some recipes call for braising the chicken in the oven, whereas I remember my mother cooking her chicken on top of the stove in a pot or large covered skillet (the method I use for my recipe here). Some cacciatore recipes I have seen call for wine, but my mother never used wine for this. If you want to use wine, I suggest using it in place of the water to deglaze the pan. And, use only ¼ cup of it to avoid changing the flavor. Oh, and use white wine when doing that.

You can use boneless chicken, if you like it better, although any cacciatore that I have ever had used chicken parts with the bones in. I think the bone-in chicken keeps the dish more in line with its rustic nature. For the sake of my good friend out there, who cannot take eating anything with a bone in it (and you know who you are), by all means go ahead and use boneless chicken.

At the very least, keep the skin on. I know people are concerned about fats these days. So am I, but let me tell you that sometimes you need to have some of these fats for the flavor it adds to the dish, flavor that cannot replicated with any spice or herb. If you want to remove all of the skin from the chicken parts, I cannot stop you, but at least keep the skin on the chicken breasts. It's needed to keep the breast meat moist and it will be enough skin to add the flavor necessary for the success of this dish. You can always remove the skin before eating it. I left all the skin on when I tested this recipe and it did not generate that much fat at all. I didn't even have to spoon any out of the pan before I threw in the onions.

CHICKEN CACCIATORE

1 whole chicken, cut into its various parts or 8 parts of your liking (cut the breasts in half if they are too big using a kitchen shears)

8 oz. can of tomato sauce

2 bell peppers, seeded and cut into chunks (can use green, red, yellow, or a combination)

8 oz. of sliced mushrooms

¾ teaspoon salt

¼ teaspoon pepper

1 tablespoon olive oil

2 garlic cloves, peeled and crushed

1 onion, coarsely chopped

1 teaspoon dry oregano

¼ cup of water

In a large covered skillet, heat up the olive oil. Cook the crushed garlic cloves in the oil over medium heat until they are just getting ready to brown (but do not burn). Remove the garlic from the skillet and discard. Add the chicken parts, arranging them so each piece is touching the surface of the skillet and not overlapping. Sprinkle with salt and pepper. Allow the chicken to sear for a few minutes on all sides, turning each piece until fully seared.

Temporarily remove the chicken from the pan. Spoon out any excessive fat, but leave enough fat to coat the bottom of the pan (about ¼ cup). Add the onion and sauté in the fat. Add the water and deglaze the pan, scraping all the chicken bits from the bottom of the pan and forming a small amount of broth. Stir in the tomato sauce and the oregano.

Add the chicken back into the skillet by nestling the pieces into the sauce. Spread the chopped bell pepper and sliced mushrooms on top of the chicken. Cover and simmer on medium-low heat for about 30 minutes, turning the chicken occasionally, allowing the peppers and mushrooms to incorporate in with the chicken and the sauce. When done, turn off the heat and let the chicken rest in the sauce for about 15 minutes before serving.

Serve on a large platter over white rice, linguini, or noodles. Makes 4 servings.

Prepare all the ingredients.

Sear the chicken parts.

Sauté the onion and deglaze with some water.

Stir in tomato sauce and add the chicken back to the pan.

Add the vegetables on top, cover, and simmer.

Allow the cooked chicken to rest before serving.

Chicken Cacciatore.

ROASTED CHICKEN WITH POTATOES

Okay folks, just to warn you, I had a really rough day today. I'm making this chicken for dinner so I can include it in the book. However, I don't have the patience to measure everything out for you (as I usually do), so you are about to get a lesson on how to create a delicious chicken dinner by using just a list of ingredients, without precise measure (the way most of my mother's recipes have been given to me over the years). I know most of you are probably saying "no sweat." I also happen to know that there are a good number of readers that may be freaked out about this. Have confidence. You are about to earn your "chicken wings" and fly solo.

This recipe, short of not using enough seasoning, is really hard to mess up. It is more about method and technique than seasonings. In fact, you can season the chicken with just about anything. I'm using parsley flakes and garlic powder, but you can use rosemary, or oregano, or lemon pepper. Anything you like, because it is going to come out good, no matter what.

Just to give you a little history about role of the roasted chicken at our house, this was the dish that my mother always had as her failsafe for most of our large family dinners. By failsafe, I don't mean that this is what she made for dinner. This is what she made *in addition* to the dinner! It was very common for us to just finish a huge meal of soup and pasta, when the next thing my mother would say was, "Okay, everybody, there's chicken." We all replied in unison, "CHICKEN?!" I guess she was always afraid that people may still be hungry.

When you think of it, this was actually a perfect thing for her to make as her failsafe. It was easy to throw together, it would cook in the oven while we enjoyed the first courses, and it made good leftovers (should nobody eat it. . . but we did). The ease of preparation is exactly why I am very happy today, given my current state of exhaustion, that this is the meal I need to make for you.

Roasted Chicken with Potatoes.

ROASTED CHICKEN WITH POTATOES

1 roasting chicken, about 3 ½ to 4 ½ pounds

3 to 4 white potatoes, peeled and cut into eighths, lengthwise

1 large onion, halved

Olive oil

Salt and pepper

Garlic powder

Parsley flakes

Paprika

OPTIONAL: Use half white and half sweet potatoes for an interesting variation.

Preheat the oven to 375 degrees. Take one of the onion halves and slice into little wedges. Remove the gizzard and neck pack from the chicken cavity and rinse the chicken under cold water. Place the chicken into a larger, non-stick baking pan, breast up. Sprinkle salt and pepper inside the cavity and place the onion wedges inside.

Arrange the sliced potatoes in the pan around the chicken. Coarsely chop the other onion half and mix in with the potatoes. Drizzle olive oil over the top of the potatoes, plus a little on the chicken, as well. Sprinkle the outside of the chicken and the potatoes with salt, pepper, garlic, and parsley flakes. Lightly sprinkle with the paprika.

Bake for about 1 hour to 1 ½ hours, depending on the size of the chicken, basting occasionally with some of the cavity juices. If the chicken appears done, remove the chicken to a dish and cover with foil to rest before cutting. Test the potatoes for doneness and return to the oven, if needed. After about a 15-minute rest period, cut the chicken into parts and place onto a serving platter. Feeds 4.

Prepare the cavity with salt, pepper, and onions. Cut potatoes lengthwise into eighths and put in the pan.

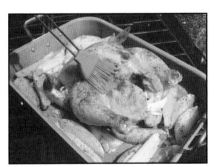

Take the chicken out of the oven to baste occasionally, then return the chicken and potatoes to the oven until they are cooked.

CHICKEN CHOW MEIN

Stop! I know what you are thinking. You are wondering how a recipe for Chicken Chow Mein made it into a book of primarily Italian style recipes (you may have even gone as far as turning to the front cover to see if you have picked up the wrong book). Relax. You are still in the right place. It is still me (Over here. . . hi!). So, what is the deal with this Chicken Chow Mein? Was this something I just threw in to see if you were paying attention? No. The deal is, my mother made it and she made it very well. Besides, you will need something to do with all that boiled chicken and stock you have hanging around from making the *Basic Chicken Stock* (page 50). This is one of my favorite meals of all time, with great flavors and textures layered on a plate; it is always a treat in our house. Here's the story (and, yes, there is a story).

My father has three cousins (all sisters) named Bernice, Geraldine, and Jeannine. These three sisters would throw huge family parties where they invited everyone they were related to in any way, shape, or form. There would be food that went on forever. The buffet table was enormous and the food would just keep coming out. Just when you thought you were done eating, something else would appear that you just had to taste. None of these parties were ever catered. The three of them did all the cooking. When I think back on it now, it was just sick (the amount of food). But we all found room in our bellies, somehow.

A featured buffet item that showed up during one of these parties was Chicken Chow Mein. I remember this vividly because my mother just raved about this dish as she was eating it. Needless to say, she obtained the recipe from the respective cousin that was responsible for this delightful concoction. My mother made it so many times for us since then, it became one of her standards (and one of her food "kicks" that I mentioned earlier). I would like to give credit to the person that ultimately came up with this recipe, but I don't know where (or who) they obtained this from. This occurred so long ago. I don't think it actually came from China, although I've ordered it in Chinese restaurants and I have to say that our American version comes pretty darn close.

One time I was in Florida visiting my parents. It was New Year's Eve and we were going to have a small gathering at my folks' house for food, drinks, and New Year's festivities. Wondering what to make, I was going through my mother's recipe box and discovered the infamous Chicken Chow Mein recipe. As I pulled it from the recipe archives, I instantly knew what I wanted. I was very excited because I had not had this in years. My mother thought this was a great idea too. It was easy, delicious, and it could be made ahead of time and just heated up before serving. It also is a very interactive food, whereas the dining participants build the layers on their plates to their own liking. I went to the store for the ingredients and she directed me as I did the cooking.

Making Chicken Chow Mein requires chicken that has been pre-cooked. It also requires the use of some chicken stock. In a pinch, if you are not a "homemade chicken stock maker" kind of person, then use canned or boxed chicken stock from the supermarket instead. For the chicken, you can steam boneless breast and/or thighs or use leftover rotisserie chicken. The results should be satisfactory if using these shortcuts.

To sum it up, if anyone has an issue with a Chinese-inspired dish in an Italian-inspired cookbook, I'll just call it Chicken "Ciao" Mein. Yes, this should set things right. Enjoy and Chow! (I mean, "Ciao!")

CHICKEN CHOW MEIN

4 onions, sliced

½ cup peanut oil

2 cups boneless chicken breast, cut into chunks (either steamed or boiled, as from stock chicken)

2 cups chicken stock

1 cup celery, sliced crosswise, slightly on a slant

8 oz. can of sliced water chestnuts

8 oz. can of bamboo shoots

1 teaspoon salt

2 tablespoons of flour

2 cups white rice, uncooked

1 package of crunchy Chow Mein noodles (as condiment)

Soy sauce (as a condiment)

Caramelize onions in a separate pan.

In a pan, caramelize the onions in the oil until clear, but not brown. Turn off and set aside.

In a separate pot, cook the celery, water chestnuts, and bamboo shoots in the chicken stock until the celery is tender (chinese vegetables will remain somewhat crunchy, which is okay). Add the salt to the vegetables, being wary of saltiness. (The chicken stock may already be salty enough, so check before adding the salt.) Add the flour to the vegetables and stock and mix in thoroughly.

Cook the vegetables in the chicken stock.

Cut the cooked chicken breast into chunks and add to the vegetable and stock mixture, along with the caramelized onions.

Cook the rice according to the package directions (2 cups uncooked rice should yield about 4 cups cooked).

Serve the Chicken Chow Mein, rice, noodles, and soy sauce separately at the table.

To build on your plate: Take some rice onto the plate and spoon on some Chicken Chow Mein over the top. Top with some of the crunchy chow mein noodles and soy sauce. Enjoy!

Makes 4 to 6 servings.

Chicken Chow Mein.

CORNISH HENS
WITH NANA'S POULTRY STUFFING

This stuffing recipe is actually an adaptation of one that Nana used for her turkey at Thanksgiving. Seeing as we mostly spent Thanksgiving with my mother's side of the family, I can count the times on one hand that I have eaten Nana's turkey stuffing in my entire lifetime. It was long ago and I was a young boy, but her stuffing did make an impression on me that I remember to this day. It was a rich, bread-based stuffing, Italian-inspired with prosciutto, pignoli nuts, mozzarella, and parsley. However, these are not the ingredients that stand out in my mind.

One ingredient that Nana used ever so sparingly in her stuffing was the liver and gizzards from the turkey itself. I remember enjoying this delicious stuffing at one Thanksgiving dinner of yore and biting into a piece of the liver. From there on in, I was not a fan of Nana's stuffing, but only because of that chunk of liver. The rest of it, I loved. The topic of a recent conversation with my cousin Sue, she set me straight and urged me to try it again. You see, Sue has been making this "Nana-inspired" stuffing for years after Nana's passing and gave me a little tip.

Sue creams the liver in a food processor prior to sautéing and mixing in (whereas Nana just chopped the liver and gizzards up with a knife). My father and I recently had an opportunity to taste Sue's version of Nana's stuffing. I can see where the grinding up of the liver made a big difference. I must say, it was delicious. The liver provided a hint of interesting flavor. With the liver being pureed, there were no surprises as it was being eaten. The liver element was totally undetectable, but it added that little something, just enough to make it unique.

Sue also told me that this makes an excellent stuffing for other poultry, especially Cornish hens. Coincidentally, I was planning to include a stuffed Cornish hen recipe in this book, as my mother al-ways made them on special occasions. My mother's poultry stuffing was good, but nothing really special, just a plain old bread stuffing. So I am taking this opportunity to demonstrate Nana's stuffing and include a Cornish hen recipe at the same time (literally, killing two birds with one stone).

The stuffing does not have to be cooked inside a turkey. It can be baked in a casserole separately as a dressing (and that is the version Sue had us taste). My father said that his personal preference is cooking it inside the bird, because the poultry juices are absorbed into the stuffing, making it more flavorful and moist. Of course, if you are a person that abhors liver, then just don't use it. Without the liver, it will still be a different and delicious variation of stuffing.

As for Cornish hens, in general, I loved when my mother served them stuffed. I was amazed at how she would take a hen and cut it in half, so each serving would be ½ of a hen with the stuffing still inside. Then she would make gravy from the pan juices to pour over the top. The presentation was beautiful. The meat was always so tender and fell away from the bone. The stuffing would pull away from the cavity in a nice, molded mound. Mmm. . . I'm salivating just thinking about it.

Cornish Hens with Nana's Poultry Stuffing.

Notice that this recipe does not call for salt in the stuffing, as the other ingredients are salty enough to carry the flavor. I know that most people already know this, but just as a reminder. . . DO NOT stuff poultry with hot stuffing and/or allow it to sit for a long period of time, even if in the refrigerator. This may cause bacteria to form inside, which can make you very sick (or dead). Again, wash all surfaces, utensils, and hands after handling poultry. Cook hens immediately after stuffing them.

CORNISH HENS WITH NANA'S POULTRY STUFFING

2 Cornish hens (about 1 ¼ to 1 ¾ pounds each), retain liver and gizzards

2 cups cubed day-old Italian bread

2 tablespoons pignoli nuts

¼ cup chopped Italian parsley

4 oz. mozzarella cheese, cubed (use the mozzarella from the dairy case, not the deli fresh)

1 egg, beaten

1 - 2 tablespoons of olive oil

1 small onion, finely chopped

6.5 oz. can of mushroom stems and pieces, well drained

6 slices prosciutto, cut into small pieces

¼ teaspoon black pepper

Remove gizzard packs and rinse the hens, inside and outside. Set them side by side in a roasting pan. Remove the gizzards from the packages and discard the necks (or use to make a small pot of stock). Rinse the gizzards and grind in a food processor or chopper until creamy in texture. Set aside.

Heat olive oil in a large non-stick skillet. Add the chopped onion and sauté until clear. Add the mushrooms, prosciutto, and the black pepper. Mix in and heat with the onions and move all to the sides of the pan (if not using the liver/gizzards, stop here). Add a little more oil to the center of the pan, if needed. Cook the creamed liver and/or gizzards in the empty center of the pan, chopping with a wooden spoon, until cooked and no longer pink. Then, mix in with all other ingredients.

Set the sauté aside and allow to cool, somewhat. Preheat the oven to 350 degrees. In a large bowl, mix the sauté in with the cubed bread. Stir in the beaten egg, parsley, pignoli nuts, and the cubed mozzarella until all the ingredients are evenly distributed.

Stuff the cavity of each hen, pushing and packing it in tightly. Flap the excess skin over the opening and secure with a toothpick, if desired. Add some water into the baking pan, about ¼ inch up. Salt and pepper the outside of the hens. Bake for about 1 ½ hours, basting occasionally, until the outer skin is nicely brown in color and the stuffing swells from the cavity. Allow the hens to rest about 15 minutes out of the oven before cutting.

To serve: Cut the hens in 2 equal halves so each portion contains a breast, wing, leg, and thigh portion, and the stuffing is still inside the cavity. Drizzle with a little homemade gravy. Serves 4.

Gravy: Strain a little of the pan juices into a saucepan. Melt in 1 tablespoon of butter. Whisk in about 1 - 2 tablespoons of flour, making a rue. Whisk the rest of the pan juices or a little chicken stock in, a little at a time, until the desired amount of smoothness is achieved. Add salt and pepper to taste.

Optional "out of bird" method: Double the recipe. (If there is no poultry, use 4 – 6 chicken livers that you have purchased or saved/frozen from previous chickens.) Use an oven safe dish that has been generously prepared with cooking spray. Bake covered for about 1 hour at 350 degrees. Remove the cover for the last 15 minutes of baking to allow the top to brown and get somewhat crispy.

Rinse hens and place in a roasting pan. Separate livers and whirl smooth in a food processor or chopper.

Sauté the onion until clear. Add in mushrooms and chopped prosciutto.

Push other vegetables to the sides, pour in liver puree, and chop fine as it cooks.

  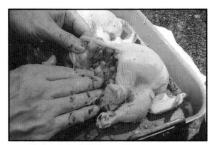

Mix all together in the pan. Cool and mix with bread, pignoli, parsley, and cheese. Stuff the hens.

Secure the opening with a toothpick. Bake until brown and puffed up. Cut in half for serving.

PORK CHOPS, POTATOES, AND VINEGAR PEPPERS

One evening, we were at my brother's house and my sister-in-law made grilled pork chops for dinner. They were wonderfully marinated and grilled to perfection. The after-dinner conversation led us to an obscure topic in which we needed to consult my father on, so we called Florida. Using speakerphone, we solved the matter at hand and delved into idle chit-chat with Dad. We told him we had just finished dinner and told him the menu. His response: "There is only one way to eat pork chops and that is to prepare them with potatoes and vinegar peppers."

Right then and there, a surge of memories overcame me as I remember my mother preparing pork chops this way quite often. My father was correct, in that it is a delicious way to prepare pork chops. As far as being the "only" way, well, I have had many a mean pork chop in my time and I could easily create an argument against that, if I so choose to (but I don't

choose to). Instead, I was very excited about him sparking this memory. This is a true resurrecting of a meal that I have not had in a very long time.

Nana would have been the perfect "go to" person for instructions about this dish, seeing that she always appeared to me to be the "vinegar pepper queen." (Nana is also the inspiration for our featured *Antipasto* and *Stuffed Vinegar Peppers*.) Since she, nor my mother, is around to ask, I only saw fit to call my father and interrogate him further on what he knows about cooking this dish. If anything, just to get a list of ingredients that I can work with. I first looked online, and there were a few recipes, but nothing like I remember. One recipe, called "Pork Chops and Vinegar Peppers," used pepperoncini. I knew this was definitely wrong for the recipe I had in mind. The one thing you're supposed to use are the same sweet peppers used for the *Antipasto* and *Stuffed Vinegar Peppers* (pages 29 and 34, respectively) recipes I described earlier. Pepperoncini is not what I meant by "vinegar peppers."

My great grandfather, Paul Bucco (center), pictured with all his children. From his left: Mario, Angelina (Nana), Furio, Vera, & Hugo. From his right: Martha, Joe, Edith, Febo, & Erklie.

Pork Chops, Potatoes, and Vinegar Peppers.

What is nice about this dish is that you can spice it up as much as you like. Throw in one hot cherry pepper just to turn the heat up a little, if you desire. Use more (or all) hot cherry peppers to make it "five-alarm." I suggest going with the sweet version first, so you can capture the true flavors without scorching your tongue off. I suppose that, if you are one that fancies pork tenderloin, you can use sliced pork loin medallions instead of chops and get the same results. Being off the bone, the meat may be a little dryer, so do not overcook. This dish is reminiscent of something called "Chicken Murphy," if anyone is familiar with that. Here, pork is used versus chicken and there is no sausage either. If one wants to use chicken instead, I do not see an issue with this except, perhaps, you may want to cook it a little longer under the lid.

If there are any *Sopranos** fans in the audience, you may remember "Pork Chops and Vinegar Peppers" as the meal that Vito served up to his boyfriend in one of the later episodes where Vito was hiding out, incognito, in Vermont. I found a recipe for this in *The Sopranos Family Cookbook*, however it does not include potatoes, nor does it call for onions, like ours. They also use whole garlic, whereas I use just a little garlic powder to flavor the meat.

My great grandparents, Paul and Carmella Bucco (Paul's brother was Vito, who was grandfather of Sopranos creator, Chase).

*Interesting tidbit: The creator of the hit series *The Sopranos* and I share some of the same blood. His grandfather is my great grandfather's (Paul) brother (Vito), both surnamed "Bucco." Vito's daughter (my grandmother's cousin, Norma Bucco) married "Chase," and David is their son. Many of the show's characters were given actual names of people in the Bucco family (Carmella, Furio, etc.).

PORK CHOPS, POTATOES, AND VINEGAR PEPPERS

4 medium-thick pork chops (preferably bone-in), at room temperature

4 medium vinegar peppers (mix red and green, if possible)

⅔ cup of the liquid from the vinegar pepper jar

2 large potatoes

1 medium onion

⅔ cup peanut oil

Garlic powder

Salt and pepper

Remove stems and seeds from the vinegar peppers and cut into ½ x 1 inch slices. Cut the onion into quarters, and then each quarter into thin slices. Peel and cut the potatoes into quarters lengthwise, and then slice them into ¼ inch slices. Set all of these ingredients aside for later use.

Heat up the peanut oil in a large skillet until very hot. Fry the potato slices (they should sizzle when added to the pan). Salt and pepper them while cooking, turning occasionally and allowing them to get somewhat brown and crispy on the outside. Remove potatoes from skillet with a slotted spoon and place in a paper towel-lined bowl to absorb any excess oil. Put a couple of tablespoons of the excess oil from the potato pan into a second skillet and heat up. Carefully discard the rest of the oil from the potato pan and return to the stove.

Lightly salt, pepper, and garlic powder each side of the pork chops. Sear the pork chops in the second skillet for about 3 minutes per side. Meanwhile, in the first (potato) skillet, turn the heat back on and deglaze with the jar liquid, scraping up all the potato pieces from the pan. Add the onion and sauté for about 3 minutes. Add the vinegar pepper slices and sauté for a few minutes more. When the pork chops are completely seared, pour the onion/pepper sauté over the top. Layer the cooked potatoes on top of that (if it looks dry, feel free to add a little water to the pan).

Cover and simmer all of this for about 15 minutes. When done, remove the pork chops from the pan and line up on a platter. Spoon the onions, peppers, and potatoes over and around the pork chops on the platter. Serve hot. Makes 2 servings at 2 chops per person.

Slice the peppers, onions, and potatoes and set aside.

Fry the potatoes until somewhat browned and set aside to drain.

Deglaze the potato pan with jar liquid, sauté onions and peppers, while searing chops in a second pan.

Cover the seared chops with the onions, peppers, and potatoes. Cover and simmer.

PORK CHOPS WITH POTATOES AND SAUERKRAUT

Just when you thought that these were mostly Italian recipes, I come up with something else that isn't. My mother didn't only cook Italian food. She cooked many non-Italian-inspired dishes, as well. This pork chop recipe is not as Far East as *Chicken Chow Mein*, but an Eastern European-inspired one. The principles are the same as the *Pork Chops, Potatoes, and Vinegar Peppers,* in that it has that briny flavor, but the preparation is different. This one is done in the oven instead of on the range top. I wanted to include it in this book because it is one of my favorite "one dish" meals that my mother used to prepare on a regular basis. It is a good recipe for those, like me, who love the flavor of sauerkraut. As a matter of fact, when it comes to topping a hot dog, it is mustard and sauerkraut for me, all the way.

The first time I made this recipe, it was because Chris became very intrigued when I told him about a little pork chop and sauerkraut dish that my mother used to prepare. Excited about trying the dish, he encouraged me to ask my mother how to make it. Being of German descent, and from a family that worshipped pork (or any meat, for that matter), Chris was elated at the notion of me cooking something that was not Italian in nature.

PORK CHOPS WITH POTATOES AND SAUERKRAUT

4 pork chops (bone-in) or 6 pork loin medallions

16 oz. package of sauerkraut, drained

2 large potatoes, peeled

1 ½ cup beef broth

1 medium onion

½ teaspoon garlic powder

1 teaspoon salt

¼ teaspoon pepper

1 tablespoon peanut, canola, or vegetable oil

Preheat oven to 375 degrees.

Mix the salt, pepper, and garlic powder together and season all sides of the chops using about half of the mixture. Set aside. Quarter the onion and then slice each quarter into small slices. Slice the potatoes into very thin, no thicker than ¼ of an inch thick pieces (you can also use a mandolin for slicing both the onions and the potatoes, if you have one). In a deep baking dish, or a casserole with a cover, arrange

Pork Chops with Potatoes and Sauerkraut.

the sliced potatoes in a flat layer and season with the remainder of the salt/pepper/garlic powder mixture.

Heat the oil in a skillet and sear each chop (or medallion) about 3 minutes on each side. When seared, arrange the chops so that they are, individually, lying flat on top of the potatoes, overlapping slightly, if at all.

Use only ¼ cup of beef broth and add to the hot pan, deglazing and loosening up any caramelized pork pieces left behind by the searing. Add the sliced onions to the pan and sauté until clear. Pour the onion sauté evenly over the pork chops. Finally, make one last layer on top using the sauerkraut. Pour the remaining beef broth over the top.

Cover the baking pan entirely, and tightly, with aluminum foil (or just use the cover, if using a covered casserole dish). Place in the oven (center rack) for 1 hour, without opening the oven door or checking under the foil. This will be enough time to allow the heat and steam under the foil to cook the thin potatoes. Check for doneness when the potatoes are cooked. Remove from the oven and serve hot with a nice rye or pumpernickel bread.

Makes 2 to 4 servings, depending on your appetite.

Slice onions thin.

Slice potatoes thin.

Layer the potatoes on the bottom and season.

Sear the pork chops on both sides.

Deglaze pan with broth and add onions.

Place chops on top of potatoes and add cooked onions.

Top with a layer of sauerkraut.

Pour beef stock over the top.

Tent with foil and bake.

YOU NAME IT* AND PEPPERS
(*SAUSAGE/VEAL/FRANKS)

Anyone that has studied U.S. History and the Industrial Revolution has heard of *interchangeable parts*, a concept that revolutionized manufacturing in our country. Without even realizing it, my mother was industrious in this way, using this "interchangeable" concept often in her own kitchen. In thinking back about this, it became apparent to me how she took one basic recipe and changed just one or two parts or steps and created a totally different, yet similar, dish.

So far, you may have even noticed that there are other recipes in this book with similarities in their basic ingredients and/or technique. However, nowhere is it more obvious than with dishes made "con pepi" (i.e., with peppers). Of course, sausage is probably the most popular single ingredient that we often see paired with peppers. In New Jersey, *Sausage and Peppers* are everywhere. Not only is it a boardwalk classic, but also a backyard barbeque standard.

Oh, those great summertime family barbeques we had, especially on the 4th of July. Everyone would make something. I remember Aunt Mary would bring the baked beans and make her delicious *Sausage and Peppers.* My Aunt Dolly would offer up some of her delicious salads. We also had American basics like barbequed chicken, hamburgers, and hot dogs. My mother baked the *Classic Sponge Cake* as the birthday cake. . . yes, *birthday cake!* You see, July 4th is not only our nation's birthday, but it is also Aunt Mary's birthday. In fact, my grandmother must have been a very patriotic woman. All three of her children were born on national holidays. My mother was born on Washington's Birthday, Aunt Mary on Independence Day, and Uncle Tony on Flag Day. You could not plan that if you tried.

On the 4th of July, Uncle Tony was our *fireworks connection.* I'll always remember him arriving with "the bag" and all the kids would get very excited about what kind of stuff was in there. He had sparklers, firecrackers, bottle rockets, cherry bombs, M80s, and Roman candles. You name it and he had it.

We couldn't wait to set them off. Of course, none of this was done without his supervision. I particularly remember once when my brother and cousins rigged up a bottle rocket with a little box in order to send an ant into orbit (That's "A-N-T", as in the bug. Not "A-U-N-T", as in Ann, Mary, or Dolly). When darkness fell, we would do fun stuff with sparklers. I think my mother even stuck them in Aunt Mary's birthday cake, in lieu of candles. To this day, the smell of a sparkler burning brings me back.

Ann (Mom), Mary, and Dolly (c. late 1960s).

My mother also made *Veal and Peppers,* but one of the more interesting things that she made with peppers was (ahem) frankfurters. Other than the Italian Hot dog, which usually includes potatoes, where else have you ever heard of such a thing? The franks are actually cooked in with the peppers. I remember her making this often for us as kids and I simply had to revive the recipe here (plus I was curious about tasting this again for the first time in many years).

All of these *Whatever. . . and Peppers* dishes can be made white (no tomato) or red. As for me, I like my *Sausage and Peppers* white, on a hard roll. I like my *Veal and Peppers* red, usually over rice or linguini. I'm neutral on the *Franks and Peppers.* Red is the only way that I can remember my mother making it, but I imagine I would like it white as well, perhaps adding some potatoes, like the classic Italian Hot dog. Please, experiment with these recipes using *interchangeable parts* of your own.

SAUSAGE AND PEPPERS

18 sweet Italian sausages

6 medium green bell peppers, stem/seeds removed and cut into 1-inch chunks

2 onions, sliced thin

2 tablespoons olive oil

1 tablespoon garlic powder

Dash of salt

Dash of pepper

1 cup of water

OPTIONAL: 8 oz. can of tomato sauce

Preheat oven to 375 degrees.

In a large skillet, brown the sausage well on all sides (sausage will still be a little pink inside). Remove from the skillet and set aside to cool slightly. (The pre-browning of the sausage serves 2 purposes: (1) To add flavor with a crisp, brown casing; (2) To firm up the meat just under the casing so slicing results in a nice, clean cut without being mushy.)

Add the onions and sauté, allowing them to cook clear and to somewhat "relax." Add the green pepper chunks and stir in to cook along with the onions (if using the tomato sauce, stir in the whole can at this time to cook with the onions and the peppers). Stir in a little salt and pepper and add the garlic powder and the water. Cook uncovered for about 15 minutes, stirring occasionally. The water should form a light gravy.

While the peppers and onions are cooking, take the pre-browned sausage links and slice each, cross-wise, on a slant, into quarters, about ¾-inch wide. Arrange the sausage slices into a suitable size baking dish. Turn the contents of the skillet into the baking dish over the sausage. Cover with foil and place into the oven (**Note:** If making for a party, it is better to do up to this point in advance, store in the refrigerator, and bake the rest of the way just prior to serving. The flavors of the peppers, onions and sausage get a chance to meld nicely together.)

Bake for a total of 40 minutes (30 minutes covered, and uncovered for the last 10 minutes). The sausage should be totally cooked and the peppers soft. Serve warm. Makes enough for a small party buffet.

Brown sausage on all sides and remove to cool somewhat. Relax the onions in the hot pan.

Add the peppers to the onions and cook until soft. Meanwhile, slice the browned sausage in quarters on a bias and move the slices to a baking pan.

Gradually add water to the peppers/onions, allowing a light sauce to form. Pour all over top of the sausage in the baking pan. Stir and bake.

Sausage and Peppers.

VEAL AND PEPPERS

1 to 1 ½ pounds of boneless veal
(usually sold already cubed for stew)

2 green bell pepper, stem/seeds removed
and cut into 1-inch chunks

1 onion, sliced thin

1 teaspoon olive oil

1 teaspoon garlic powder

½ teaspoon of salt

Dash of pepper

½ cup of water

8 oz. can of tomato sauce

Remove any thin layers of fat or grizzle from the veal. If the cubes are thick, slice into thinner slices, no more than ½ inch wide. (**Hint:** Sometimes veal can tend to be tough or chewy in this dish. To help tenderize, slice the veal cubes across the grain. Also, you may want to pound the cubes down to size between sheets of plastic wrap, which will help tenderize the veal further.)

Once the veal is prepped, toss the veal slices with the garlic powder, salt, and some black pepper.

In a large skillet (one with a cover), heat the oil. In a stir-fry fashion, quick sear the veal slices in the hot pan. Once all sides are browned, remove the veal from the skillet and set aside.

Add the water to the skillet to deglaze. Add the sliced onions and sauté, allowing them to cook clear and to somewhat "relax." Add the green pepper chunks to the pan and stir in to cook along with the onions. Stir in the whole can of tomato sauce and cook with the onions and the peppers. Bring back to a boil, lower the heat, cover and cook for about 15 minutes, stirring occasionally.

After the vegetables cook for 15 minutes, throw the pre-cooked veal slices (along with any run-off juices) back into the skillet. Mix in well with the sauce and vegetables, cover and simmer on low for another 15 minutes, stirring occasionally. You can make this

ahead of time and reheat, or serve immediately over rice or linguini. Makes 2 to 3 servings

**Remove fat or grizzle from veal and slice
(pound to tenderize, if desired).**

**Sear the veal slices in a hot pan and remove.
Sauté the onions and the peppers.**

**Add the tomato sauce, cover, and simmer,
stirring occasionally until the peppers are cooked.**

Veal and Peppers.

FRANKS AND PEPPERS

1 lb. of all beef frankfurters (package of 8)

2 green bell pepper, stem/seeds removed and cut into 1-inch chunks

1 onion, sliced thin

¼ teaspoon garlic powder

Dash of salt

Dash of pepper

½ cup of water

8 oz. can of tomato sauce

OPTIONAL: Leave the tomato sauce out, but increase the water to ¾ cup. Remove the cover during the last 5 minutes of cooking to allow the water to dissipate.

Cut the frankfurters crosswise into five slices, each about 1-inch wide.

In a large, non-stick skillet, sear the frank slices, about 3 to 4 minutes, until they start to brown and caramelize. Add the onions and cook in with the franks, allowing the onions to cook clear and to somewhat "relax" and take on some color (about 2 minutes). Mix in the green pepper, salt, pepper, and garlic powder.

Stir in the whole can of tomato sauce and the water with the franks, onions, and peppers. Cover and cook on medium heat, stirring occasionally, for at least 20 minutes or until the peppers are the desired tenderness.

When done, uncover the pan and cool for 5 minutes. Serve warm on a hard roll.

Makes 4 sandwiches.

Slice the frankfurters crosswise.

Brown and caramelize the franks.

Add the sliced onions, green peppers, and cook together. Add the sauce.

Mix all together, cover and cook for about 20 minutes.

Franks and Peppers.

STEAK PIZZAIOLA

I am going to admit, right up front, that my mother never made this recipe with steak. She always made it with shoulder cut lamb chops. It has to be, let's see, at least 25 years that I have had Lamb Chops Pizzaiola (Yes, at least, because I'm sure I haven't had it since I moved out of my parents' house). I also have to admit that Lamb Chops Pizzaiola was not one my favorite meals, nor was it my brother's favorite (he actually shivers at the mere mention of it). But, for all the criticizing we do, I remember always eating it up and walking away from the table satisfied. You might be wondering, if I don't care for pizzaiola, why I am including it in this book. The answer to this is *"I just have to."* Call it nostalgia, I guess. My mother made it so often I felt compelled to recreate it.

Here's the thing. The pizzaiola sauce she prepared the lamb chops in was delicious, without a doubt. What we objected to most was the cut of meat itself. The shoulder cut lamb chop, whatever meat you can find on there, has a chewy texture. I don't mean to insinuate that you should use loin lamb chops for this (they are WAY too expensive for this application).

I originally tested this recipe with shoulder lamb chops, thinking that I could fix the chewy texture issue somewhat, but I was unable to. I saw some shoulder lamb chops in the store and they looked nice, fresh, and lean, so I bought them. I thought I could minimize the chewy texture by not over-

cooking the meat. I think I was successful in making a better finished product (not perfect, but better). Aside from buying the leanest chops I could, I seasoned the meat first and let it stand awhile prior to searing. I also did another thing Mom did not do. I removed the chops from the pan after searing them off. I then deglazed with the tomato and added the spices, building the sauce before returning the chops to the pan. She built the sauce in the pan, right on top of the seared chops.

In tasting these after such a long time, I have to say that the flavor I remembered was spot on. Even better, there was an actual person who never had them before that I could test them on (Chris). He is a meat lover, so this was a true test. I chose to serve them with mashed potatoes. He liked the flavor. (A light tomato base with just the right amount of spices and the sauce made a nice topping for the mashed potatoes.) He liked the presentation. (Nice and earthy looking on the serving platter, with a bright red color. He wanted to dive right in.) The texture, though, was not so good. (The lamb chops had some nice tender spots. Other spots were still very tough and chewy.) I am convinced that it is just the nature of this cut of meat, because they looked absolutely beautiful when I bought them.

Now, I was faced with a dilemma. When you are a cookbook author, you want to supply recipes that people are going to like. I could have scratched this one, but I thought it was still a worthwhile recipe. With that, I decided to trade out the shoulder lamb chops and make the same recipe with sirloin steak instead (for *Steak Pizzaiola*). That was the answer. It was a BIG improvement on the tenderness factor. I suppose a nice bone-in pork chop would work nicely with this recipe, as well. My father told me that my grandmother used to make "Veal Pizzaiola" and she did it in the oven. Any meat you choose, I think you will enjoy the fresh flavor of the tomato and herbs paired up with the meat, along with the nice, bread-dipping juices.

Steak Pizzaiola.

STEAK PIZZAIOLA

2 top round or sirloin steaks (about 1 lb. each)

1 14.5 oz. can diced tomatoes

2 garlic cloves

3 tablespoons fresh parsley, chopped coarsely

2 tablespoons olive oil

Salt and pepper to taste

OPTIONAL: For other meat options, use veal chops, pork chops, cubed steak, or lamb chops.

Tenderize each steak by pounding with a meat pounder. Rub a little salt, pepper, and olive oil on both sides of each steak. Allow steaks to reach room temperature, about 30 minutes. In a hot skillet (with a cover), large enough to fit each steak flat on its surface, drizzle the olive oil in the hot pan and sear each steak for about 4 minutes per side. Meanwhile, remove the skin from the garlic and cut each clove into thin slices.

Remove the seared steak from the pan and set aside on a separate dish. Open the can of tomatoes. In the same pan, sauté the garlic slices, but do not burn. Put all the diced tomatoes into the pan and stir in with the garlic. Add the chopped parsley, salt, and pepper. Bring to a boil, cover, reduce heat, and simmer (sauce only) for about 5 minutes.

Return the steaks to the pan. Nestle them into the sauce (spooning some of the sauce on top of each steak). Cover and simmer for 5 minutes. After the first 5 minutes, turn the chops over, cover, and finish for another 5 minutes. When done, turn off and allow to rest (covered) for about 5 minutes more.

Place the steaks on a serving platter and spoon the tomatoes and juices over the top. Best if served with a plain side starch like a mashed potato, white rice, or noodles. You will want to spoon the additional juices onto your starch of choice. You may also want to have some bread handy to dunk into the juices. Makes 2 servings (1 steak per person).

**Tenderize and season the meat.
Sear on both sides and set aside.**

**Build the sauce base.
Add the herbs and simmer the sauce.**

**Add the meat back into the pan and nestle into
the sauce. Move to a serving platter when done.**

STUFFED MEATLOAF

Stuffed Meatloaf.

Riddle: What came first, the chicken or the egg? Well, whatever your answer is, you're wrong. The correct answer is: The *Meatloaf* came first (well, in Nana's house, anyway). Here is an example of an American, blue plate classic with an Italian spin. Leave it to my grandmother to come up with something like this.

What I am referring to is a meatloaf that contains onion, parsley, and mozzarella cheese and includes a surprise center. . . hard boiled eggs and salami. Yes, the eggs are rolled up in the salami and embedded within the meat. They are positioned, as such, so that the innermost center slices of the meatloaf contain this very attractive round of white and yellow. The meat itself is moist and contains just a hint of the salami flavor, which is released into the meat as it cooks. Also, the mozzarella melts into the meat, providing yet another layer of flavor. To say the least, comfort food as its finest. When you think of it, the ingredients are reminiscent of her poultry stuffing, only with meat instead of bread as the main ingredient (and, of course, no chicken livers).

This recipe is what I would classify as quintessential Nana. When I tasted this recipe, all I had to do was close my eyes and I could imagine that she was physically there, cooking it, and placing the dish in front of me. Bittersweet as this is, I could also imagine my grandfather there at the table clutching his heart. My God, a meatloaf made with meat, eggs, and salami. No wonder it tasted so good, but you could just feel your arteries hardening with every bite. It was so good though, I didn't care. I could always go back to the oatmeal tomorrow.

The next test is how well meatloaf fares the next day, sliced on a sandwich. I wasn't sure which topping would complement it best, so I divided my sandwich into quarters. The first quarter I ate plain, just to see how the flavors melded in overnight. The other three quarters I spread with mustard, ketchup, and mayonnaise, respectively, to see which tasted best. Plain was good, definitely moist enough to eat on bread by itself, but it still needed something.

Both the mustard and the ketchup I used sparingly, as to not overpower the meat, and I liked them both equally. They complemented the sandwich nicely in their own way. When I got to the last quarter, the one with the mayonnaise, I prepared to take a bite by picking up the phone and strategically positioning my thumb on the "9." Of course, the one with the mayo is probably the worse for you, but it tasted the best. It's always the way. Luckily, I made it through the test without having to call 9-1-1!

It's funny. We are so used to making meatloaf using ground turkey (and we have mastered the art of actually making it moist and delicious), that I was not used to seeing so much fat runoff when using the beef. For the sake of tradition, and recipe testing, I tried to ignore the fat. However, I curiously tried this recipe using ground turkey instead and it came out really good. So, I will leave it up to you. Either way, it's a winner. I suggest trying it with meatloaf mix (beef/veal/pork) first, as the recipe calls for. This way you can get to experience the authentic flavor that meatloaf was meant to have.

Not intending to insult anyone, I do include a procedure for hard boiling eggs. Oh, I could hear you right now, "What, is this guy kidding here with a recipe for *hard-boiled eggs*?" Believe it or not, as well as I know my way around the kitchen, I could not hard boil an egg right. My sister-in-law gave me a tip about hard boiling eggs. I just wanted to share that tip with you, as it was successful for me.

STUFFED MEATLOAF

1 ½ to 2 pounds of meatloaf mix
(ground beef/veal/pork), or ground turkey

1 egg (raw)

1 medium onion, chopped fine

¼ cup fresh chopped parsley

¼ cup of plain bread crumbs

1 teaspoon garlic powder

½ teaspoon salt

¼ teaspoon pepper

4 ounces of mozzarella cheese, cut into ½-inch cubes

4 to 6 thin slices of Genoa or hard salami

2 to 3 hard-boiled eggs, chilled and peeled

(**Note:** Recipe shows 2 eggs, but adding a third egg will yield more slices that have egg in them.)

How to hard boil the eggs: Place the eggs in a small pot of water so that the surface of the water is above the eggs. Place the pot on high heat. When the water reaches a rolling boil, reduce the heat and boil for at least 5 minutes. Shut off the heat and let the eggs stand in the hot water for about 10 minutes. With the eggs still in the pot, run cold water into the hot water until the water in the pot turns cold. Add some ice cubes to the cold water to shock the eggs. To peel, take the cold egg, tap the fat end on a hard surface, and break the shell (there is a little air pocket at this end). Gently, with the ball of your thumb, pull the shell away from the egg at the break point. Do this while under running cold water, allowing the water to help separate the shell from the egg.

Preheat oven to 350 degrees. Combine all the ingredients in a large bowl (including the raw egg) except the salami and the hard-boiled eggs. Allow the mixture to rest for about 10 minutes.

Form the meat mixture into a long loaf. Lay into a baking pan. Use a small ladle, a cup bottom, or other egg-shaped utensil to press two well-like holes into the meat. Do this so the egg will sit in the meatloaf, lengthwise, in the same direction as the loaf so

when sliced, you will get a cross-section of the egg.

Take a peeled egg and wrap it in a piece of salami. Wrap it a second time with a second piece of salami until the egg is wrapped completely. Place it into a hole and repeat this with the second egg. Bring some meat up from the sides so that the eggs are completely sealed in by the meat, working and reforming the loaf. (Push any stray mozzarella cubes inside and seal the whole with meat.) Place, uncovered, into the oven and cook for about 45 to 60 minutes. Allow to rest for 5 minutes before cutting.

Makes 4 servings of meatloaf.

Combine all ingredients in the bowl, except the hard-boiled egg and salami. Mix well. Form the loaf and indentation for the hard-boiled eggs.

Wrap the hard-boiled egg in salami and place into the holes.

Bring the meat up and reform the loaf with the eggs embedded inside. Bake.

BAKED FISH WITH HERBS

This recipe is an adaptation of one of my mother's all time standard fish preparations. I know this much about it, she got this technique from Nana. Although I know all of the ingredients by heart, I was still unable to get my recipe to taste exactly like theirs, but I am very pleased with the turnout of this recipe. It was definitely worthy of including, as they were the inspiration for what I came up with. What I love about this recipe is its simplicity. The herbs and the crumbs strike a nice balance with the fish, taste-wise and texturally. The small amount of butter used is just enough to make it yummy without overpowering the other flavors. It is a fast recipe, too. If you are a busy person, you can get home from work and have this fixed up and out of the oven within a half an hour. Serve with a steamed vegetable and baked potato, and you have yourself one healthy meal.

My mother always used flounder for this, but any light, white fish will fare well. I found I love it best with cod because of the way the fish holds up firm and flakes apart. I would steer away from tilapia, as I have tried making it with that and it always seems to shrink up too much when I use this recipe. With tilapia, I usually do a quick pan sear with butter and herbs, or steam it on the grill in a foil pouch with some butter, lemon pepper, and assorted vegetables.

The mega supermarkets of today have extensive fish departments, where I'm sure you will be able to find fresh fish for this recipe. I find that they usually have most kinds of fish I am looking for, and the product seems to moves fast enough. Back in the day, when the supermarkets were not so specialized, our family went to an actual fish market to get fish. The market we went to was over on Franklin Avenue in Nutley, NJ. I can remember, on many occasions, my mother taking me for a haircut over there. (You see, my father's Uncle "Doc" had a barber shop over on Franklin Avenue.) On the way home, as my mother obsessed about how they took "too much off the sides," she would say, "Let's stop at the fish market to see what kind of fish they have for supper."

The only words I can come up with to explain this fish market are "to the point." There was no mistaking that this was a very serious place where fish commerce transpired. A big, minimalistic space with open stainless steel bins containing ice-covered fish, a door to a back room, a scale, a lobster tank, and a cash register (the "optimal business model" for selling fish). Any attempt at décor, at most, was a fish net on the far wall with plastic nautical *thingies* wedged into it. I loved their homemade Manhattan-style clam chowder. It was such a treat to get a container of that every time we stopped. My mother would often buy bluefish. She prepared it on a sheet pan in the oven, smothered with thinly sliced potatoes. Bluefish is an oily fish, so the skin and potatoes would get really crisp in this natural oil. It wasn't one of my favorite meals she made, but I liked it. The potatoes were the saving grace. Not a recipe that I do here, but one I would definitely like to try and recreate someday.

I'm not sure if that little fish market is still in existence today (I would guess not). It doesn't matter, as my hair no longer exists either, thus I no longer require the services of that barber shop. Sorry I do not have any more riveting fishing stories for you that I might have experienced as a young lad. I never really was a fisherman. I mean, the closest I have ever came to actually catching fish was Chris tossing me a can of tuna from the pantry, and I think I even dropped that one. (Ah, yes, the proverbial "One that got away.")

BAKED FISH WITH HERBS

2 lbs. of any white fish fillets
(such as flounder, cod, or haddock)

½ cup plain bread crumbs

2 garlic cloves, chopped fine
(or 1 teaspoon of garlic powder)

½ teaspoon dry oregano

¼ cup of rough chopped, fresh parsley leaves

¼ teaspoon salt

Dash of fresh ground pepper

2 tablespoons of olive oil + an additional ½ teaspoon

1 to 2 tablespoons of butter

**Oil and season the bread crumbs.
Cut thicker pieces of cod into thinner fillets.**

Preheat oven to 400 degrees.

Prepare the crumb topping by combining the bread crumbs, garlic, oregano, parsley, salt, and pepper in a bowl. Add the 2 tablespoons of olive oil and moisten by using your fingers to incorporate the oil evenly throughout the crumbs (they should look somewhat crumbly).

Flounder fillets are fairly flat, and should be fine as is. However, if you are using cod or haddock, some parts of the fillet can be quite thick. If so, make additional, thinner fillets by carefully running a non-serrated edge knife horizontally through the center of the thick end of the cod or haddock.

Layer the fish and sprinkle crumbs in between the layers.

Grease the bottom of a 2-quart glass casserole with the ½ teaspoon of olive oil. Arrange one layer of the fillets on the bottom of the casserole. Sprinkle generously with some of the crumb mixture and dab a little piece of butter on each fillet. Repeat by making another layer of fish/crumbs/butter on top of the previous layer. Keep doing this until all of the fish is used and you end with a layer of crumbs and butter.

Bake for about 20 minutes at a high temperature.

Cover and bake in the oven for 20 minutes. Remove the cover and bake uncovered for another 5 minutes. Remove the fish and cover. Allow to rest for 5 minutes before serving. Serve by cutting a wedge of fish out of the casserole with a spatula. Spoon some of the buttery renderings over the top of each portion. Makes 4 servings.

Baked Fish with Herbs.

BOB'S PORK CHOPS "ON THE FLY"

This wasn't one of Mom's or Grandma's recipes, but it was one that I came up with "on the fly" (hence the name). It happened on a cold, winter's day in January. It came out so good, that I posted a note on Facebook and it got an overwhelming response. I'd like to share it with everyone else. Feel free to substitute the pork chops with chicken or fish (**Note:** If using fish, cut back the 15-minute simmer time until the fish is just cooked.) Here is exactly how it was posted:

1/13/2010

It was still too cold to use the barbeque grill yesterday, so I needed to come up with a way to cook pork chops indoors. I went to the pantry and saw a jar of marinated artichoke hearts. Went to the fridge for other ingredients and here is what I came up with. . . they were delicious!

Grandpa's personal salt shaker still lives on in my cupboard

I have no pictures to post for this recipe, but since we are on the subject of pork, it may be a good time to tell you about my grandfather's *piggy* salt shaker. Ever since I could remember, he had to have his personal salt shaker next to his place at the supper table. I could still hear him today. "How is it Grandpa?" "It needsa salta." That salt shaker still lives on my shelf, and I think of him every time I look at it.

BOB'S PORK CHOPS "ON THE FLY"

2 bone-in pork chops. medium thickness

1 jar marinated artichoke hearts

1 medium onion, sliced

6 cherry tomatoes

1 cup sliced mushrooms

Salt, pepper, garlic powder to taste

Olive oil

Season both sides of the pork chops with salt, pepper, and garlic powder. Heat a non-stick skillet to very hot. Drizzle a little olive oil into the hot pan. Sear the pork chops on both sides (about 3 minutes per side) until nicely browned. Remove the seared chops from the pan and set aside on a platter. Open the artichokes and pour all of the juice only into the pan to deglaze (do not add the artichokes yet). Add the chopped onions and cherry tomatoes. Sauté the onion and tomato in the juice for about 2 minutes, crushing the tomatoes in the pan. Nestle the pork chops back into the onions/tomato. Add the artichokes and the sliced mushrooms on top, cover, lower the heat, and simmer for about 15 minutes (to finish cooking the pork inside). Turn off and allow them to rest for about 5 minutes.

To serve: Place the pork chops back onto the platter and pour all of the pan ingredients on top.

Side suggestion: ½ pound of buttered penne, rotelle, or bow tie pasta (juices from the pork chops will converge with the pasta on your plate, making a nice, light sauce).

COOKIES
AND DESSERTS

BISCOTTI COOKIES / KNOT COOKIES

Ah yes, *Biscotti*! Everyone loves them, topping off a good meal in a fine Italian restaurant, or alongside a $4.99 cup of specialty coffee. We've seen them in many varieties. . . chocolate chip, chocolate dipped, raisin, cranberry, almond, macadamia nut, even savory, garden herbed versions. We've seen them maxi and mini. . . You name it and someone has created biscotti out of it. Today's purchased biscotti is just another perfect example of an Italian classic food that started out as plain, simple, and economical, and has somehow turned chic and expensive. I grew up on biscotti. In fact, the recipe is so basic, that I bet that you have all the ingredients on hand right now to make a batch.

This particular recipe calls for walnuts, but you can leave them out. If you are using the walnuts, resist the urge to chop them. As this is a sliced, loaf cookie, you will see cross sections of the walnuts, which makes them look somewhat pretty. If you are serving to guests, you can lightly dust them with confectioners' sugar, which will dress them up a bit. Oh, and if you want to dip them in chocolate, by all means do so.

Biscotti Cookies.

If there is anyone reading this that does not know biscotti, they are crunchy, delicately sweet and buttery cookies, formed by slicing from a loaf. They last a long time in a covered container. In fact, rumor has it that these "biscuits" were developed many years ago when there was little means of preserving food. It's true. I can make a batch of biscotti and still be eating them out of the cookie jar two weeks later. They are still as delicious and crunchy as the day I made them. And, they ship very well, too! When I was in college, my mother would include biscotti in every care package she sent. The first time I got one, I made the mistake of introducing the biscotti to my dorm buddies. They demolished the whole batch. Subsequent to that, I needed to hide a stash for myself before offering any up. I would have hid them all, but it was very difficult concealing the box as I walked from the campus post office. Besides, it was not fair to keep Mom's biscotti hidden from the world.

Mom's influence spilled over in other ways at school. You see, my mother made sure that she taught me very well about how to take care of myself in her absence. We'd stand at the washer/dryer, her teaching me how to do laundry "properly". . . *"You separate the whites from the colors, whites in hot and colors in warm, etc., and avoid ironing by removing shirts from the dryer damp and hang them nicely on hangers to dry the rest of the way."* I applied this rule diligently in our dorm laundry room, where I remember this poor girl sighing at the folding table. After about 5 minutes of this, she finally looked up at me and said, "Can you please tell me how on Earth you got your whites so white?" I proceeded to relay the *Anna Vendetti Method.* That girl was so intently interested in what I had to say, almost as if I was revealing the secret to world peace. I never knew laundry could be so interesting to someone. She was very cute but, as I am telling you this story, I am just realizing now how much an episode like that was wasted on a guy like me. Well, anyway, back to the cookies. . .

Because biscotti are so crunchy, they are best enjoyed by dunking them in milk. The *Knot Cookies* use the same exact dough as the biscotti, but they are a spoon-dropped cookie instead of a loaf cookie. They have a more cake like, soft center than biscotti because they are not cut and toasted. They are also capped with lemon icing.

BISCOTTI COOKIES

3 ½ cups all purpose flour

6 eggs at room temperature

1 cup sugar

½ cup (or 1 stick) of butter, softened

7 level teaspoons baking powder

1½ teaspoons vanilla extract

¼ teaspoon salt

½ cup walnuts (optional)

Preheat oven to 375 degrees. In one bowl, combine the flour, baking powder, and salt. In a second bowl, beat the eggs well with an electric mixer while adding the sugar, vanilla, and butter. Stir the flour mixture into the egg mixture and incorporate thoroughly to form a sticky dough. Stir in the walnuts at this time (if using).

On a greased cookie sheet, form the dough into 4 loaves, 2 inches wide, about 3 inches apart. (For larger biscotti, divide the dough and make 2 larger loaves, about 3 inches wide, about 4 inches apart.) Make sure you allow for expansion, especially along the sides of the loaves.

Bake for about 15-20 minutes, checking frequently. When the loaves are light brown in color, remove them from the oven and carefully place them on a cooling rack.

To toast: Increase the oven temperature to 400 degrees. On a cutting board, cut the loaves on an angle into ½-inch slices. On the cookie sheet, lay the slices on their side. Place in the oven for about 5 - 10 minutes, but keep checking for a light toasting on top. Careful. . . do not burn! Remove from the oven and turn them over onto the other side. Place back into the oven and then *really watch them* carefully. When done, cool them on a rack.

Beat the eggs with the sugar, vanilla, and butter. Pour in the dry ingredients and mix into a sticky dough.

Fold in the walnuts, divide the dough, and spoon into loaves on a greased pan (space far enough apart for expansion).

Cool the loaves slightly. Slice. Return to the sheet for toasting.

Toast on both sides. Cool completely on a rack before storing.

KNOT COOKIES

Use the same dough as the *Biscotti* recipe (minus the walnuts). Instead of making loaves, dab heaping teaspoons of dough in rows on a well-greased cookie sheet. Bake at 350 degrees until light brown in color. Cool on a rack when done.

Knot Cookies.

Lemon Icing: Start with some confectioners' sugar and mix with fresh lemon juice until a smooth icing forms (adjust consistency by adding more sugar, as needed). "Ice cap" the cookies by dipping the peaks into the icing. The cookies are ready when the icing hardens.

Making Knot Cookies.

ANISE COOKIES

This is the lighter, crispier descendent of the biscotti cookie. The dough is actually a light, loose batter instead of a heavy, sticky dough. The original recipe calls for oil or butter (one or the other, not both). I think my mother opted for the butter. I already knew they were good, so I decided to test the recipe using the oil. The results were great! I could not even tell that there was no butter in there. They were lightly sweet and the taste of the anise was very slight.

I think you will find that these cookies are nice when you want something a little more delicate than biscotti. Perhaps for dessert after a hearty meal, or during afternoon tea with your neighbor ladies. (Do neighbors even get together for tea or coffee anymore?) It definitely is not as manly a cookie as the biscotti, although I am sure any guy would gobble them up in a heartbeat, if placed in front of them.

As a kid, I remember my grandmother (Victoria) always had these at her house. It is specifically the shape and the smell of anise that strikes the memory. She kept them in these big, yellow metal tins in her butler's pantry. (Yes, her house in Montclair actually had a service area between the kitchen and the dining room.) I'd love to see what that house looks like inside today.

ANISE COOKIES

3 eggs (room temperature)

½ cup sugar

1½ cups flour

½ cup oil (can substitute with 1 stick butter, melted)

2¼ teaspoons baking powder

3 drops anise (and 1 or 2 more drops if you want a stronger anise flavor)

Preheat oven to 350 degrees.

Using a hand or stand electric mixer, beat the sugar, eggs, anise, and oil (or butter, if using instead)

together well. Combine the flour and the baking powder. Slowly incorporate the dry ingredients into the wet mixture until a thick batter forms. Grease two baking sheets and, using a large spoon, spoon the batter onto the pan to form loaves (you should get about 4 or 5 loaves, depending on whether you make them long or short).

Bake for 15 minutes until they are a little firm and springy in the center. Remove from the oven and, using a flat, flexible spatula, gently loosen the loaves from the pan. Cool lightly before slicing.

To toast: On a cutting board, slice the loaves on an angle into ½ inch slices. On the baking sheet, lay the slices on their side. Place in the oven for about 5 minutes. Toasting will occur on the bottom side of the cookie. Remove from the oven and turn them over onto the other side. Place back into the oven for about 5 more minutes, but watch them carefully, as not to burn. When done, cool them on a rack. Serve with tea or espresso. Lightly dust with powdered sugar for an elegant look.

Slice and toast similarly to the Biscotti.

Anise Cookies.

CLASSIC SPONGE CAKE
(ANGELINA'S BIRTHDAY CAKE)

If I was ever asked to pick one recipe that has stood the test of time in our family, it would have to be, hands down, this *Classic Sponge Cake*. It came from Nana, and this was my mother's favorite cake to make. My mother then passed the baton to my sister-in-law, Judie, who helped me demonstrate the cake for this book. (Seeing as I had never made it before, and Judie makes it so well and often, it only seemed right for me to not try and reinvent the wheel.) My cousin Sue also picked this recipe up from Nana.

This is the lightest and freshest tasting cake I've ever eaten. Most people that taste this cake for the first time would agree. Prior to assembling, the layers are sprinkled with pineapple juice, which adds additional moisture, flavor, and density to the cake. Using fresh whipped cream as its topping, instead of a buttery/sugary icing, it becomes the ultimate blank canvas for other fillings or toppings. Pictured here with whipped cream and mixed berry filling, my mother applied various fillings and toppings over the years, such as:

> Custard or vanilla pudding
> Lemon pie filling
> Crushed pineapple (drained well)
> Canned or fresh peaches
> Fresh strawberries (like a shortcake)

There are so many possibilities, but I think that the one thing you would not want to use with this cake is anything chocolate. Chocolate definitely would not go well with the general makeup of this cake. The key is to keep the fillings and toppings fresh and light in nature. You can also cover the sides with whipped cream. My mother usually added whipped cream to just the top and center, as pictured.

Called *Angelina's Birthday Cake*, aptly named after Nana who passed it down to her children, this cake has taken on quite a few names over the years in our house. It has been referred to as the "Cuppa-Cuppa" cake, because it uses a "cup o' this," and a "cup o' that." Because it is a "cup o' this and a cup o' that" type of recipe, it is very easy to double and triple the recipe. If you were making a larger rectangular cake, you would double the recipe and use two 9" x 13" pans (or bake all of the batter in one pan, and slice horizontally into two layers).

Written recipe, originally shown with a crushed pineapple filling.

Speaking of Angelina's birthday, Nana was born in 1900, so her age always went along with the current year. I, personally, don't think I would have liked that (being reminded how old I was going to be every New Year's Day). I remember in 1966, on her 66th birthday, a 7-year-old me asked Nana, "How old are you?" She replied, "Oh, how old am I?. . . I'm 16," and she laughed. Well, I'll never forget that day. Every birthday she had since then I would say, "So Nana, are you 17 now?" (Or 18, 19, 20, or whatever followed.) Right up into my adulthood, it was our little private joke between us. At her 80th birthday (pictured next page), I said, "Happy 30th Birthday,

Nana" and winked. She laughed, as always, and it made it all worth it. I suppose I would have been wishing her a happy "60th" this year (only 10 years older than my actual age, which would have made her 110 in real life). Okay, this is scaring me now, so let's move on. . .

There are a few important tips when making this cake. As with any baking, the eggs must be at room temperature. The egg whites and the yolks are mixed separately, and mixed back in gradually with the yolks and sugar. When combining the flour with the other ingredients, you need to start with flour and end with flour, which is a point that my mother could not stress enough when making this cake. If you have a stand mixer with both a wire beater and a paddle attachment, making this will be a breeze. Finally, it helps to put wax paper in the bottom of the pans before pouring in the batter. It not only helps free the cake from the pan, but will keep it from drying out and allow the pineapple juice to absorb without having to poke holes into the cake.

Me (left) getting ready to "dig in" to Classic Sponge Cake, with brother Randy and Judie (c. 1975).

Angelina's (Nana) 80th Birthday Party (August 1980) Nana (center); Standing from her left – My mother, my father (son), Aunt Norma (daughter), Randy (grandson) & wife Judie; Standing from her right – Aunt Sandra (daughter) & husband Mike, Eddie (grandson) & wife Rosalie. Down in front, from left – Uncle Eddie (son) with Mark (great grandson), Chris (grandson), Nancy, Joanie, and Sue (granddaughters), Robert (me, grandson). Back row: Steve (grandson), Aunt Marcella (peeking over), Ronnie (grandson).

CLASSIC SPONGE CAKE (ANGELINA'S BIRTHDAY CAKE)

Note: The steps to making this are not difficult, but they are specific and purposed. For that reason, I wrote this recipe different from the others, in that the pictures are incorporated into each step.

1 cup of sifted flour (sifted first and then measured)

1 teaspoon baking soda

6 eggs at room temperature

1 cup of sugar

1 teaspoon vanilla extract

1 cup pineapple juice (½ cup per layer)

WHIPPED CREAM (FOR TOP AND CENTER ONLY):

½ pint heavy cream

1 tablespoon sugar

½ teaspoon vanilla extract

(Double the above amounts if applying to the sides of the cake)

Preheat oven to 350 degrees. In a bowl, sift the flour first before measuring, and then measure out accordingly. Whisk in the teaspoon of baking powder. Set aside and follow the directions and illustrations below.

Take two pieces of wax paper and score around the bottom of your baking pan to make a pattern. Cut around the scored line and place the wax paper cutout at the bottom of the ungreased pans.

Separate the eggs, putting the whites into the bowl of your mixer. Set aside the yolks. Using the wire attachment, beat the egg whites until stiff (start the mixer on a slow speed and increase the speed gradually).

Move the beaten egg whites to another bowl and put the egg yolks and sugar into the mixer bowl. Using the paddle attachment, begin blending the sugar and the yolks on slow speed, adding vanilla. Increase the speed of the mixer and mix until the contents are a light, lemony yellow color.

Starting with about ¼ of the flour, add to the yolk/sugar mixture and blend slowly (do not over blend). Add about ⅓ of the egg whites and blend in slowly. Repeat with flour, then egg whites, then flour, then egg whites.

Finally ending with flour (remember, start with flour/end with flour), blend in one last time. Scrape down the sides of the mixing bowl into the batter and separate the batter evenly between 2 pans, pouring right on top of the wax paper liner. Bake for 20 – 25 minutes until light brown in color and a toothpick comes out clean (do not let it get too brown or burnt).

Cool on racks in the pans. Work the sides loose and flip out of the pans onto the rack.

Continue to cool with the wax paper on. Just before assembling, peel away the wax paper.
Take pineapple juice (½ cup for each layer) and soak the entire surface of the layer.

Prepare the fruit filling. In a clean mixer bowl, add heavy cream, sugar, and vanilla, and whip into cream.

Spread the middle layer with cream and top with fruit filling. Place the second layer on top and spread the whipped cream over the top layer. Add some fruit to the top as a garnish, if desired.

Classic Sponge Cake.

MOM'S SIGNATURE LEMON MERINGUE PIE

Question: What happened when Mr. Reese accidentally dropped the chocolate in the peanut butter?

Answer: The Reese's Peanut Butter Cup was invented.

Many of us remember those funny commercials that Hershey put out showing two guys unknowingly approaching and getting ready to round the same corner. . . the chocolate lover and the peanut butter lover. . . then, CRASH! Instant discovery! Maybe it didn't really quite happen that way, but it did for my mother when she discovered her *Signature Lemon Meringue Pie.*

Now, if you remember in the Introduction, I talked about "gourmet chef vs. good cook" and I tried to establish how to tell the difference. Well, there was one more type of gourmet out there that I failed to mention. In addition to the "chef" and the "cook," there are some people that I like to call "GBA" (i.e., Gourmet by Accident). The GBA is one that devises a dish that tastes totally wonderful by, either being forced to substitute certain ingredients for others, or throwing together something unexpectedly delicious as a result of a mistake.

I think we all have been a GBA, at one time or another. My mother definitely was. One day, she was making a lemon meringue pie using 2 packages of lemon filling. She accidentally cooked in one box of vanilla pudding with one box of lemon pie filling (instead of using two boxes of the lemon filling). The result was what I like to call, her *Signature Lemon Meringue Pie.* She had made this pie many times before that and knew what the filling was supposed to look like. She discovered her error while cooking the filling on the stovetop. With the pie shell already baking, she had no choice but to continue making the pie with the erroneous filling. What it really turned out to be was pure genius, and became her recipe for lemon pie from that day forward. . . and discovered all *by accident.*

So what made it a "signature" pie? First off, it was the uniqueness of the flavor. The vanilla pudding cut the acidity and "burn" that you can sometimes experience with lemon pie filling. At the same time, the tart lemon cut the sweetness of the pudding, as well. Secondly, because she invented it totally by accident, she owns the technique, as far as I am concerned. But, since she was such a giving person, I am sure that she would want the world to enjoy it.

Now, I'm sitting here thinking, "What the heck does one need to do in order to recreate a lemon pie in which there is no recipe documented and whose filling was created completely by accident?" Okay, well, let's see. . . the crust part is easy (basic), and the meringue part is easy (also, basic). I guess the only question is how to make the filling the way my mother did. I suppose I'll just pretend that the box of vanilla pudding is a box of lemon filling. I'll follow the recipe for the lemon filling, doubling all the other ingredients as if I am making two boxes of that, as I sure she did that day. Then, to the pot, I will add the one box of lemon, and then the box of vanilla pudding and say, "Whoops!" (I hear it does not come out the same unless you say, "Whoops!")

Well, this is exactly what I did and I believe I nailed it first time out. It tasted just like Mom's. So folks, without further ado, I present to you *Mom's Signature Lemon Meringue Pie.*

Lemon Meringue Pie.

MOM'S SIGNATURE LEMON MERINGUE PIE

1 package (2.75 oz.) lemon pudding and pie filling

1 package (2.75 oz.) vanilla pudding and pie filling (must be "cook & serve," not instant)

1 pre-baked pie crust shell (9 inch pie plate), cooled

Egg yolks (number per lemon package directions, doubled)

Sugar (amount per lemon package directions, doubled)

Water (amount per lemon package directions, doubled)

PIE CRUST:

(You can use ready crust from the dairy case or this quick crust that works for any pie)

¼ cup of flour

1½ teaspoons sugar

Pinch of salt

6 tablespoons butter, firm and cubed

2 tablespoons vegetable shortening

¼ cup ice water

Sift (or pulse, if using a food processor) together the flour, sugar, and salt. Work in with your hands (or pulse in) the shortening and the butter cubes until the mixture is crumbly. Work (or pulse) the water in until a dough is formed. Form it into a ball. Do not overwork the dough. Wrap in plastic and chill for 20 minutes. On a floured piece of wax paper, use a rolling pin and roll the dough from the center, outward and evenly around, so a round sheet is formed. Pick up with the wax paper and flip onto the pie dish. Carefully peel the wax paper away. Gently work the dough against the bottom and sides of the dish. Pinch the edges to form an outer crust. Pierce the bottom and bake at 400 degrees for about 20 minutes, or until brown. Remove and lower the oven temperature to 350 degrees.

PIE FILLING:

While your pie shell is baking, make the filling by following the directions from the lemon filling package, doubling all the other ingredients, such as the water, sugar, and egg yolks. (**Note:** When separating the eggs, save the whites for the meringue.) Add the lemon and vanilla pudding mix. Cook, stirring constantly, until it comes to a full, bubbling boil and cool, as directed on the lemon package.

MERINGUE TOPPING:

Egg whites (saved from extracting the yolks for the filling)

½ teaspoon cream of tartar

¼ cup sugar

With an electric mixer, beat the egg whites, cream of tartar, and sugar until stiff peaks form. (**Note:** Make sure you do not have any yolk in the whites, as you will have trouble forming the meringue.)

PIE CONSTRUCTION:

Pour the cooled pie filling into the baked/cooled pie shell. Spread the meringue over the warm pie filling, sealing well up to the outer crust. Bake at 350 degrees until the meringue is light brown (about 10 minutes). Remove, cool, and chill in the refrigerator for at least 8 hours, allowing the filling to set firmly before slicing.

Make the dough and chill. Roll on wax paper, flip onto the pie dish, trim, and form a crust. Bake.

Prepare the lemon filling (using 1-1 vanilla pudding to lemon filling). Pour into the baked and cooled pie crust.

Beat the egg whites until stiff and top the lemon filling to the edge, pulling up to form peaks.
Bake until lightly browned on the peaks.

ICE BOX CAKE

Neither my mother nor grandmothers originated this dessert. If they had, I'm not sure they would have called it a "cake" of any sort. For that matter, I don't think they'd call it a pie either. Well, whatever it's called, I'd definitely call it "good." For anyone that has never seen *Ice Box Cake* before, it is made with two flavors of pudding (usually vanilla and chocolate) with layers of graham crackers in between. It is not baked. It is a refrigerated cake. Picture, if you will, "pudding lasagna." I can still see the big, square-covered CorningWare that my mother used for making this (you know, the classic one with the blue cornflower). If I'm not mistaken, that very piece probably still exists in her kitchen down in Florida.

You can also use one flavor of pudding for both layers, if you like, but it is more interesting (and fun) with two different flavors. Oh, and it MUST be the "cook and serve" style of pudding and not instant. The cooked pudding sets better and forms that "pudding skin" on top. When my mother wasn't making *Ice Box Cake*, she would always make two flavors of pudding at once and combine them into individual servings. The vanilla ones had a little circle of chocolate in the center and the chocolate had a little circle of vanilla. Sometime she'd do butterscotch and chocolate. Whatever way, it always had that "pudding skin" on the top and tasted so much better than instant pudding.

As for the graham crackers part, it is not your usual crushed graham cracker crust that you see for a pie crust. The crackers are layered whole between the layers of pudding. My favorite part is when the moisture of the pudding penetrates into the graham crackers, causing them to expand somewhat. When eaten, they take on a shredded coconut texture in your mouth. Served with a dollop of whipped cream, I am in heaven eating this. I don't even need to test this recipe out. I know it so well that I can just sit here and give it straight out to you. Give it a go!

ICE BOX CAKE

1 small box of cook & serve chocolate pudding

1 small box of cook & serve vanilla pudding

1 package of graham crackers

1 quart of milk, divided in half

OPTIONAL: Add a shot glass of rum to the bottom of the dish before putting the first layer of graham crackers for a special twist)

Cook the chocolate pudding and the vanilla pudding separately, according to the stove top directions on the packages. When done, allow the puddings to cool somewhat. Line the bottom of a deep, heat proof dish (preferably square or rectangular) with a layer of whole graham crackers. Gently pour all of the vanilla pudding evenly over the first layer of graham crackers (use a rubber scraper to clean out the pot). Float a second layer of graham crackers over the top of the vanilla layer, butting them up close to the sides of the dish. Pour the chocolate pudding over the second layer of crackers. Take one graham cracker, crumble it in your hands, and sprinkle over the top of the chocolate layer. Allow to cool further before placing into the refrigerator. Refrigerate until fully set (about 2 hours). Serve using a spatula to cut individual squares. Garnish with a dollop of whipped cream, if desired.

Ice Box Cake.

Cook two puddings at the same time, in separate pots, stirring each constantly until done.

Assemble a single layer of graham crackers.

Pour vanilla pudding on top.

Float another layer of crackers on top of the vanilla layer and add the chocolate layer.

Spread the chocolate pudding out evenly.

Crumble graham crackers on top and chill.

THE CHRISTMAS COLLECTION OF CONFECTION

The Christmas Collection of Confection (Ricotta Rum Cheesecake, Struffoli, Chinese Chews, and Castagna Dolce).

Christmas has always been a good excuse for us to over-indulge on certain foods, specifically foods only made at Christmastime. This is especially true for baked goodies. They are all over the place. It seems like everyone's *inner baker* surfaces around the holidays. No matter how good or bad of a cook they normally are, there is always someone that has no business in the kitchen handing you a cookie at Christmas. . . *"Have a cookie. I baked them myself. . ." "Oh, okay, thanks. Mmm, yummy, oh is that Santa I see over there (here doggie!). . . Mmm, delicious. Thank you, again."*

Our family was no different, with the exception that we had phenomenal cooks throwing their hats into the ring, all making the same foods. Each outcome was truly delicious, but each individual result had something different about it and we got to taste each version as we visited, or were called on, by our kin folk. This comparison occurred, especially, with two of our family holiday standards: *Ricotta Rum Cheesecake* and *Struffoli*.

There were two other holiday cookies that popped up in our house at Christmas, as well. The first was a sweet, buttery, and chewy date and nut bar cookie, made by Nana, called *Chinese Chews.* The other was the cookie of all cookies, made by Grandma Victoria. It was an encrusted, chestnut, chocolate, orange-filled, honey-coated cookie called *Castagna Dolce* (and also the one that started this whole "recipe recovery" nonsense in the first place).

Ricotta Rum Cheesecake, Struffoli, Chinese Chews, and *Castagna Dolce. . .* These four confections came to be known as our families' *Christmas Collection of Confection* (and you can bet that each one comes with a story of its own). As for the family "bake off" competition, Nana and Grandma win by default for the *Chinese Chews* and *Castagna Dolce* category. In fact, after Grandma Victoria's passing in 1963, nobody really attempted to recreate those chestnut cookies until many years later. The *Chinese Chews,* on the other hand, persevered due to the longevity of Nana, who lived to the age of 94.

Randy and Me visiting Santa at Levy Brothers.

Our tree at Christmas (c. 1959).

I insisted on a real tree, with tinsel, for my last Christmas at home (1984).

A Typical 21st Century Christmas Day at our house (2009).

I will never forget the great Christmases that we had at home. We'd do most of our shopping at the local stores. The closest we had to online shopping was via catalog, over the phone, or by mail. In Clifton, there was (and still is) a shopping center that was near our home called Styertowne Shopping Center. It was made up of a bank, a pharmacy, a card/gift store, a liquor store, a shoe store, a record store, a "five & dime," a jewelry store, a bakery, a barber shop, a hairdresser, an ice cream/fountain shop, and a Chinese restaurant, to name a few. An offshoot building housed the Berra-Rizzuto Bowling Lanes, a place I frequented much as a youth. The anchor stores for this shopping center were a supermarket (Grand Union), and a department store called Levy Brothers, which later became the building for the infamous Rowe-Manse Emporium. None of these stores are in existence today.

At Christmas, a portion of the Styertowne parking lot was roped off for selling Christmas greens. Wreaths hung and trees leaned against wooden racks under the glow of a string of bare light bulbs. Every year, Santa's "elf," dressed as Santa, would stand on the sidewalk and ring the Salvation Army bell. (It had to be an elf, right? I mean, the REAL Santa was sitting on his throne on the top floor of Levy Brothers). I can still hear that bell ringing. To this day, I get a little misty every time I hear my favorite Christmas song, *Silver Bells.* To me, this old shopping center scene that I described to you is my quintessential memory of *"Christmas time in the city."*

As a young child, I loved to help my mother pick out and put up the tree (although they enjoyed the tree, my father and brother never really seemed to get deeply involved in the whole tree "process"). In the beginning, our trees were real, lit with those big "screw in" bulbs, and draped with tinsel. It was that old heavy, leaded tinsel, too. (You would not see that around anymore, would you?) Every year, we would remove the tinsel from the tree and save it for the next year in an old Bamberger's gift box. By the time the 1970s arrived, our tree was artificial, the lights tiny, and the tinsel replaced with cheesy gold garland. So, for my last Christmas living at home, I insisted on having a real tree and one draped with tinsel. I was now out of college and working, so I bought the tree. It was so much more beautiful than our artificial one, but still not like the trees I remembered as a youngster.

RICOTTA RUM CHEESECAKE

Ricotta Rum Cheesecake is my favorite holiday dessert. We would always have this cheesecake for dessert on Christmas Eve, but the best part was waking up on Christmas morning, lopping off a chunk, and enjoying it with coffee as we opened our gifts. I never attempted to make this cheesecake while my mother was around. I never had to, as she gave away pieces of her own cheesecake. A few years after she moved to Florida, I was starting to miss the cheesecake and felt compelled to make it. The first time I did, as involved as it was, it came out pretty well.

This version of an Italian ricotta cheesecake was originated by my great grandmother, Carmella (Nana's mother). My grandmother passed this recipe on to us, and many different versions have emerged as a result of the various cooking styles in our family. Some added citron (dried fruit), which I believe Nana did (but, my mother didn't). Some left out the rum and replaced it with either lemon or orange zest, which I believe Aunt Mary does (but, my mother didn't). My mother would make a lattice design on the top with left over crust dough (but I don't). No matter what occasion my mother was making this for (Christmas or Easter), she always made it with the rum. She would also sprinkle the

Ricotta Rum Cheesecake.

top with those tiny colored candies to give it a festive look. If you like, sprinkle the top with some confectioners' sugar just prior to serving to give it a more elegant look.

The fact is that you can do whatever you prefer, but one thing holds true for anyone making this cheesecake. . . you MUST hand-mix the eggs in with the ricotta cheese, one at a time, using a wooden spoon. (I personally don't think the material the spoon is made of matters, however, Nana's directions say "stir with a wooden spoon," so. . . just do it!) Electric hand or stand mixers are out of the question! Here is why: If the ricotta/egg mixture is too loose, your cheesecake is going to be runny. What you want is for the mixture to "puff up" in the center when cooking. Using an electric mixer (no matter how slow the speed) is going to make this mixture too smooth. Remember, you are making a loose, Italian-style cheesecake and not a tight, New York-style cheesecake (Which reminds me to mention, since I have been making this, I find that people either like this style of cheesecake or they don't).

Another interesting thing to note is that the crust is made by using the same recipe as the *Biscotti* cookie dough, but made with more flour, which makes stiffer dough for rolling (instead of the normally sticky dough used for the *Biscotti*). My mother always made her cheesecake in a large, regular cake pan. I am not as daring as my mother, nor should you be. I use a springform pan with removable sides, and I don't make such a big one. My mother always made a huge cheesecake (about 15"). It was amazing the way she was able to flip the cake on a rack and then flip it back onto a cake plate without it falling apart. She used to give pieces of it away to everyone. I make a smaller 9" size.

Let's talk about the rum. When making this cake, you need to be generous with it. The number one answer we always gave my mother when she asked, "How's the cheesecake this year?" was, "It's good, but it NEEDS MORE RUM!" One year I was helping her make it and, after tasting the mixture, I snuck more rum into it behind her back. So, it's no wonder that she said, "Mmm, the cake came good this year, didn't it" (yep!).

My favorite part is the center. You see, when cutting this cake, you make a circle in the center and cut the pieces as "spokes" off of that. Once all the sides

are eaten, the rum-soaked, cheese center remains and it is just the best. The longer this cake stays in the refrigerator, the better it tastes, so make it a couple of days ahead of when you plan to serve it.

Another interesting thing I noticed about this special holiday cheesecake is that we had more pictures that included this cake than any other food. It has to be the most photographed cake in history. This cake has been photographed more than Princess Diana, herself. Take a look. . .

Ricotta Rum Cheesecake . . .

and a cheesecake. . .

and cheesecake (notice how it is cut). . .

and a cheesecake (again). . .

. . . and, yet again, cheesecake. . .

. . . and, finally, a cheesecake!

RICOTTA RUM CHEESECAKE

This recipe is for one, 9-10 inch cheesecake. For both the crust and the filling, the eggs need to be room temperature, and one stick of butter needs to be softened.

CRUST:

3 cups flour

3 large eggs (at room temperature), beaten

1 stick of butter, softened

1 cup sugar

3 teaspoons baking powder

Pinch of cinnamon

Note: The crust ingredients above make two crusts that fit a 10-inch springform pan. Freeze half of the dough for later use.

Mix all of the dry crust ingredients together first, then cut in the softened butter with a fork and add the beaten eggs. The mixture will be crumbly. Transfer to a floured board and knead into soft dough. Cut the dough in half and wrap one of the halves in plastic, label, place in a freezer bag, and freeze.

Take the other half of the dough and form into a round disk. Place on some wide wax paper that has been well floured. Roll out evenly, not too thin, so the circle will fit the bottom surface of the pan, plus up the sides (use the pan to judge the measurement). Grease the pan well. Place the pan next to the rolled crust. Hold one edge of the wax paper and quickly, but carefully, flip the dough on top of the pan, centering it as best you can. Peel back the wax paper. Lift the edges of the rolled dough, creating enough slack to allow the dough to fall into the corners of the pan. Square off the dough with your fingers and pinch the edges, forming a thick, high crust. Do not overlap the crust, as you do not want it to interfere with the removal of the springform. If any of the crust tears or gets a hole, just patch it up with some of the excess dough (you don't want it to leak).

RICOTTA CHEESE FILLING:

3 lbs. of whole milk ricotta cheese

12 large eggs (at room temperature)

1½ cups of sugar

½ to ¾ cup of rum

2 teaspoons vanilla extract

¼ teaspoon cinnamon

OPTIONAL: If you do not want to use rum, it can be substituted with the zest of one orange or lemon, depending on which flavor you prefer.

Preheat the oven to 350 degrees.

Add the ricotta cheese to a large mixing bowl. Break one egg into the ricotta cheese and mix in well with a large wooden spoon. Do this with each egg, breaking and mixing in *one at a time,* until all 12 eggs are used and the mixture is smooth (**Important:** DO NOT use an electric hand or stand mixer for this. Eggs must be stirred in by hand).

Mix in the sugar, cinnamon, and vanilla. Add the rum last (or citrus zest, if substituting for the rum). The original recipe calls for ½ cup of rum, but adding an extra ¼ cup makes a better cake.

Pour the entire contents of the bowl into the crust prepared earlier. Open the oven door and pull the center rack out before picking up the pan and transferring to the oven. Do this very carefully, as it will be very heavy and the contents will slosh around. Once on the rack, slide in slowly. Bake for 1½ to 1¾ hours. About ½ hour into the baking, the crust will begin to look brown. To avoid burning, cover with a little foil that has been formed to fit over the crust, without touching the filling (see photo). Foil protectors can be removed when there is about 20 minutes left to cook.

This is what crust should look like prior to filling.

When the cheesecake is done, it will nicely brown and fully puff up in the center. Remove from the oven and cool completely before refrigerating. Refrigerate with the springform on and remove it after the cake has had a chance to chill and set.

This cheesecake is best when made a few days ahead of when you plan to serve it, and it tastes better the longer it is left in the refrigerator.

To serve: Dust with powdered sugar prior to serving, if desired. Cut a circle in the center, about 4 to 5 inches in diameter. Then, cut "spokes" off of the circle to make the individual serving slices.

Mix the crust ingredients, form into dough, and divide (wrap and store the other half in the freezer).

Roll on floured wax paper, measure, and flip onto the springform pan.

Work the crust into the pan and seal any holes. Mix eggs into the ricotta one at a time.

Mix until smooth, add the rum, pour into the crust, and bake on the center rack.

Cover the crust to keep from burning. The cheesecake will puff up in the center, but will fall back in when cooled.

STRUFFOLI

On our Christmas dessert table, right alongside our *Rum Ricotta Cheesecake,* was something called *Struffoli*. This is an Italian confection that is made up of tiny pieces of dough, fried crisp, and coated with honey. As with the cheesecake, this would be around for us to enjoy for the entire week between Christmas Eve and New Year's Day.

In the beginning of this book (when I was discussing how the various cooks in our family had there own versions of antipasto), I made mention of something called the *Great Struffoli War of the 20th Century.* Before I tell you about this, I'll first give you a bit of Struffoli history (as it pertains to me). I'm not sure how far back Struffoli goes in our family, but my first introduction was from my grandfather's second wife, Connie. She made them sort of oblong in shape, mixed them with whole almonds, and coated them in a hard, candy-like coating. I'm not sure if she added caramelized sugar to the honey to make it harden, but it certainly resembled that. Soon after Connie came on the scene, my mother began making them. Then, my Aunt Mary (Mom's sister) joined the ranks of Struffoli makers.

From that point on, the *Great Struffoli War* began, but this war had a different twist. In this war, the "Generals" stood in allegiance to the opposing sides. *"Oh, Ann, yours are better. . ." "No, Mary, yours are better. . ." "No, yours, are. . ." "No, yours are better. . ."* etc. At some point, others were called in for their opinion (as for me, I played it like Switzerland. . . neutral). That was regarding the taste. Then, the time came to battle on quantity. They did this by revealing the "egg count." To understand what this was all about, one only needs to understand that the basic Struffoli recipe is made with 3 eggs (double the recipe, 6 eggs; triple the recipe, 9 eggs, etc). The more the eggs, the more the Struffoli you would get. My aunt would ask, "How many eggs did you make?" My mother would reply, "Oh, 6 eggs, how about you?" "I made 12 eggs." My mother would gasp, "12 eggs! Mary, are you crazy?" (Aunt Mary made large quantities so she could give them as gifts.) Ah, yes, the *Great Struffoli War*, how I miss that.

Let's talk a little bit about the technique in making Struffoli. Once the dough is made, how do you get them into little pieces? My mother used to roll pieces of dough into strands on a floured board. Then, she would cut off little pieces with a knife, as you can see in this vintage photo below.

Mom, preparing for battle in the Great Struffoli War and, no, the whiskey is not for drinking! (Lo and behold, is that another picture of a cheesecake I see, cooling on the stove?)

This was a daunting task, one in which I remember my mother describing as "backbreaking." So I, being a traditional-style cook in a 21st Century world, said to myself, "no way" and found a better, faster, and easier way to do this. I roll the dough out fairly thick (about ¼ of an inch) on a floured board. Then, I take a pizza cutter and cut it into ¼-inch strips. Then I cut again on a bias, across the last cut, about another ¼ inch, to form little diamond shapes. The pieces may seem small, but they need to be because they are going to puff up when they are fried. If they are cut into the actual size you think they should be, they will end up huge.

Struffoli is served on a large plate and passed around, people taking individual portions by using a serving spoon or a knife. I sometimes make individual portions using baking cups (as used for cupcakes), putting them on a tray so a portion is easily obtainable. Decorate with colored candies, or colored, crystallized sugar sprinkles.

STRUFFOLI

3 eggs, beaten

1½ cups flour

1 shot glass of whiskey

1 cup shelled walnuts or almonds

12 oz. jar of honey

Pinch of cinnamon

24 oz. of vegetable, canola, or peanut oil
(or other oil suitable for deep frying)

Mix the flour well with the eggs and whiskey. Transfer to a floured board and knead into stiff dough. Cover with plastic and set aside to rest for about 15 minutes.

Take about ¼ of the dough and roll out to about ¼-inch thick. Taking a pizza cutter or a sharp knife, cut into ¼-inch strips, then cut again, crosswise on a bias, creating little diamond shapes. Separate the pieces and move to a well-floured surface to dry.

Repeat this process until all the dough is cut and drying. Allow the pieces to dry out for about 30 minutes.

Place all of the oil into a deep pot. Heat the oil thoroughly. (Test readiness with one piece of the dough. When it sizzles, the oil is hot enough.) Carefully, slide all of the dough pieces into the hot oil, and stir frequently to allow even browning. It may take about 10 to 15 minutes, but the oil will begin to foam up. Once this happens, you will know that they are nearing doneness. When lightly brown, but not too dark, move to a colander with a slotted spoon. (Do not pour out. . . oil is very HOT!)

In a large bowl, toss the dry Struffoli with the walnuts or almonds. Heat the honey in a pot with a pinch of cinnamon until it becomes a hot and loose liquid. Mix the hot honey with the Struffoli and the nuts. Make it at least a day in advance to allow the honey to penetrate the Struffoli.

To serve, make individual servings in cupcake cups, or mound onto a decorative dish. Garnish with tiny multi-colored nonpareil candy sprinkles.

Add all the ingredients together and knead into stiff dough.

Roll out, cut into small diamond shapes with a pizza cutter, and dry on a floured surface.

Fry in a deep pot, stirring frequently. The oil will begin to foam up when nearing doneness.

Move to a colander with a slotted spoon. Stir in the walnuts and toss with hot honey.

Struffoli.

CHINESE CHEWS (DATE & NUT BARS)

Okay, you must be saying, "First this Italian guy gives us a recipe for *Chicken Chow Mein*, now he's giving us something called *Chinese Chews!*" The funny thing is, even though they are called "Chinese," there really isn't any one ingredient that warrants them to be called Chinese *anything*. However, chewy they are, indeed. I'm pretty sure that Nana got this recipe from one of her neighbor ladies at the senior citizens apartment complex where she lived. Soon after moving there, they turned up one Christmas and appeared every year and afterward.

I was curious about the name, so I *Googled* "Chinese Chews" and came up with a ton of hits, so that tells me that this was not one of Nana's original recipes. I found that not one recipe was identical to the one that Nana passed down to us, but most of them had many similarities in that they contained butter, flour, eggs, sugar, fruit and nuts, and were cut into bars dusted with confectioners' sugar. My recipe features chopped dates and walnuts as the two key ingredients. One recipe I found online called for "date paste" (whatever that is). Another called for pecans instead of walnuts. Yet another recipe even called for prunes instead of dates. So, all of this leads me to believe that "Chinese Chew" is nothing but a generic name for a fruit and nut chewy bar cookie.

Every time I watch someone taste one of these for the first time, I watch them casually pick it up, take a bite, look down at the remaining piece in their hand, squint their eyes, and go "Mmm!" I love making these even more than I love to eat them. You don't even know you are eating fruit, because it takes on the characteristic of a chewy candy. Any they are kind of pretty, all rolled up in the confectioners' sugar. I picked up on Nana's tradition and I now make these every Christmas.

CHINESE CHEWS (DATE AND NUT BARS)

2 eggs

1 stick butter, softened

1 cup sugar

1 cup flour

1 cup chopped walnuts

8 oz. package dates, chopped (or use the pre-chopped)

1 teaspoon vanilla extract

Confectioners' sugar (for dusting)

Preheat oven to 350 degrees.

Cream the butter and sugar together and add the eggs and vanilla. Fold in the flour, walnuts, and chopped dates until all are evenly combined. Grease and flour a 9" x 13" pan. Bake for 30 minutes.

Cool halfway and cut into bars (about 3" x 1" in size). Roll in powdered sugar. Makes 3 dozen bars.

Chinese Chews (Date & Nut Bars).

Chop whole dates (or use pre-chopped). Cream together the butter and sugar, and add eggs and vanilla.

Fold in the flour, dates, and walnuts. Press into a greased and floured 9" x 13" pan and bake.

Cut into bars, roll in confectioners' sugar, and store in a wax-papered tin.

VICTORIA'S CASTAGNA DOLCE
(CHESTNUT & CHOCOLATE PILLOWS)

This is it. This is the recipe that started the whole family "recipe recovery" kick. To me, this fabulous confection is my Grandma Victoria's legacy. Don't get me wrong. I'm sure that the woman did much more in her life than just make these Christmas cookies. Please understand that I was very young (Only five, to be exact) when she died. I never really got the chance to know her better. If she spoke any English at all, it was very little. I always remember her conversing with my mother in Italian and I would say how they talked that "scribble talk." I identified with this grandmother more so via actions and not words. The best memory I have of her is that she had a kind face and a gentle disposition. I guess if anyone should have a final memory, this is a good one to have.

Grandma Victoria (right) laughing with Mom, as both my grandfathers look on (mid-1950s).

So what about these cookies? After making these for a few years now, it occurred to me that they have quite a sophisticated flavor. I'm surprised that I liked these as a child, as the sweetness is derived mostly from the honey coating and the filling is made with bittersweet chocolate kissed with a hint of orange. If you do not like the flavor combination of dark chocolate and orange, you may not like this recipe, as written. I suppose that the sweeter milk chocolate could be used instead.

The other thing to note is that they are definitely a labor of love. Yes, they're a bit of work, but well worth the effort (I think). How much work exactly?

Let's just say that Rachael Ray would probably never make these. Besides the fact that she always says baking is not her forte, there are just too many steps that make the task well exceed 30 minutes of time. I always make the filling a day in advance. I do this for two reasons: First, to separate the steps; second, to allow the filling to chill overnight, which makes it easier to apply. Making the dough itself is not hard, but the rolling and cutting, and rolling and cutting, rolling and cutting! Cooking and pulling the meat from the chestnuts is no walk in the park, either.

We always question if Grandma fried them. I honestly don't know. My brother seems to think that she fried them, similarly to the Struffoli. I have been baking them, and with great success, so that is the method I am sticking to. I find that the thinner the dough is rolled, the better. When the dark brown of the chocolate is seen through the dough, it allows the honey to absorb better and seems to result in a tastier cookie. Just as with the *Struffoli* and the *Rum Ricotta Cheesecake*, these are a Christmas morning staple with my coffee. If I could sum it up in two words. . . They Satisfy!

VICTORIA'S CASTAGNA DOLCE (CHESTNUT & CHOCOLATE PILLOWS)

CHESTNUT AND CHOCOLATE FILLING:
(**Note:** Filling can be made in advance and refrigerated)

1 lb. chestnuts, boiled and shells removed

¼ lb. semi-sweet chocolate (bar or morsels)

4 oz. grape jelly

Zest of ½ an orange

½ teaspoon cinnamon

¼ teaspoon ground clove

½ cup honey

Boil whole chestnuts (about 1 hour). Cool in cold water. Cut a chestnut in half. If it looks rotten or moldy, discard it. With the tip of a paring knife, carefully insert and twist. Some will come out easier than others. Scrape any chestnut meat out from the shell (pick out any shells as you go). Repeat until all the chestnuts are shelled. Chop the walnuts fine in a chopper or food processor.

In a saucepan, melt the chocolate in hot honey, mixing in the cinnamon, clove, and orange zest. Stir frequently and when bubbly, remove from the heat. Pour the chocolate mixture into the chopped chestnuts and add the grape jelly, mixing it all together thoroughly. The mixture must cool before applying as a filling (it should tighten up when chilled in the refrigerator, at least one hour).

Boil chestnuts whole. Slice. If rotten or moldy, discard. Only use nice ones.

With paring knife, carefully insert and twist, scraping out the meat. Chop fine. (You may also find shelled chestnuts in the supermarket and can try using those).

Melt chocolate in honey with spices. Mix with chopped chestnuts and jelly. Allow to cool and set up in the refrigerator before using.

CRUST:

2 cups flour	½ cup of shortening
1½ teaspoons baking powder	1 teaspoon lemon juice
2 eggs	¼ cup white wine
½ cup sugar	½ teaspoon vanilla extract
	15 ounces of honey

Mix all of the ingredients together, except the honey, and knead on a floured surface into stiff dough. Allow the dough to stand for about 30 minutes before rolling.

Take ¼ of the dough and roll out thin and flat. Using a teaspoon, dab some filling in rows about 2 inches apart and about 1 inch from the edge (on one side of the flattened dough). Take the side of the dough that has no filling and flip over the top of the filling row, matching the edges the best you can. With a pizza cutter, cut out in neat half-moon shapes, leaving the folded side intact. Using a fork, crimp the edges of the dough together, sealing in the filling. Place each completed cookie on the baking sheet. When done with a row, take the scrap dough and roll out (should have enough for about 3 more cookies).

Repeat this process until all 4 quarters of the dough and the filling are used up. Bake at 350 degrees for 30 - 35 minutes. When they are lightly brown, they are done. Remove from the oven and cool completely on a rack. Place in a large plastic container with a tight lid. Pour honey evenly over the top. Every once in awhile, turn the container over to allow the honey to disperse itself. It is better to serve these after the honey has had a chance to fully coat and absorb into the cookie. These can be made well in advance of serving them and will last for days in an airtight container.

To serve, arrange on a dish. Sprinkle with some colored sugar crystals or confectioners' sugar. Makes about 3½ dozen *Castagna Dolce.*

Mix all crust ingredients into the dough. Roll out thin and make dabs of filling with a teaspoon.

Fold the flap over, trim with a pizza cutter, and crimp with a fork.

**Bake and cool completely on a rack.
Pour honey over the top and coat well, allowing it to absorb.**

**Castagna Dolce
(Chocolate & Chestnut Pillows).**

DON'T LET THIS HAPPEN TO YOU

Back in the very early 60s, when I was just a pre-school tot, I can remember my mother and me sitting in the living room of our little house watching our black and white console television. For anyone old enough to remember, it was the kind that, when you turned off the TV, the screen disappeared into a little dot that faded into the background until it totally disappeared (I remember thinking that the people were fading into oblivion).

One of the shows we used to watch together on this television was *I Love Lucy*. Starting out my life by watching Lucy, it's no wonder that I have been a lifetime fan. I wasn't even born yet when the series aired in prime time, between 1952 and 1957. However, by 1961, the show was in syndication and CBS used to run it every weekday morning at 10:00. At that young age, I may not have understood everything that was going on in the show, but my mother used to laugh a lot so I knew I liked it.

(c. 1961) Me, in front of our Magnavox 3-way entertainment center.

So, why do I even bring this up? There is one episode where Lucy decides that she's going to embark on some writing (you may know it. . . Episode #90: "Lucy Writes a Novel"). Well, poor Lucy, amid her slandered friends and husband, tries frantically to get her book published, but no publisher will have her. Finally, a publisher calls and tells her that there is someone that is VERY interested, after all, and gives her the number of the interested party. Excitedly, Lucy calls the number. It turned out that this gentleman was writing a textbook about "How to Write a Novel," and he wanted to use excerpts of Lucy's book for a chapter called "*Don't Let This Happen to You.*"

It's not that I originally planned to include such a chapter in my own book, but I only saw fit to add one after what happened to me one night. For the sake of you wanna-be cooks, rest assured that even folks that know their way around the kitchen can goof up from time to time. So, for the sake of my own book, I present to you my *"don't let this happen to you"* story.

Before I tell you about my mishap, I'll need to tell you another story. It is a story that my mother has told me many times as a young lad. She usually told me this story when she was trying to knock some sense into me about something. This story will help you understand my mishap much better.

When my mother was a young girl (probably in her teens), there was a cookie recipe that she had gotten from a friend. These cookies were so delicious, that she just had to make them and wanted to make them to taste exactly like her friend's. Well, she in the kitchen with her mother (my grandmother, Victoria) and was getting ready to add the sugar. My grandmother stopped her and said, "Wait. Where are you going with all that sugar?" My mother showed her the recipe and it said "12 cups of sugar." To my grandmother, an experienced baker, this was absurd. "Ann, call your friend and ask her if that is right." My mother, being an obstinate teen, did not want to call and insisted that this was a correct measurement. She began adding the sugar. My grandmother, after begging her to double check, finally threw her arms up and said to herself, "The girl has to learn the hard way," and let her go. Well,

Ouch! (But, they still tasted pretty good.)

long story short, the cookies melted into a molten mess. A pool of melted sugar, so bad, they had to throw the cookie sheet into the garbage. Fast forward to 2010. . .

I was sitting around the other night and I had a real hankering for something sweet. Mmm. . . What can I make? Ah, yes. . . oatmeal cookies will do the trick. I have a really good recipe that I use, too (the Quaker Oat's "Disappearing Oatmeal Raisin Cookie Recipe"). You have to understand, I really needed an oatmeal cookie badly, so I whipped them up quickly. Maybe just a little too quickly, though. Not wanting to make a whole batch, I decide to cut the recipe in half. I halved all the dry ingredients in a bowl. When I went to cream the butter with the sugar in a second bowl, I forgot I was halving and accidentally added enough sugar for a whole recipe. Here's what happened . . .

You can only imagine what went through my mind when I looked through the window of my oven door. When I figured out what I did wrong, flashbacks of my mother's story of molten cookies filled my head. Luckily, my episode was not as critical (I was able to save the pan). Mine was just a small mistake. In my mother's case, that "12 cups" was most likely "½ cup," or "2 cups" (with a little pen mark in front of it that looked like a "1"). 12 cups is a lot of sugar for one batch of cookies!

Ergo. . . My own, personal chapter of, *"don't let this happen to you!"* What can be learned from all of this? . . . I learned that the next time I multiply or divide a recipe, I will take my time, pre-measure each ingredient, and double check. As for my mother's story, there is a moral, as well. . . *"Don't be so smart and listen to those that are older and wiser than you."* They know things from experience and they may be trying to give you advice on something that can result in an outcome much more serious than just melted cookies.

IN CONCLUSION

I have to admit, I had fun writing this book. It not only gave me the opportunity to document the family recipes, but it made me better understand myself as it forced me to think about things that I have not thought about in ages. That said, I think the most important accomplishment of this book, for me, is in knowing that my mother's, grandmothers', and great grandmothers' efforts were not in vain. There is an ultimate, true, positive, physical outcome that was produced out of their efforts, one that you are holding in your hands at this very moment.

As for the book's impact on my own life, it represents a significant chapter in itself. . . a milestone. I never intended to write a book. It happened on a whim, which makes me believe more and more that it was something meant to be. When you think of it, life's best moments always come about in that way. . . naturally, without being forced.

Even though I say it was fun to write, it was in no way an easy task. The writing part was dependent on the success of the recipes. Some recipes had to be done more than once in order to get them to a point where I thought they were an acceptable match. Recipes, normally very easy to do, became cumbersome when I had to stop at each step to write notes or take photos. Dinner was delayed many a night because I had to get just the right light or angle in photographing the finished product. This represents over a year's worth of work, as the seasons changed from spring to summer, summer to fall, fall to winter, and now spring to summer again.

Most of the joy I've gotten out of this project involves family and friends that I have brought along on the journey. These are people that have encouraged me and tasted and tested recipes on behalf of it. Now that I am finished writing, all that remains for me is the journey forward. Wondering where this endeavor will go next is a very exhilarating feeling. For as exhilarating as it is, it is equally terrifying that it can fall flat and become a big flop. Either way, I still can say that I finished something of a significant nature and, flop or not, it is a project that I can be proud of. I know that my ancestors would have been very proud and that is what is most important to me.

So, let's all raise our glasses now and say, "Cheers to good family, good friends, good times, and good food. . ." "Here, Here!" (clink)

HOLIDAY MENU IDEAS

EASTER

Appetizer: Easter Salad (Orange, Oil Cured Olive, and Onion)
Paired with Pastiera Di Grano

Soup: Stuffed Escarole Soup

Entrée: Roasted Chicken with Potatoes
Served with Early Peas and Caramelized Onions

Dessert: Ricotta Rum Cheesecake

FOURTH OF JULY

Entrée: Sausage and Peppers on an Italian Hard Roll

Sides: Hot Potato Salad
Classic Coleslaw
Tomato and Cucumber Salad

Dessert: Classic Sponge Cake (Served "Red, White, and Blue"
with Whipped Cream, Strawberry and Blueberry Filling)

THANKSGIVING

Appetizer: Antipasto

Soup: Italian Chicken Vegetable Soup with Meatballs

Entrée: Turkey Stuffed with Nana's Poultry Stuffing
Served with Candied Sweet Potatoes and Assorted Vegetables

Dessert: Mom's Signature Lemon Meringue Pie

CHRISTMAS EVE

Appetizer: Stuffed Vinegar Peppers

Entrée: Linguini with Shrimp, Scallops, & Stuffed Calamari
Paired with a Salad of Mixed Greens

Dessert: Assortment of Struffoli, Castagna Dolce,
and Date & Nut Bars (Chinese Chews)

CHRISTMAS DAY

Appetizer: Antipasto

Entrée: Chicken Cordon Bleu
Paired with Linguini Aglio e Olio and Fresh Green Beans

Dessert: Ricotta Rum Cheesecake

INDEX

IN MEMORY

To those that have been a positive influence in my life, but are no longer with us. . .

Anna Vendetti — Mother (2006)

Angelina Vendetti — Grandmother "Nana" (1994)

Angelo Vendetti — Grandfather (1966)

Carmine Miscia — Grandfather (1992)

Victoria Miscia — Grandmother (1963)

Wilhelmina Ondrak — Chris' Mother (1996)

Eddie Ondrak — Chris' Father (2001)

Norma (Vendetti) Hantson — Aunt (2005)

Sandra (Vendetti) Cerulli — Aunt (2010)

Michael Mastropietro — Uncle (2006)

Edmund Vendetti — Uncle/Godfather (1992)

Jane Krietz — Mother of Judie (2004)

Rudy Krietz — Father of Judie (1977)

Al Cuzzi — Friend and Neighbor (1974)

Bill McCormick — Second Uncle and Neighbor (1992)

Dolly Christiano — Friend and Neighbor (2004)

Sonny Christiano — Friend and Neighbor (2004)

Robert Turon — Partner and Friend (1993)

Kathleen Balunis — Friend and Neighbor (2000)

Diane Peters — Friend (2006)

Joseph Sbano — Friend (2008)

Bob Young — Friend (2000)

Ted Donaghy — Friend (2007)

Chuck Heinz — Friend (2007)

Carol Frascella — Friend (2009)

Dr. Jeannette Ritzenthaler — Professor of English and Poetry (1999)

Made in the USA
Lexington, KY
09 February 2011